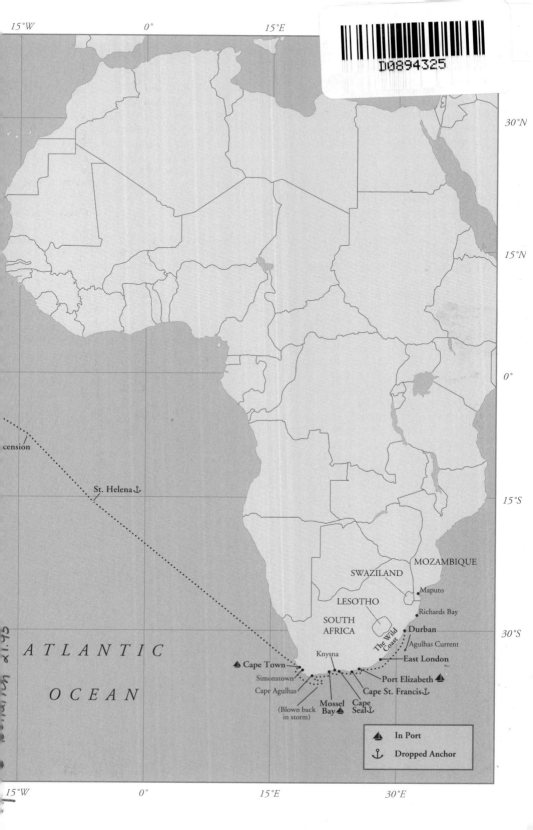

15°W   0°   15°E

D0894325

30°N

15°N

0°

...cension

St. Helena ⚓

15°S

MOZAMBIQUE

SWAZILAND

Maputo

LESOTHO

Richards Bay

SOUTH
AFRICA

Durban

ATLANTIC

Agulhas Current

30°S

Knysna

East London

OCEAN

Cape Town ⚓

Port Elizabeth ⚓

Simonstown

Cape St. Francis ⚓

Cape Agulhas

(Blown back
in storm)

Mossel
Bay ⚓

Cape
Seal ⚓

	In Port
⚓	Dropped Anchor

15°W   0°   15°E   30°E

SMALL BOAT
TO
FREEDOM

SMALL BOAT
TO
FREEDOM

A Journey of Conscience
to a
New Life in America

JOHN VIGOR

THE LYONS PRESS
Guilford, Connecticut
An imprint of The Globe Pequot Press

The Lyons Press is an imprint of The Globe Pequot Press.

10 9 8 7 6 5 4 3 2 1

Printed in the United States of America

Endpaper maps by Stefanie Ward

910.45
V V6

ISBN 1-59228-226-1

Library of Congress Cataloging-in-Publication Data is available on file.

To June, Trent, Terry, and Kevin

Contents

So many good friends and acquaintances have helped us on the journey that started fifteen years ago that it would be impractical to name them all. Nevertheless, there are a few deserving of special mention.

First and foremost I acknowledge with deep gratitude the help and guidance of my editor, Tom McCarthy, of The Lyons Press. His skill, unflagging enthusiasm, and constant encouragement made my task much easier.

My sincerest thanks also go to:

Carol and Al Stoddard, my sister- and brother-in-law, who kindly afforded us practical help with our immigration and helped us clear many hurdles.

Bernadette Bernon, former editor of *Cruising World* magazine, and Jonathan Eaton, editorial director of International Marine Publishing, for allowing me to earn a freelance living by writing and editing articles and books for them.

Julie Fallowfield, formerly of the literary agency McIntosh & Otis, New York, and now retired, who encouraged me to write my first book—and then sold it.

Angelo Lavranos, firstly for a designing a wonderful boat that carried us safely halfway around the world from the Indian Ocean to the United States, and secondly for permitting me to reproduce her lines in this book.

Jonathan Raban, for a chance suggestion that the story of our voyage from South Africa might be made into a book. This is probably not the book he would have envisaged, but I am grateful for the spark that started my fire.

FLEEING APARTHEID

I knew from the beginning that I would be frightened, badly frightened, sooner or later. I had read about it many times, and talked with people who'd done it, and thought I was prepared. But no amount of reading can really prepare you for the brutal reality.

Yet what I remember now is not so much the fear—though, heaven knows, I was paralyzed with fear—as the helplessness of it, the feeling of inevitability, of not being able to do anything about it. That was somehow more frightening than the raw fear.

We had been lucky so far. The storm waves had grown with the howling wind as the hours passed, but, as fate would have it, the real monster waves, the widely spaced graybeards with their fiercely plunging crests, had laid down their acres of seething white foam on either side of us.

Now, for the first time, we were in the direct line of one, and there was nothing I could do about it. None of my careful preparations could stop that malevolent mountain of water from collapsing and smashing into our side.

Already the wind was shaking our thirty-one-foot sailboat as a terrier shakes a rat. Tight-stretched shrouds and stays moaned with unearthly shrieks that rose and fell with the vicious gusts. Flapping halyards battered the metal mast. Atop the mast, a small nylon burgee fluttered so hard it made a frantic metallic buzzing noise so loud you could hear it above everything. Noise, unnerving noise, was everywhere on deck and in the sea around us.

Pellets of salt water snatched from the sea's surface racketed against the hull and stung my face. As I turned to avoid them, warm puffs of air escaped from the neck of my oilskins. They reeked of the private, acrid stench of fear. But as I clung, immobilized, to the tiller, it was not fear but the helplessness that made my stomach tighten. I was convinced we would capsize and there was nothing I could do about it. Inevitably, unavoidably, three seconds from now we would capsize, as many had done before us off this Cape of Storms at the bottom of Africa.

The mind does strange things at times like this. I had none of the grand, majestic thoughts. I didn't ponder on life and death. My past existence didn't flash before my eyes. I didn't think of sending loving thoughts to my wife and son in the cramped cabin below decks, or even of warning them to hang on tight. Instead, my mind plummeted into the ridiculous.

Frozen and fascinated like a snake's victim, I watched the tumbling, frothing mass pour down the wave slope toward us and I wondered if my fingers, tightly gripping the tiller, would leave prints in the six-month-old varnish. I wondered if I'd be able to swim with my toes curled so tensely in my sailing shoes.

And, just before the wave struck, I closed my eyes, crouched down in the cockpit, and wondered if fish would gobble up the precious gold coins we were trying to smuggle out of South Africa, as they swallow the shiny lures of fishermen . . .

It had all begun two years previously on a typical summer's day in the subtropical city of Durban, on South Africa's southeast coast. I was standing shirtless in the blazing sun, mixing cement mortar with a shovel, when a black man came past. He wore a white, long-sleeved shirt and dark trousers. He had the athletic build and handsome features of a Zulu.

"Got a job, boss?" he asked.

I shook my head. "Sorry," I said.

The mortar was for a brick garage I was building at home. I enjoyed laying bricks. I was a humor columnist and editorial writer for the *Daily News,* a metropolitan daily newspaper, so my life's work was thrown away every day after breakfast—or used to line the parrot cage. But brickwork remained solid and tangible, to be patted and admired years later.

"Why are *you* making dagha (mortar), boss?" he asked.

"I like to do it."

He stiffened and scowled. "That's black man's work," he said belligerently. "Why are you taking a black man's work away from him? You must give that job to a *black* man."

The next day, I found African National Congress graffiti sprayed in my backyard. I had been marked for special attention.

At that time, Nelson Mandela's ANC was a full-blown black terrorist organization supported by Libya's Moammar Gadhafi, the Palestine Liberation Organization's Yassar Arafat, and the Kremlin, among others. The ANC not only planted land mines on white farms and blew up white military barracks but also attacked what they called "soft" civilian targets. They placed bombs in white schools, supermarkets, and mailboxes.

But although the appearance of ANC graffiti in my yard was a defining act, it did not panic us. Terrorism was nothing new to South Africans, and we had learned to live with it. The *Daily News* frequently received bomb threats from the ANC. I constantly worried about whether it was safe for my wife, June, to drive to her job as editor of a national parenting magazine, because the freeway passed a black township where ANC recruiters often sparked fights and rioting among members of the Zulu and Xhosa tribes.

Deaths from the intertribal warfare that we called "faction fighting" were so common, especially after weekends of prolonged beer drinking, that Durban's white-controlled newspapers seldom bothered to report them unless their numbers were particularly significant—say fifty or more. It was no more than what we whites *expected* blacks to do.

The ten major black tribes and the two white tribes of South Africa had been at each other's throats for centuries. There was always violence of one sort or another in South Africa and not just the faction fighting among the rural blacks in the hills. The ruling white tribes were hopelessly split, too. White political meetings became roughhouses and often broke into physical fights between right-wing Afrikaners and more liberal English-speaking South Africans. Whites were even murdered by other whites, including secret police and government agents, for political reasons.

Afrikaans-speaking whites, who made up 60 percent of the white population of about four million, dominated everyone else. They ruled the country through their Nationalist Party with ruthless and passionate determination born of steadfast conviction of their moral virtue. They literally believed they were the chosen race, and their Dutch Reformed Church was kept busy feeding them with biblical references to prove it.

Most English-speaking whites, on the other hand, were much less bothered with politics or the morality of restraining black dissent by brute force. English-speakers in general concentrated on making money and enjoying the fruits of cheap black labor that brought them a standard of living equaled nowhere else on the continent. There were, of course, many brave English-speaking souls who publicly objected to the Nationalist government's inhuman policies. Among them were the dedicated women of the Black Sash movement, women whose job was to stand solitary on downtown street corners wearing their sashes, silently mourning the blacks' loss of freedom. They were spat on by Nationalist supporters, arrested by the police, and jailed, but they always came back. Their silent protest pricked the white public conscience, but while the good times lasted—while there were still servant "girls" to bring them tea in bed in the morning, and garden "boys" to cut the lawn and wash the Mercedes—the white public had no difficulty keeping its conscience at bay. And what little political protest did come from such sources as my home province of Natal, the country's main English-speaking province, only made the Afrikaners despise the English-speakers more.

The British and the Dutch had been fighting over South Africa since 1652, when Jan van Riebeeck set up a revictualling station in what is now known as Cape Town for the ships of the Dutch East India Company. Dutch settlers followed, as did French Huguenots fleeing religious persecution, and Germans. These whites stole land from the indigenous blacks and took them as slaves.

Then the British realized the strategic importance of South Africa's position at the foot of Africa, controlling the sea routes to the riches of India and the Far East. They, too, sent settlers and vied with the Dutch for possession. These squabbles came to a head in 1900, when the outnumbered commandos of the Boers (the Dutch-speaking inhabitants of South Africa) were defeated in a bitter war against the mighty British army. That war scored the psyche of the Dutch settlers so deeply that to this day many of their descendants, the Afrikaners, hate their English-speaking compatriots for no better reason than the fact that they speak English. Afrikaners still refer to English-speakers with contempt as *rooineks* (rednecks). The English-speakers, in turn, refer to the Afrikaners as hairybacks.

It was the overwhelming power wielded by the Afrikaners after their accession to power in 1948 that held together a country fractured into small warring tribes. That, and the country's enormous natural wealth. South Africa was a storehouse of gold, diamonds, coal, and precious metals such as uranium and chromium. Fertile soils, good weather, and advanced farming methods made South Africa the greatest producer of agricultural products on the continent. In many respects, South Africans were world leaders in science, industry, medicine, education, and sport. We journalists knew that government scientists even had the capability of making a nuclear bomb, though we were forbidden to write about it. In short, South Africa was so far ahead of other African countries that if it weren't for the preponderance of black and brown faces, you might think you were in Europe or America.

But if political dissent was suppressed inside the country, it was flourishing outside South Africa's borders. The African National Congress opened offices in Europe and in countries adjacent to South Africa. There they solicited financial aid and recruited volunteers to carry out terrorist missions to bring down the apartheid government. Countries in Europe and America, concerned about the oppression of blacks and the lack of human rights, began to impose sanctions and embargoes. But white South Africans made light of them. We started making our own planes and guns. We swapped military secrets with Israel, whose troubles with the Palestinians we equated with our own black problem. We became self-sufficient. In the face of an oil embargo we made oil from coal. We thumbed our noses at the world, cursed it for its hypocrisy, and clamped down even more harshly on protests in black townships. Only in the field of sport was there much grieving. White South Africans hurt badly when their national Springbok teams and Olympic athletes were banned from international competition.

Like many other white South Africans, June and I realized that the ANC— our fellow Xhosas and Zulus—had turned to terrorism because they had no other way of making their voices heard in South Africa. Blacks outnumbered whites six to one, but they had no vote in Parliament. They could not live or work where they wanted. They had no freedom of speech or demonstration, no way to air their grievances against the many evils of apartheid. Any dissent on their part was met with martial force and crushed immediately.

Because blacks were tolerated in large cities only to the extent of their usefulness to white employers, they had to obtain special permission to move from their home kraals in the countryside. To this end, each was issued with a passbook, or *dompas,* that had to be endorsed on a regular basis by government officials. In that way, whites retained complete control over the black labor pool, bringing it in to the cities when needed, and ordering it out when it wasn't. But the task of applying the law overwhelmed the white-controlled police force.

Passbook offenses were legion. Blacks were constantly found working in unauthorized areas, or sleeping overnight in white suburbs where they were not allowed. Blacks flooded the jails. Zulus and Xhosas, Vendas and Sothos, Ndebeles and Shangaans, considered it a badge of honor to have been jailed for a dompas offense. It was a rite of black manhood.

The heart of the Nationalist government's grand scheme for apartheid, or "separate development," was the homeland program. This involved giving blacks their own ministates within South Africa's borders. There they would be issued with their own passports and consequently deprived of South African citizenship, thus ensuring they could never vote the whites out of power in South Africa. But the twenty-four million blacks were to be shoveled into "countries" whose combined total area amounted to about 11 percent of the area of a pure-white South Africa.

The Nationalist government insisted the blacks would have "separate but equal" amenities and the freedom to govern themselves and work where they liked. But in reality the homelands were some of the most arid, undeveloped land in the country with few natural resources. There was little likelihood they could attract foreign investment, so their inhabitants would still have to rely on finding work in South Africa—now a foreign country from which they could be deported at the whim of any white official, even though they were born there.

This grand scheme took a long time to get under way. It involved the usual coercion and bribery of black leaders and the unexplained disappearance of opponents. Meanwhile, blacks everywhere were outraged.

That still left the problem of the country's two other racial groups, the mulattos or Coloureds, as they were known, and the Indians, both Hindu and Moslem. The Coloureds, most of whom lived in the Cape Province, numbered nearly three million. The Indians, mostly in Natal Province, numbered about one million. Until the black problem was solved, nobody had any idea where Coloureds and Indians would end up. But their numbers were relatively small. The four million whites did not feel threatened by them, as they did by blacks.

So when the ANC terrorist attacks began, it was really no surprise. The only question most of us had was when the full-scale black uprising would start. Years before, my old high-school geography teacher, Miss Pamela Hudd, had told us in class one day that she had asked her black maid if she would kill her when the revolution started. Miss Hudd wanted to know because she'd always understood that there was a surprising amount of goodwill between whites and Zulus in our part of South Africa, the English-speaking province of Natal. Other South Africans, especially the hard-line Afrikaners, regarded the Natal English as "very soft" when it came to dealing with black people. So Miss Hudd found it difficult to believe that the faithful Zulu maid who had lived in a small room at the bottom of her garden for twenty years would suddenly rise up one day and murder her.

"Would you *really* do that?" she asked.

"Oh no, missus," said the maid. "Never! The maid from next door will do it. And I will kill *her* missus."

It was a naive response, of course, and I have no idea why Miss Hudd found it necessary to share this information with us, but it does illustrate the swirling undercurrents of an iniquitous social system that appeared quite smooth on the surface for decades after the Afrikaner Nationalist government swept into power in 1948 with a grand plan of discrimination based on skin color.

When we saw the ANC graffiti in our yard we knew it was time to leave South Africa. It wasn't so much the unfairness of the threat—I had worked for antiapartheid newspapers all my life—as the realization that, when the revolution came, no black was going to pause to ask if you were a good white or a bad white.

It didn't matter that a surprisingly large number of whites had fought to right the wrongs of apartheid; it was apparent that in the chaotic end, everything would come down to black versus white. There would be neither time nor opportunity for cross-questioning. Already we were living in a state of constant apprehension, though outwardly we didn't show it emotionally. It was a siege mentality that had crept up on us so gradually that it seemed quite normal. We had grown accustomed to the armed guards who sprung up in the foyers of downtown buildings, who required you to sign a book and show photo identity before you could step into the elevator. It seemed quite natural for supermarkets to employ security personnel supplied with revolvers who insisted that you check all your parcels with them before you could enter the store proper.

Despite the security, ANC operatives had no difficulty finding targets. They planted bombs in white girls' schools, department stores, and mailboxes in busy downtown streets. Toward the end of our life in South Africa, June, who was editor of the women's pages of the *Daily News,* landed a plum job as editor of the country's largest parenting magazine, *Living and Loving.* One afternoon, as she sat in her office in the suburb of Mobeni, the building reverberated to the shock waves of an explosion about a mile away. A bomb had been detonated in a supermarket.

A little later, a woman colleague walked into her office. She was pale and shaking, obviously still in shock.

"I was there," she said.

June made her sit down.

"I heard the bang and I saw the shelves falling, toppling, one after another," she said. "They fell slowly, deliberately, and all the cans and boxes spread over the floor. But it was in slow motion. Very slow. It seemed to take forever. It was like time was standing still."

She didn't know if anyone had been killed. She thought several people had been injured. But she really didn't want to know. She had fled to her car and driven straight back to work.

At home, our windows were barred, as were those of all our friends' homes. Our doors were double-locked. I had built six-foot brick walls all around our house. It was all perfectly run-of-the-mill. When the graffiti appeared in our backyard, the next logical step was a gun. I hadn't ever owned a gun, but June and I sat down on the living room couch one night after the kids had gone to bed and talked about it.

"I think a shotgun is what we need," I said.

"Not a rifle? A rifle shoots farther."

"No, a shotgun. A rifle only shoots one person at a time. They'll be coming in a mob. A shotgun will get a whole bunch of them at once."

"What about an automatic rifle?" said June.

"Like the military? I don't know if you can buy those."

"Well, OK, a shotgun, then."

"Double-barreled," I said. "Or pump action."

"Where will you stand?"

"On the stoep upstairs. I can shoot down on them, and hide behind the pillars."

Neither of us could get to sleep that night. It was hot and humid and we lay on the double bed tossing listlessly. But it wasn't the weather that was keeping us awake.

"Did we just say we're going to shoot people?" June whispered. "Did we just say that?"

"Uh-huh."

"What were we thinking? You couldn't really shoot anybody, could you?"

"Maybe. If I had to."

"In cold blood?"

"I guess not," I conceded.

It was a turning point in our South African lives. If we weren't going to fight, we had to leave.

English-speaking whites like us were irrelevant in this struggle against apartheid because we had almost no political power. The Afrikaners ruled. We were in the minority. The liberal English speakers were, in any case, less politically active. We tended to overlook social injustice as long as we could continue to enjoy our drinks at sunset on the stoep or beside the swimming pool in one of the world's loveliest countries.

June and I concluded that the future of South Africa would be decided (either in direct talks or bloody conflict) by Afrikaans-speaking whites (the Nationalist Party government) and representatives of the black majority.

Neither of us could envisage a peaceful transition to black majority rule. We foresaw long and bloody clashes as whites sought to preserve their wealth and privilege, and blacks fought bitterly among themselves for the political power denied them during more than three hundred years of white domination. We didn't want to grow old in the chaos of a civil war, and we could see no future for our kids or any other white children in a black society rightfully taking over the social and economic privileges that whites had reserved for themselves for so many decades.

We had flirted for several years with the idea of leaving South Africa as the political situation worsened and the Nationalist government became more intractable, but we had good jobs and a lovely home.

For nearly twenty years I had written a humor column six times a week for two leading Durban newspapers, first for *The Mercury* and then for the *Daily News*. I had two hundred and fifty thousand readers daily, and I was syndicated in Johannesburg, Cape Town, Pretoria, and Bloemfontein. I was well known everywhere I went. And I knew people. I had been to the races with former Miss World, Penny Coelen, and I had made friends with Harold Evans, editor of the British *Sunday Times,* while we were peeing next to each other in the men's room of a Durban hotel.

As the editor of *Living and Loving,* June flew to Los Angeles to shoot fashion for kids, and she flew to Camden, Maine, to interview Dr. Benjamin Spock. We owned a large old colonial house opposite Mitchell Park, a fashionable part of the city, and we had a Zulu housemaid and an Indian gardener. We owned two cars, a seagoing yacht, and five cats. Life was easy. We might have been living in any civilized subtropical city, say somewhere in Florida or on the Gulf of Mexico. But as the years went by, and the terrorist attacks increased and came closer to the cities, we added bars to the windows. Brick walls took the place of our beautiful bougainvillea hedges. And whites started leaving the country.

In an attempt to stem the flight of well-educated whites to other countries, the government introduced draconian exchange-control regulations. Emigrants were severely restricted as to the amount of goods and money they could take out of the country, and any amount in excess of the limit had to be left behind in South Africa.

Looking back now, it's hard to believe that one little burst of graffiti from an ANC spray can could have galvanized us into action that would result in one of the biggest upheavals of our lives. But the time had come. Our youngest son, Kevin, would finish high school in eighteen months. Our two elder sons, Trent and Terry, had recently flown off to the United States, where they had to live for a certain number of years to avoid losing the American citizenship they had inherited from June. They also avoided two years of compulsory duty in the South African army. They were sorry to leave, but relieved that they wouldn't have to do the army service and use firearms against helpless black demonstrators calling for basic human rights. We saw them off with one-way tickets to the States, naively told them to find jobs, and wished them luck. They went to stay with a friend in Chicago. They did well. They found jobs, and settled in. June and I presumed we could do the same.

There was no doubt about it. The time for hedging was past. If we were ever going to break free from the insidious evil of apartheid, now was our chance.

The sadness that followed is indescribable. All I can say is that we decided with heavy hearts to leave the home, the country, and the friends we loved so dearly and to start a new life in the United States while we still were able to work and earn money.

At that time, the South African economy was in the doldrums. The management of the *Daily News* decided to reduce the number of staff and asked for volunteers to resign. They offered a small cash incentive.

June and I discussed it and decided that although it was eighteen months until Kevin finished high school and we could emigrate to America, this might be an appropriate time for me to quit my job.

News of my resignation was received with astonishment by my editor, Michael Green, and my colleagues. "This was meant for people nearing retirement age," Green explained. "Not you."

Nevertheless, once I assured them that I wasn't going to work for the rival *Mercury* newspaper, they accepted my resignation. I told them I was going to freelance, writing books and articles for magazines. My colleagues shook their heads and informed me I was mad. I told nobody that I was planning to leave South Africa, not even my widowed mother or my sister, Sandra. I wrote a painful last column, saying good-bye to my fans without explaining why I was quitting. It was our big secret. Whites who left South Africa at that time were treated almost as traitors. All able-bodied whites were supposed to stay and fight the blacks when the big revolution came. I didn't want my family to suffer eighteen months of insults and harassment, so June and I didn't breathe a word about emigration.

I settled down to work from home. I started the Newscraft Press Bureau, a one-man-band that supplied canned editorials and news fillers to little country newspapers all over South Africa. It earned me very little, but it gave me the spare time I needed to attend to the myriad details of emigration.

We were, in fact, lucky to have the option to emigrate. I had been married to an American for twenty-five years, so I was eligible for a U.S. immigration visa. We knew, of course, that emigration from South Africa was financial suicide. Besides the exchange-control regulations, international trade boycotts against South Africa had caused the local unit of currency, the rand, to fall to thirty-nine U.S. cents, when just a few years earlier it had actually been worth more than a dollar.

As a settling-in allowance, the South African Reserve Bank allowed emigrant families to take with them a maximum of 100,000 rands, or US $39,000. It was an effective deterrent.

Could we start all over again in America on $39,000, with no jobs to go to, and no way of knowing if we could earn a living? Especially at the age of fifty?

"We'll never know unless we try," said June.

So we tried.

It was my idea to go in our own boat. I reasoned that when we got to America, we'd have a home to live in and a mobile base from which to start looking for work. If we couldn't find work in one city, we'd simply sail on to another.

June wasn't as enthusiastic as I was about living aboard the boat once we'd got to America. She was born in Utah and grew up in Idaho, the eldest of seven children, and her father was a genuine cowboy. She said she would want to go West to see her family as soon as we arrived in the States. I heard her, but I didn't listen well enough. I thought I could persuade her, after she'd tried it for a bit, that living aboard a sailboat would be the most practical way to start a new life in a strange country.

Perhaps I was blinded by the fact that I'd wanted to live on a boat ever since I was a schoolboy. Durban was on the tradewind route for round-the-world sailors, and I had met many of the great names in ocean cruising. Sailing was my passion—when I wasn't laying bricks—and June sailed with me, but perhaps a little more reluctantly than I realized in those days. Nevertheless, she agreed to be my crew on a voyage to America, along with seventeen-year-old Kevin.

We sold our house, again to the surprise of our friends and family, and bid tearful farewells to our five cats. We sold our twenty-eight-foot racing sailboat and bought a slightly bigger one. She was a sturdy, five-year-old cruiser, a Performance 31 sloop, designed by the Cape Town naval architect Angelo Lavranos. She was just over thirty feet in length and weighed a little more than five and a half tons. She was not very big.

Two retired Swedish sea captains living in Durban had originally bought her as a bare hull. They had finished her off strongly but simply down below. They had planned to cruise north in the Indian Ocean, but on their first voyage they had run into a bad storm. One of them was washed overboard and had a hard time getting back, so they returned to Durban and sold the boat.

When I first looked her over she was owned by Hughie Wannenburg. She lay on a mooring on palm-fringed Durban Bay, near the Point Yacht Club, and Wannenburg was busy trying to add a little comfort to her Spartan accommodation. He and his large Zulu handyman were squeezed into the forecabin with sheets of plywood, lengths of mahogany stringers, tools, pots, and paintbrushes. On the cabin sole, stamped with a smudged footprint, lay a ruled page from a notebook with a long handwritten list of jobs still to be done.

I asked Wannenburg if he would sell her to me. He brushed a sleeve across his sweaty brow. "If I sell her to you, can I stop working now?"

I nodded, and the deal was done.

Like most of the boats I've bought in my life, she hadn't actually been for sale. My method of buying is to look for a boat I really like, and then to keep nagging the owner to sell her to me. Wannenburg had capitulated with surprising speed, but I found out later that he actually had his eye on another, bigger boat. I hadn't done any of the usual things boat buyers do. I had never sailed this boat, never even heard her engine run, never seen the sails, and never had her surveyed. When you've been around boats for a while, you develop a feel for a particular craft. A quick glance around the deck will yield a dozen clues to her strength and the way she's been sailed and maintained. A little crack in the fiberglass gelcoat near a chainplate, or a slight bump in the otherwise fair curve of a sheerline, are clear messages for those who can read the signs. I had looked over her deck quite thoroughly, and this boat had a good solid feel about her.

Wannenburg and I drew up our own purchase agreement and bill of sale. I gave him a deposit but I couldn't pay him the full price for a month because the money was on thirty-day call at my bank. He, being a cautious businessman, refused to let us sail the boat until we owned it outright. So, for a whole month we sat on the boat at moorings in our spare time, patted her decks, and dreamed of how she'd sail.

We changed her name from *Our Way* to *Freelance* and spent the next few months fitting her out for a long voyage. We applied for, and received, official permission from the South African Reserve Bank to take her out of the country; but it meant that her value—85,000 rands—was deducted from the 100,000 rand settling-in allowance. Thus, we'd arrive in America with a thirty-one-foot boat and 15,000 rands (US $5,800), less whatever we might spend during the six-month voyage.

Now, I've always had great respect for the law. I don't cheat on income tax and I even left a note once when I backed into a parked car. But something about the South African government's arrogant exchange-control regulations got my back up.

Any funds an emigrant possessed in excess of 100,000 rands had to be handed over to a commercial bank that placed the money in a "blocked" account. It meant the money could be spent only in South Africa and was in effect trapped in the country forever.

The more I thought about it, the more it irked me. I had money left over from the sale of our house, in excess of the 100,000 rand allowance. It amounted to about $15,000 in American money. I figured it would give Kevin a good start in college in America, where we'd have to pay heavy out-of-state tuition fees for the first year. It was, in any case, my hard-earned and heavily taxed money.

Furthermore, the South African government had deducted hefty tax and social security payments from June's paychecks, and mine, for a combined total of well over forty years. Neither of us would get a penny of that back in the form of a pension or any other benefit now. All that money was forfeited.

So for eighteen months after we'd made the decision to emigrate, I bought one-ounce gold coins, Krugerrands, in small quantities. They cost an average of $375 each. In the end I had forty of them in little plastic coin packets and no idea what to do with them. It was illegal to smuggle them out of South Africa and it was illegal to import them into the United States because of trade sanctions against South Africa.

I needed two miracles. One to get them out of the country and another to turn them into dollars that could legally be taken into the States. In the meantime I kept them hidden, and told nobody about them except June.

* * *

As emigration day drew nearer, we cautiously began revealing our plans to my family and our closest friends. We didn't say much. It was just too emotional a subject. The word got around, despite our precautions. People we didn't know particularly well just waved good-bye and smiled. They knew, and we knew, we wouldn't see each other again.

The weeks leading up to our departure from Durban were some of the most stressful I've ever experienced. Saying good-bye to lifelong friends in a city where you're well known after eighteen years of writing a daily newspaper column is not easy. Our good-byes were complicated by suggestions that we were deserters taking the easy way out of South Africa's troubles—taking the "chicken run" they called it. "Decent" white folk didn't run like chickens. They were supposed to stand up like fighting cocks.

The truth was that the great majority of white South Africans had no hope of emigrating, even if they wanted to. They were stuck there, no matter what happened. Although you could gain entry to countries such as Canada, Australia, New Zealand, and (most sought-after of all) the United States, it wasn't easy unless you were highly educated, your skills were in demand, and you had a great deal of money. We were among the privileged few.

As usual, there were scores of things to do to get the ship ready for a major cruise and scores more to get me ready. June and Kevin, who would be sailing with me, were already American citizens, of course, but I had a British passport. I was born in Plymouth, England, a stone's throw from the Mayflower Steps, and although I'd lived in South Africa from age thirteen, I'd never taken out South African citizenship. As far as the Afrikaners were concerned, I was a *vreemdeling*, an alien, or a "salty prick" with one foot in South Africa, the other in England.

I had to go to the U.S. consulate, four hundred miles away in Johannesburg, to pick up an immigration visa. I caught the overnight bus and arrived there in the morning, only to discover that Americans, too, suffer from bureaucratic inefficiency. They hadn't informed me about some of the documents I'd need for a visa application. I booked into a nearby hotel, used my room as an office, and started organizing color portraits, medical examinations, X-rays, cash from Durban, and various other bits and pieces.

As a journalist, I understood the South African system well. Almost anything was possible if you were white and willing to pay the price. After many telephone calls and taxi rides in a city I hardly knew, I was able to get everything done—color pictures, chest X-rays, the lot—in a matter of four hours, albeit at exorbitant expense. I reported back to the U.S. consulate that afternoon and a young American woman issued my visa.

There was just one problem, I quickly discovered. It was valid only for three months. It would be outdated by the time we got to the States. I mentioned this to the young woman and she said she couldn't help me; it was the law. Two of her colleagues joined the discussion but every consular official I spoke to was adamant: there was no way an immigration visa could be extended.

I caught the bus back to Durban, half-elated and half-dismayed. I wrote to the U.S. consulate, pointing out that the famous American circumnavigator, Captain Joshua Slocum, the first man to sail alone around the world, had taken six months over the passage I was contemplating, and he didn't hang about.

I kept at it, and eventually the matter got attention in Washington, D.C. The U.S. State Department sent instructions for a letter to be attached to my visa. It was addressed to immigration officials in Boston, our planned port of arrival in the States, and it said my visa should be regarded as valid when I arrived, provided I had made the voyage with reasonable dispatch. Such bureaucratic flexibility was almost unheard of in South Africa. I was impressed.

At this time, I was teaching myself the art of celestial navigation for the second time. I hadn't handled a sextant for sixteen years, since I was the navigator on a thirty-three-footer racing from Cape Town to Rio de Janeiro. I knew it would take some practice to get back into the swing because it is no easy matter to take an accurate sextant sight from a small boat being tossed around in waves at sea.

But another matter caused me even more concern: neither June nor Kevin had ever been to sea overnight on a yacht before. Both were experienced dinghy sailors. Kevin was an expert singlehander and June had been my crew when we

won the South African National Championships in our eleven-foot Mirror
dinghy in 1972. But neither had any deep-sea experience, apart from day-sails
off Durban.

June asked several times why we didn't take a practice run up the coast to the
nearest port, Richards Bay, eighty miles away, but I always stalled. I was afraid
that if we ran into rough weather she and Kevin would change their minds about
sailing to America with me. My plan, therefore, was virtually to kidnap them and
set sail straight for Cape Town, by which time they'd be committed. But the
eight hundred nautical miles of hostile coast between Durban and Cape Town is
known for good reason as the Cape of Storms, and all three of us were prone to
bad bouts of seasickness. Even during day-sails off Durban, where the Indian
Ocean often turns mean, we would turn green and hang over the rail. The last
time I sailed from Durban to Cape Town I was sick for six days out of nine.

Luckily for all of us, June had discovered an antiseasickness drug called
Scopolamine during a vacation visit to the United States, and brought back
enough for a small army. But the patches behind our ears gave us all side effects.
June got a headache. I got blurred vision and a dry mouth, and Kevin got depressed. Nevertheless, we all agreed the side effects were preferable to seasickness.

The stress of departure and the responsibilities of getting my boat and my
family to America I had inherited, began to work on me. For the first time in
my life I suffered from nightmares. The theme was always the same—an
untested crew on an untested boat with an untested skipper. I had some deep-
sea experience, but always as crew, never as skipper. I had never been in full
charge of a boat from port to port. I dreamed time and time again that we were
all seasick and incapable, drifting in the shipping lane around the Cape, about
to be run down by a ship and sunk. Night after night I woke up in bed rigid and
soaked with sweat, my heart pounding madly.

So I planned a route from Durban to Cape Town that would take us straight
out to sea for fifty miles and then parallel to the coast. That would keep us away
from the shipping routes, which tended to hug the coast. I drew the course on
the chart in pencil, and made sure June and Kevin knew about it and understood
why it was necessary. If we all got sick, we would simply drift in comparative

safety outside the shipping lanes until someone got well enough to handle the boat again.

As it happened, the Scopolamine June brought back from America was a lifesaver. We didn't need to implement such a melodramatic plan after all. But we didn't know that then, while I was having nightmares.

A month or so before our departure date, we moved aboard *Freelance* permanently and leased a slip for her at the floating marina dock in front of Point Yacht Club. A few days later, we were woken in the early dawn by the noise of a great fire crackling downtown. It was in a street where our house furniture had been taken to be auctioned. "Wouldn't it be funny . . . ?" I said to June.

It wasn't funny. I pulled on some clothes and hurried across the Esplanade to the auction house in downtown Gardiner Street. With lights flashing and sirens screaming, fire engines were converging on the thick black column of smoke and leaping flames. A police cordon stopped me from getting close, but I could see enough. The building was ablaze from top to bottom. Our furniture had indeed been destroyed in the conflagration.

We learned later that day that the auction house accepted no responsibility. They hadn't insured our furniture, and we hadn't thought to insure it independently. Too bad. We had planned to use the proceeds to buy yachting gear such as a refrigerator, a pressure-water shower, and other luxuries that would add to *Freelance's* value when we got to America. I wondered for a moment if the ANC had had anything to do with the fire, but decided that was too fanciful. All the same, it seemed as though we were being tested. If this was the "chicken run," what was a difficult emigration like?

As our sailing date grew closer, *Freelance's* engine transmission failed in dramatic fashion. A group of friends with boats had been discussing the difficulty of maneuvering their vessels in the close confines of the marina. I foolishly insisted it was quite easy if you knew what you were doing, and offered to demonstrate how to slide a boat bodily sideways into her berth.

Accordingly, I took *Freelance* out under power and circled back to her slip, where four of five of them were waiting expectantly. *Freelance* has a long keel, and does not turn quickly, so my plan was to come in quite fast and initiate the turn that would take her into her berth. We all knew that she wouldn't have sufficient space to complete the turn before she crashed into the floating concrete pier, but I knew that if I slammed her into astern gear after she had started her turn, and gave the engine full power, she would tighten the turn, slow down, and slide gracefully sideways into the space alongside the finger pier.

All went well until the crucial moment when I slammed her into reverse. I revved up the engine, and nothing happened. I tried astern gear again immediately, and still nothing happened. She wouldn't go into reverse. Meanwhile we were approaching the pier almost bows-on at five knots. I could see the faces of my audience now, and their eyes were wide open with alarm. They knew that a collision was inevitable.

"Just push off the bow!" I screamed.

Four hefty men sprang forward and shoved our bow pulpit sideways as we came boring in, and by a miracle she swung around and shot past them, missing the pier by inches and careering out into the fairway. I came creeping back five minutes later and tried to explain what had happened to the gearbox, but those who weren't wiping tears of laughter from their eyes were expressing serious skepticism about my boat-handling abilities.

It was a Hurth gearbox, a normally reliable German make that worked off our auxiliary engine, a twelve-horsepower BMW diesel, but after several abortive attempts, the local agents announced that it couldn't be fixed. All they could recommend was that they should import some expensive spare parts from Germany. But it had already cost me more than $300 to find out they couldn't fix it, and I just couldn't afford to have parts airfreighted from Germany.

I was relating my woes to friends in Charlie's Bar, in Point Yacht Club, when someone mentioned the name of a gearbox mechanic who worked on fishing boats at Maydon Wharf. He was reputedly a Scottish engineer with magic hands.

"But whatever you do, don't leave the gearbox with him," I was warned. "Make sure he fixes it there and then while you watch."

I realized why when I tracked him down and found his workshop walls lined with gearboxes that had been torn apart and never put together again. Untidy piles of gears, springs, shims, nuts, bolts, and casings lay on dirty benches.

To my untrained eye it appeared impossible that this huge jumble of parts could ever be resolved into separate and complete gearboxes.

He was a taciturn man, not easy to speak to. I showed him my transmission, a gray-painted box the size and shape of a small loaf of bread.

"It won't go into reverse," I explained.

He glanced at it and nodded.

"I was hoping to leave for America next week," I said.

"Och, aye," he said, wiping his hands on overalls that could only have made them dirtier.

"Could you take a look at it for me?"

He nodded. "Just leave it on the bench."

The alarm bells went off in my head. "I noticed an Atomic 4 engine outside," I said, desperate to keep him talking until I could entreat him to open up my gearbox. Atomic 4s were American engines, quite rare in Durban. "Where did it come from?" I asked.

"Found it at the bottom of the bay," he said.

"What gearbox did it have?"

"None that I know of."

Damn. My mind went into overdrive.

"Would this Hurth fit an Atomic 4, as a matter of interest?" I asked.

"Aye, I dare say it could be made to fit," he said, taking it from me and squinting at it through the lower half of his grubby bifocals. "What did you say is wrong with it?"

"Reverse gear. The agents say it can't be fixed."

That got him. His eyes gleamed. "Agents say a lot of things," he said. "Let's have a quick look."

He cleared a space on the bench by brushing everything aside with his sleeve, and opened the gearbox. He put his hands inside and let his callused fingers run all over the fine machinery. He pushed and pummeled it, as a doctor might a sick patient. Then he started to take it apart. He was plainly concentrating on the major faults, and not at all concerned about the petty details. Small springs and washers started popping out and falling on the floor or landing among the mess of parts on the bench. I leaped upon them and rescued all I could find, putting them carefully together in the cleared space.

"Just needs a couple of shims," he announced eventually. "Somebody put it together wrong. Agents, I would'na doubt."

His magic fingers fitted the shims, rearranged everything else, and closed the box. He charged me thirty dollars for his time and nothing for the shims. Fifteen minutes later I was on my way back to *Freelance* with the repaired gearbox. So once again we had astern gear and would no longer run into jetties at five knots. Now we were ready to sail to America.

I went to say good-bye to my widowed mother in her stark room at the Natal Settlers' Memorial Home, on the cool leafy slopes of the Berea. She was pinched and frail and very brave.

"Well, good-bye, John," she said, holding out her hand and trying to smile.

I swept her to me and hugged her tight and we both burst into sobs.

"When will I see you again?" she asked.

"I don't know," I said. "I'll write."

"Yes," she said, "that would be nice."

I walked out to the car, and the nurse at the reception desk smiled and asked how I was doing, but I couldn't talk, and hurried past her.

I said good-bye to my sister Sandra, her husband Robin, and her daughter Sharon. I forbade them to come down to the marina to say good-bye. I couldn't have coped with tearful dockside farewells. We said good-bye, too, to our dearest friends and explained that we couldn't set an hour for our departure, or even a day. It all depended on the weather. We needed to wait until one of the lows spinning off the great storm tracks in the Southern Ocean had passed us, and a northeasterly wind had filled in.

Some of our dearest friends, like Dave and Penny Valentine, colleagues from the *Daily News,* used to come secretly to the yacht club every day to check whether we were still in our berth. I knew because I saw Dave early one morning. We both turned and looked away, each pretending not to notice the other. *Partir, c'est mourir un peu,* the French say. To part is to die a little. How true that is.

2

ADVENTURE BY DEFAULT

Like many famous voyagers had done before us, we waited impatiently in our berth for a favorable wind. As a teenager in Durban I had met and made friends with many of the early circumnavigators. There were comparatively few of them in the 1950s, and their daring voyages were still making newspaper headlines wherever they went.

I sat on their boats, happily feeling the hot subtropical sun burning my bare arms and legs, and letting the evocative smells of tarred hemp, red lead, and linseed oil wash over me. I listened, entranced, to the tales of their adventures, and I began for the first time to dream of crossing an ocean under sail in my own boat.

For anyone sailing around the world in a small boat, Durban is a natural port of call on the westbound tradewind route. It's also a wonderful introduction to the continent of Africa. It's a strikingly beautiful city of 2.5 million people, filled with the sweet scents and blazing color of the subtropics. I say *strikingly*, because some cities evince a pale, soft beauty, like a delicate watercolor painting; but Durban is not one of those. Durban hits you right between the eyes with a sudden rush of colors, forms, and fragrances.

Lustrous blooms of the frangipani tree flourish there and vivid bougainvillea spill over burnt-brick garden walls. In this gardeners' paradise, rustling palm trees vie for elbow room with the bird-of-paradise flower, hibiscus, and wild bananas. Clusters of delicate mauve jacaranda blossoms carpet the neighborhood sidewalks, and on the horizon the araucarias, the tropical conifers, stand out like tall Christmas trees on the cool breezy hills of the Berea.

This is the melting pot of South Africa, filled with vibrant people, Zulus and Xhosas, Indians and Coloureds, Afrikaners and English-speaking whites, talking in many different tongues. Mostly, they use English and Zulu, but you'll also hear Xhosa and Afrikaans, as well as the Indian languages of Tamil, Hindi, Telegu, and Urdu.

The Indians were brought here more than a century ago as indentured labor to work as coolies in the rolling sugarcane fields on the coast a few miles north of Durban, and now outnumber the whites two to one. The ratio of blacks—the Zulus and Xhosas—to whites is six to one or more, but the race South Africans call "Coloureds," the mixed-race mulattoes, numbers only one-fifth of the white population.

In Durban's casual downtown markets, strewn between Muslim mosques, Hindu temples, Christian chapels, churches, and a cathedral, the Far East blends with Africa. There are aromas to make your nose curl. Tables piled high with mounds of exotic, brightly colored powders and pungent spices (imported from the Orient to make curry and breyani) jostle cheek-by-jowl with the stands of native witch doctors selling traditional medicines made from tree bark, roots from the veld, and parts of animals that most people don't like to discuss.

Downtown, modern air-conditioned skyscrapers and shopping malls cram densely into the desirable area around Durban Bay, and high-rise, high-class hotels line the Marine Parade that borders the rolling white surf of the warm blue Indian Ocean. For mile after mile, golden beaches spread north and south of Durban. The thunder of the surf never stops, for the swells are built up as the wind travels unhindered over the thousands of miles of open sea between Durban and Australia. In the world of international surfing, Durban is well known.

Durban Bay, which ships enter through a long narrow harbor mouth, is one of the best natural harbors in the whole of Africa, and certainly the busiest in terms of cargo handled. It is five miles long, by two across, and while much of it is taken up with sandbanks, it still provides good sailing waters for the local yacht clubs, which date from the 1890s.

As you travel inland from Durban, the landscape rises in a series of hills and plateaux, becoming drier and more continental in climate until, after about one hundred miles, you find yourself in the foothills of one of Africa's great mountain ranges. The early Dutch settlers, the Voortrekkers, who had to find a way through it for their oxwagons, called it the Drakensberg, or Dragon's Mountain.

It is actually an escarpment, for the land on the far side of the ten thousand-foot mountains is a plateau that leads to the famous gold-bearing reefs of the Witwatersrand, the ridge of white waters, whose commercial and industrial center is Johannesburg, South Africa's biggest city. When I was a press photographer working for *The Mercury*, there were winter days when, flying over Durban at nine thousand feet in a light aircraft, I could see clear across the province of Natal from the beaches to the 'Berg, from a curtain of surf to a blanket of snow.

But many years before that, when I was still a schoolkid, it was Durban Bay that attracted me. In my spare time, I explored every inch of Durban's dockland on my bike. These were the most efficient docks on the whole continent, so that cargoes for places as far away as the Belgian Congo passed through Durban. There never seemed to be fewer than twenty or thirty cargo ships loading or unloading between Point Road, where all the sailors' dives and whorehouses were, and the dry dock at Congella. Each ship was romantic and fascinating to me, but none more so than the lavender-colored Union-Castle passenger liners, the mailboats, that called once a week on a regular run from Southampton, England.

Durban Bay was also the home of Point Yacht Club. It occupied a prime site on the water's edge a few blocks from the city center, but it had none of the standoffishness that has come to be associated with modern yacht clubs. This was a working man's club, and the members and flag officers were largely men who had fought the Germans in the desert of North Africa in World War II. They had no false pretensions or delusions of grandeur. They just wanted a place that would enable them to build, repair, and race small sailboats, a place where they could have a shower, a meal, and a drink with friends afterward.

They mostly sailed dinghies, flat-bottomed scows capable of twenty knots, and hard-chined sharpies that could slice to windward through a chop like a knife through butter. They built fourteen-foot Sprogs in the club's workshop and little Dabchicks for their kids to learn on. Later, the current Olympic classes started appearing, too: the singlehanded Finn, and the superb two-man nineteen-footer, the *Flying Dutchman.*

I watched all this from the fringes at first, riding down to the club every Saturday and Sunday to watch the dinghies being launched, and the keelboats trying out their racing sails on the chain moorings just off the club. My family was poor, so we didn't have a boat, and I had no expectations of being invited to join the club or to go for a sail. But people must have got used to my hanging around. One Sunday the owner of a Royal Cape One-Design yacht, a twenty-five-foot wooden keeler called *Lapwing,* saw me watching him get the boat ready.

"Want to come for a sail?" he shouted. And then, as a curious afterthought: "Do you like egg-and-onion sandwiches?"

I didn't know about the sandwiches, but I yelled back "Yes, please," parked my bike, and scrambled aboard. I sailed with Alan Byrd many times after that, and we always had egg-and-onion sandwiches for lunch. His housemaid made them, he told me, and he couldn't get her stopped.

He introduced me to other members of Point Yacht Club, including a fellow schoolmate, David Cox, who was to become a lifelong friend. I joined the club as a junior member and discovered a passion for boats and sailing that has absorbed me and delighted me to this day.

It was on Durban Bay, flying the Point Yacht Club burgee, that I lost my first command under sail. I was fifteen then, and the boat was probably a lot older, a rickety fourteen-foot wooden catboat of an Olympic singlehanded class from years gone by. Nobody at the club seemed to know who owned her, and nobody seemed to care, so I sailed her to death. She leaked like a sieve, even though I had plastered the inside with rubber paint.

One day while I was sailing her alone on Durban Bay, an extra-hard gust of wind from astern tilted her bow down. The bilge water rushed forward, pushing her bow completely under water. She dived down, and sank. The waterlogged wood was no match for the heavy metal centerboard plate. Luckily, the shore wasn't far away. I swam to a thin strip of beach in front of a mangrove swamp on Salisbury Island. I don't remember now how long I waited, but eventually a small fishing boat passed by and I waved and yelled until they saw me and took me back across Durban Bay. Nobody at Point Yacht Club ever asked where that old boat had gone and I never volunteered any information.

This was the club that greeted many of the great long-distance sailors of the post–World War II era and introduced them to Africa after a tedious voyage across the fitful Indian Ocean. Their names were later to become famous in the annals of world cruising, but they were mostly unknown then.

Jack Polson and his wife, Holly, owners of a Tahiti ketch called *Jaho,* were the honorary port officers in Durban for the Little Ship Club, and used to row out to each new arrival with a gift basket consisting of a loaf of fresh bread, butter, eggs, milk, and fresh fruit. Every round-the-world sailor who arrived in Durban were made honorary members of Point Yacht Club, which entitled them to free use of the club's showers and lockers, the dining room and bar, the reading room, and the long jetty against which they could lean their boats while they repainted the bottoms with antifouling paint.

The Durban newspapers invariably interviewed these intrepid adventurers and published their pictures and stories. They made news then, when so few people dared to cross oceans in small boats of thirty-five feet or less.

As a teenager, I fell under the spell of these sailors, especially the singlehanders. They represented the glamour of bluewater voyaging, the tropic seas, and exciting islands with waving palm trees and dusky beauties in grass skirts. They represented freedom, and escape from authority and regimentation of everyday life—what Henry David Thoreau called the life of "quiet desperation," and what the South African sailor and author Frank Wightman referred to so aptly as the "long littleness of life." And they represented the intense satisfaction of going where you please, when you please, while carrying with you your own snug little home and your most treasured possessions.

* * *

My hero then was Marcel Bardiaux, a brash, daring Frenchman in his thirties, who had sailed his home-built thirty-foot cutter, *Les Quatre Vents,* around Cape Horn the wrong way—against the prevailing wind and current—in the middle of the Antarctic winter. He was tough as nails, a superb seaman, and physically the fittest man I had ever seen. He thought nothing of diving in freezing cold water to pick up his ninety-pound anchor and walk it along the sea bottom to find a more secure holding ground. He stayed on watch for sixty hours at a time. He pushed his boat and himself to limits that had never been reached before. I doubt that they have ever been equaled since.

He capsized twice near Cape Horn in subzero weather, and almost lost his boat on rocks and reefs dozens of times during his voyage around the world. The adventures and mishaps he relates in his book, *The Four Winds of Adventure,* make all other small-boat voyages seem tame by comparison. Bligh, Shackleton, and even Smeeton take second place to Bardiaux. But strangely enough, although he was fêted and revered in France and South America, he was largely unknown in the English-speaking world, and has remained so to this day.

He spoke little English, and I was too shy to try out my schoolboy French on so exalted a character, so we never spoke, but I watched him at work on his boat whenever I could, and wondered whether some day I would have a boat of my own like his sleek white cutter.

Ironically, another French singlehander I met in Durban, Bernard Moitessier, later became the world's darling when he dropped out of the first nonstop single-handed race around the world while he was leading by a great margin—for the sake of his soul, he said—and carried on many thousands of miles more to Tahiti.

Contrary to popular opinion, Moitessier was a lousy sailor in some ways. He lost his first and second boats, the two named *Marie-Thérèse,* on reefs because he fell asleep, and he lost his third boat, the famous *Joshua,* because he anchored in the wrong place at the wrong time.

He was, nevertheless, a carefree, charming character, well built and deeply tanned, with the profile of a Greek god. He was to become one of the most highly respected singlehanded sailors in the world, and a national hero in France, but when he arrived in Durban he was a maritime hippie, or a vagabond as he preferred to call himself. He was broke, having spent all his money on having his wooden twenty-eight-foot sloop *Marie-Thérèse II* built on the Indian Ocean island of Mauritius. She was shoddily built of poor materials, and had practically no accommodations to speak of. I was amazed to find that most of her interior was taken up with one enormous bed stretching from front to back and side to side of the cabin. It was apparently a cheap and easy way to finish her off.

My friend Ray Cruickshank, an expert shipwright who had built his own seagoing twenty-four-foot sloop, found Moitessier a well-paying carpenter's job at Louw and Halvorsen's, one of the local boatyards. Cruickshank was under the impression, which he conveyed to the foreman, that Moitessier had built his own boat. They soon found out that, no matter what else he might be, the easygoing, smiling Frenchman was certainly no shipwright or carpenter. But they covered up for him, as people will do when they see another daring to achieve the things they only dream about, and set him to making wooden cargo partitions on big ships—hard work, but not fancy.

Then they discovered that he was an excellent swimmer, and had invented (through necessity) a method of stopping leaks in wooden planking by caulking the seams under water. So they used him to repair leaks on fishing boats that would otherwise have had to be pulled out of the water in cradles on a marine railway. Moitessier saved them time and money that way, for the railway was always busy and expensive to use. At the end of six months, Moitessier had saved enough money to continue his voyage to Cape Town.

Point Yacht Club was just one stop of many for the round-the-worlders, but each one I met made me more interested in the sea and voyaging. Nevertheless I knew, even in my teens, that I didn't have the confidence of Bardiaux and Jean Gau, or the devil-may-care attitude of Moitessier. I was a worrier by nature and timid with it. I was secretly scared by the physical challenges of handling a boat at sea. I had not the heart for big adventures. Yet sometimes, in the still hours of the night, I would wake up dreaming of crossing an ocean in a boat under sail.

Jean Gau, a French-born American in his sixties, arrived in a thirty-foot Tahiti ketch called *Atom* on a solo circumnavigation. He thrived on long passages, and had sailed for eighty days nonstop from the Cocos Islands in the Indian Ocean. He was wiry, grizzled, and crew-cut, and his aquiline profile was deeply tanned. He was in a hurry to get back to the United States, he said, because they were keeping open for him his old job as a chef at the Waldorf Astoria in New York. But he had been delayed in Tahiti, where dusky young maidens had swum out to his anchored boat and offered their services.

"They would do anything," he marveled, "anything. Even for an old man like me. I knew it was time to go, but I just couldn't tear myself away."

In Durban Bay he leaped overboard from his moored boat and showed me how to survive in the water while awaiting rescue by bobbing up and down in a natural rhythm that coincided with drawing breath. He swore you could do it in your sleep if you had to.

Gau was a gifted artist, and painted on his travels. He carried several completed oils on board, and would willingly show them to visitors, setting them out in his small cockpit and happily explaining their creation with much animated conversation and waving of arms.

Another famous cruising couple who called at Durban were Eric and Susan Hiscock, a British couple, in their wooden thirty-footer, *Wanderer III*. They were quite the opposite of the laid-back Moitessier and the intrepid Bardiaux. They were well-mannered and almost invisible. They were perfect guests, and never complained. They hated to make waves. They were self-sufficient to a fault and always considerate of other people's feelings. They had so many good qualities and so few shortcomings that one almost felt guilty to be in their company.

Eric Hiscock had the pinkish look of a white albino and his eyesight was not too good. Susan, a strong-boned woman, was capable of doing all the heavy work on board, and she had excellent eyesight. They were quite plainly devoted to each other. Eric Hiscock, in fact, disclosed in an article in a yachting magazine that he used to tiptoe below to place a special cover over a porthole when his wife was sleeping during the afternoon at sea, to prevent the sunbeams from shining in her eyes.

Wanderer III was impeccable, of course, a pretty little heavy-displacement sloop, and they were so proud of her that they would sometimes heave to at sea before entering a port and touch up her paintwork so she could arrive looking her best. Both the Hiscocks were superb sailors, acknowledged experts in the English-speaking world and authors of acclaimed books, but their seamanship was based on caution. Their brand of navigation avoided, as far as is possible, the near-disasters and brushes with death that made the voyages of Moitessier and Bardiaux so newsworthy. Whereas Bardiaux went to sea to see the land, and called at as many ports as he could, the Hiscocks went to sea to get away from land, for that was where the gravest danger lurked. It's fair to say, however, that caution is a comparative word in this respect. No really cautious person would willingly cross an ocean in a thirty-foot sailboat. All the early circumnavigators were practicing extreme sports long before the term was invented.

These and other long-distance voyagers such as Tom Steele in *Adios* and John Guzzwell, in his tiny twenty-foot yawl *Trekka,* were the background to my life as a teenager and young man but it was to be many years before I found the guts to follow them to sea in my own boat.

Perhaps guts is the wrong word, though. There was no conscious act of bravery on my part that finally got us aboard *Freelance,* ready and provisioned for a long deep-sea voyage. It was like the end of a long, slippery slope that I had been sliding down for decades—not consciously wishing to reach the logical conclusion, but not resisting it either. This was really adventure by default. Nevertheless, *Freelance* was as ready as a boat ever can be, and her crew were about to find out whether they were ready or not.

There was one subject June and I didn't like to speak about, although it occupied our thoughts a lot of the time, and that was our planned passage down the Wild Coast. The waters everywhere between Durban and Cape Town have an evil reputation for gales and freak waves, but the one hundred fifty miles of the Wild Coast had the worst record of all, and it began just one hundred miles south of Durban. We would be there in a day.

We knew that most yachts going that way managed to survive the Wild Coast. But we also knew of small yachts and even large ships that had been lost there. It was the graveyard of hundreds of people. I could only hope that my untried skills were great enough to avoid a similar fate. June could only hope that her faith in my book-learned seamanship was justified. And Kevin—well, nobody could tell what Kevin was hoping. He was seventeen, fresh out of boarding school, and kept his thoughts pretty much to himself.

Freak waves in the open ocean, and their counterparts, freak troughs, or holes in the sea, are not really freak at all. They are the result of certain physical effects, and their rate of occurrence can be calculated mathematically. Sea systems are composed of many different wave trains, each with its own speed and height. In layman's terms, freak waves happen when one wave rides on another's back, or perhaps coincidentally and momentarily on the backs of two or more waves. It's no old wives' tale that every fifth or seventh wave is bigger than the rest.

Dr. Laurence Draper, a marine physicist at the British Institute of Oceanographic Sciences, says 1 wave in 23 is over twice the height of the average wave. One in 1,175 is more than three times the average height. One in 300,000 exceeds four times the average height. And there are equal chances, he adds, that an unusually low trough will occur.

The average height of an ocean wave is nine feet, and the biggest waves recorded in storms are about sixty feet high on average, according to the Institute of Oceanographic Sciences. But when a strong wind blows against a fast current, waves may become much higher, steeper, and closer together. It's the effect you get when you push a rug from one end and it rears up into a series of sharp folds.

A current is an invisible river in the sea, and one of the fastest currents in the world runs down the southeast coast of South Africa for hundreds of miles. It's known as the Mozambique Current to the north of Durban, and the Agulhas Current to the south. It runs consistently at three or four knots until it spreads out, slows down, and changes direction over the Agulhas Banks, a huge shallow area south of Cape Agulhas, the southernmost tip of Africa.

When a gale-force wind blows against this current, the sea becomes a true maelstrom of leaping, vertical-walled waves whose unstable tops plunge as powerful foaming breakers. It's one of the most dangerous sea states imaginable for ships and boats of all sizes. And off the Wild Coast, southwesterly gales that have spun off the Roaring Forties at the bottom of Africa frequently come raging up the coast against the current. They are South Africa's equivalent of the infamous "Northers" that create havoc off the East Coast of the United States when they blow against the Gulf Stream.

In Durban, we knew these southwesters as "busters" because of the suddenness of their arrival. When we were getting *Freelance* ready for sea, I thought about the Wild Coast every time a buster came through and the palm trees along the Esplanade touched their toes. I cringed at the thought of what might happen if we were caught in a buster off the Wild Coast.

In July 1909, the passenger liner *Waratah* disappeared without trace off the Wild Coast. She was the newly built flagship of Lund's Blue Anchor Line, a vessel of 9,339 tons, and declared "unsinkable" because of the eight watertight compartments built into her hull. The *Waratah* was on the return leg of her maiden voyage from England to Australia with 211 passengers and crew on board, and had just left Durban for Cape Town. Nothing was ever found of her, not even a trace of floating debris. Three years before the *Titanic* (another "unsinkable" ship) met her fate in the North Atlantic, the *Waratah* just disappeared from the face of the earth. But, significantly, when she disappeared a southwesterly buster was blowing.

It wasn't until ninety years later that the wreck was discovered by an expedition from the National Underwater and Marine Agency of South Africa. In June 1999, side-scan sonar finally located the final resting place of the legendary *Waratah* off the Wild Coast in three hundred and seventy feet of water, lying upright with her bow facing northeast—the opposite direction to her course. The assumption is that she was capsized by a giant wave.

The *Waratah* was 465 feet long. *Freelance* was 31 feet long.

While the mystery of *Waratah* gained most publicity worldwide, she was only one of many ships known to have been sunk or been badly damaged there. On October 7, 1925, the Greek cargo steamer *Margarita* left East London, about two hundred and sixty miles southwest of Durban (and the first place of shelter along the way), and set sail toward Cape Town. Early next morning she sent out a distress signal, saying "heavy seas breaking through." Like the *Waratah*, she disappeared without trace.

During World War II, the British cruiser HMS *Birmingham* was one hundred miles south-southwest of Durban when she suddenly "hit a hole" in the sea, plummeted down into the next sea, and plunged bow-first into an enormous wave. Her captain, Commander I. R. Johnston, said: "The sea came green over A and B turrets and broke over our open bridge. I was knocked violently off my feet, only to recover and find myself wading in two feet of water at a height of sixty feet above normal sea level. The ship was so jarred by the impact that many of the watch below thought we had been torpedoed and went to emergency stations."

Later, in August 1964, the Union-Castle liner *Edinburgh Castle* fell into a deep trough that opened in the sea ahead of her very near the spot where the *Waratah* was lost. The liner was seven hundred and fifty feet long. She was steaming southwest, straight into a southwesterly buster, and making heavy weather of it, so her master, Commodore W. S. Byles, decided to take a knot off her speed and close with the coast. Byles had a healthy respect for this coast, having completed hundreds of voyages between Durban and East London.

He reported later that the distance from one wave top to another was about one hundred and fifty feet, and that the ship was pitching and scending about ten to fifteen degrees. And then, out of the blue, it happened. Having scended normally, a great hole appeared in the ocean ahead of the ship and she charged downward at an angle of thirty degrees or more, eventually plunging into the face of the oncoming wave and burying herself in it to a height of fifteen or twenty feet before she could recover. A wall of water coursed over the foredeck, sweeping away rails and ladders, and the passenger accommodation was flooded. Luckily, no one was swept overboard.

June and I happened to know the *Edinburgh Castle* well. We had sailed aboard her from Southampton, England, to Durban, just a few months before that incident occurred. She was a big ship, displacing 28,600 tons gross. Our boat, *Freelance,* displaced five and a half tons gross. I couldn't help wondering what would happen if we met one of those freak troughs. Would we simply be swallowed whole? When I was awake, I could dismiss the prospect as highly unlikely and melodramatic. But in my nightmares it was very real.

* * *

Meanwhile, back at our berth in Durban harbor, we waited ten days for a gap in the parade of southwesterly depressions spinning off the Roaring Forties and rampaging up the coast toward us. Our friends Chris and Libby Bonnet, owners of a sailing school, kept an eye on the facsimile weather charts issued by the government department of meteorology. Every day I would cross the busy, traffic-clogged Esplanade to the school and study the isobars with Chris, and we would shake our heads.

Then, on the tenth day, in midmorning, Chris came along the jetty to where we were moored.

"This is it," he said. "Here's your chance. Go for it."

There wasn't a southwesterly wind in sight. "You can expect favorable north-easterlies for at least two days," he added. Then he turned on his heel and left.

Two days of northeasterlies. If that came true, we'd be blown safely past the Wild Coast. June poked her head up through the main hatchway and looked at me expectantly.

"OK, I said quietly. "Let's go."

Kevin and I started the engine and cast off our mooring lines. I was very conscious of the fact that it was the last time we'd cast off in Durban. I was nervous of what was to come in the following days and weeks. I moved stiffly. For a minute or two I had the strange feeling that I was detached from my body, looking on from some floating position up above, and watching myself and Kevin.

We turned slowly into the Silburn Channel and motored past the yachts moored on either side. A friend of ours, Mel Field, was aboard one of them. He looked up, waved enthusiastically, and stared at us for a long time after we'd gone by. He had recently returned from a round trip to Australia in his small yacht. He knew what we were in for. Only later did we realize that he was the only person in the whole of Durban to wave us good-bye.

With a lump in my throat, I called up Durban Harbor Radio on the VHF radio and asked for permission to leave harbor, bound toward Cape Town. It was Thursday, January 8, 1987.

The little BMW diesel pushed us out of the long, narrow harbor mouth. I felt a tightness in my chest, and tried to take one last look around as we left the harbor I knew so intimately. I didn't have to look, though. I could sense the old Union Whaling Company slipway over to starboard, where the little Norwegian whalers used to land their catches in the old days, with sharks thrashing and snatching great hunks of flesh, turning the sea red with bloody foam. My dad had worked for Union Whaling in their factory on the other side of the Bluff, not as a whaler but as a coppersmith and plumber, trades he'd learned in the British Royal Navy long before my mother brought him back to her homeland after World War II.

Behind us was the old coaling wharf, and the tug basin, and Salisbury Island where the South African navy hid its lethal little missile-carrying patrol boats, and behind that the new container terminal, acres of concrete and cranes that seemed suddenly one night to spread over the golden beaches and mangroves where we used to picnic as kids after sailing over from Point Yacht Club in our dinghies.

On my right, the south pier. To the left, the north breakwater, and the spot where Bernard Moitessier, bumbling along as usual, ran onto the rocks on his way out of harbor, and had to be pushed back into midchannel by his friend Peter Gibson who had come to see him off, and who was luckily standing on the breakwater.

Freelance curtsied to the first swells of the Indian Ocean as she neared the end of the long entrance channel. Over to the left was Addington Beach, and the big hospital, the beginning of three miles of soft golden sands, world-renowned surfing spots, and luxury hotels along the palm-fringed Marine Parade. Subtropical Durban was South Africa's year-round playground. We had many happy memories of racing our ten-foot Mirror dinghy from Addington Beach, out through the surf into the huge offshore swells.

I tried greedily to absorb it all in one last look—and then I stopped abruptly. I suddenly felt that I didn't want it to be a *last* look. I stared ahead instead, out to sea, and for a long while saw nothing but a blur of two blues where the horizon split the sky from the water.

3

PAST THE WILD COAST

As Chris Bonnet had promised, the wind was blowing from the northeast when we left Durban. It was a humid, sticky, fretful wind, irritable after a long hot midsummer trip across the Indian Ocean. It was blowing without enthusiasm, but I didn't mind that. I had sailed *Freelance* at sea for only a few hours, and never overnight, so I didn't yet know how she handled in heavy weather. I was content to start off quietly, and this wind was blowing in the right direction. A low, rounded swell was sweeping in from the northeast but there were no large waves to speak of. Shadowy ripples grew into cat's-paws and chased each other over the jade-green inshore waters.

I switched off the engine, and with Kevin's help I raised the white mainsail and tidied up the fall of the halyard.

"Big jib?" he asked. He was young and keen.

"Not yet," I said, feeling very wimpish. "Let's take it easy at first."

He fetched the smaller working jib up on deck, and while he took the tiller I fastened the jib hanks to the forestay and hauled the jib up tight. *Freelance* was obviously undercanvassed but I didn't care. She was making three knots through the water and heading obliquely offshore. Good enough. Soon we would get a boost from the south-flowing Agulhas Current. Meanwhile, I wanted everybody to get accustomed to the motion of the boat and the rhythms of our new life aboard her.

We jogged along quietly while the Aries self-steering vane on the transom sensed the wind direction and guided us out to sea, away from the coast that the early Portuguese explorer Vasco da Gama had named Natal in honor of Christmas Day. All three of us sat in the cockpit in the warm sunshine as if we were on an ordinary day-sail, but we were consumed by our own thoughts.

It's difficult to describe the sensation of being at sea on a small boat, but it begins with a turning inward as your whole world shrinks into a patch of deck thirty feet long and ten feet wide, and a cabin ten feet long by ten feet wide. This tiny world contains everything you need to sustain life and to protect you from a hostile environment. Hostile is the wrong word, of course, because neither the wind nor the sea has emotions, nor are they capable of evil intentions. But it's only natural for humans to translate their intentions as hostile, for there are times when they seem hell-bent on obliterating you. When you go to sea, you do so on their terms, and you had better know what those terms are before you leave port.

After you turn inward from the sea, you turn inward upon yourself. The beginning of a voyage in a small boat is a period of intense self-examination, both physical and mental, particularly if you begin to feel the stirrings of seasickness and wonder if this was such a good idea after all.

With any luck, this introspective phase doesn't last long. The work of running the ship is nonstop and quickly assumes priority over all else except seasickness. We had each forearmed ourselves against seasickness with a little patch behind one ear. These patches were the size of small Band-Aids and they were moist with the antiseasickness drug Scopolamine, which our skins absorbed in minute quantities. Each patch was good for three days, by which time we should be accustomed to the boat's motion. But they had their limitations as were soon to find out.

It was very quiet with the engine stilled, and for a long time we could hear the roar of the surf to leeward as it pounded the shoreline of the steep Bluff. After that noise faded there was just the gentle sigh of the breeze through the rigging as *Freelance* rose and fell with the passing of each swell. Our reveries were broken by the brass clock on the cabin bulkhead sounding eight bells surprisingly loudly. Normally I didn't notice the noise. I had learned to tune it out. But now it surprised me. Noon. It was time to start the watchkeeping schedule, and stop acting as if this were a pleasure jaunt. It was important that we should all be properly rested, for sailors make bad mistakes when they're fatigued.

I had figured out a watch system under which Kevin and I would take alternate watches, four hours on and four hours off. We would do all the steering, navigation, sail changing, and deckwork. June, the self-appointed Ship's Welfare Officer, was to stand a two-hour watch in the morning, and another in the evening, so that both Kevin and I could get a six-hour sleep once in every twenty-four hours. She was to do all the cooking, washing up, housework, doctoring, and a score of little jobs that had no official title. I suspected she had the hardest job on board, but she didn't complain because she didn't know that, and I didn't enlighten her. She imagined she was getting off lightly because she could sleep all night—or thought she could. Little did she know.

"I'll take the first watch below," I said. "Kevin, she's all yours. Call me if you need help with the sails or anything." I picked up the grease pencil and wrote our proposed course in degrees on the fiberglass cockpit bulkhead right next to the steering compass. I had decided to keep *Freelance* ten miles offshore, just to seaward of the one hundred-fathom line, taking advantage of the south-flowing Agulhas Current.

"OK, Dad," he said with a serious face. "I've got her."

I felt confident about leaving him in charge, despite his lack of deep-sea experience. He knew how to sail small dinghies and he was observant and quick to react. He was also becoming increasingly independent, as I was to find out later.

I went below and lay in my bunk, the settee berth in the main saloon, listening to Kevin and June talking quietly in the cockpit, but I couldn't sleep. The wind stayed light, and I could hear the water trickling past *Freelance*'s side, just a few inches from my head. Sunlight poured in through the transparent hatch overhead. A spare halyard was tapping softly against the hollow mast. The blocks of the mainsheet were squeaking every few seconds as the mainsail lifted and fell with the swells. The burgee, flying from the top of the mast, made an irritating rattling noise as the mast swayed back and forth. I thought I heard water swishing in the bilge, and only just managed to stop myself getting up to investigate. I was too tense to sleep. None of us had yet learned the sailor's trick of ignoring noise, light, and movement. None of us yet had the ability to fall asleep in minutes.

Scientists who study human biorhythms say that shift workers mostly take about a week to adjust to new sleeping schedules. But some people take so long to adjust that they gradually become more and more fatigued until they finally fall unconscious on the job. I hoped that wouldn't happen to any of us.

None of us ate anything that first day. Even the smell of the chicken breasts and creamy soup that June had thoughtfully prepared in advance turned our stomachs. The Scopolamine patches stopped us from retching, but we were left with the other dreadful symptoms of seasickness—the headachy, washed-out feeling, the nausea, the scratchy feeling behind the eyes, the inability to focus— all the symptoms of a hangover without the fun of the binge.

Toward evening, the wind went even lighter and started switching direction from time to time. Light showers started to fall, and we huddled in the shelter of the canvas dodger that spread over the main companionway hatch like the domed tent of a Voortrekker wagon.

Down below in the cabin, the feeling of seasickness intensified after dark. We didn't switch on a light because whoever was on watch in the cockpit would lose his night vision, which can take as long as twenty minutes to recover. The only light I allowed down there was a small red one over the chart table. Red light doesn't affect your ability to see in the dark.

Then there was the noise. Our galley stores, the cans and bottles of food and condiments, kept up a constant racket as they slid on their shelves and collided with each other. June had stowed the lockers and cupboards with great care, but even in fairly calm seas like this, little *Freelance* pitched and rolled enough to get things moving. It only took one can to move slightly, and the others, sensing freedom, would enthusiastically push and shove in the space created, setting up a chain reaction of clinks and clanks.

June hadn't expected that constant, irritating clamor, and in truth it wouldn't have mattered so much if we hadn't had to sleep with our heads right next to the galley lockers. But in a boat as small as *Freelance,* you really couldn't get far away from *anything.*

"Everything changed for me that first night," she told me later. "I hadn't thought about it before, but suddenly I realized that we weren't going back to port. It wasn't an afternoon's sail. This was it. The real thing. I was going to have to go down into the darkness of the cabin and stay there."

She soon discovered that she could sit or stand for about thirty seconds before nausea overtook her. Then she had to lie down flat on her back until she recovered.

So she did everything in thirty-second bursts, hopping up from her bunk, working like a whirling dervish, stuffing clothes and dish towels into the food lockers to jam things tight and stop the noise, and then flinging herself back down again until the nausea subsided. She learned, too that you daren't open a locker door if the boat were heeling over toward you.

She hadn't anticipated the jerkiness of *Freelance's* motion, even in this light weather. She didn't think she could stay upright long enough even to change her clothes. It will sound ludicrous to anyone who has never been to sea in a small boat, but it takes a surprising amount of time and effort to step out of a pair of jeans when you have to hang on constantly with one hand to stop yourself being flung across the cabin. So June wore the same jeans, sweater, and underwear day and night for the whole of the first two days. Kevin and I did, too, of course— but we didn't even think to complain about it.

On the second day, the sun flung itself over the horizon too enthusiastically for my liking, as if it were eager to start the morning's work. I am never at my best in the morning, and I'm at my worst when I'm feeling seasick. Nevertheless, I was concerned for the welfare of my kidnapped crew.

Kevin looked gray and wan.

"How are you doing?" I asked.

"Fine," he said. "I'm OK."

It was plain that he wasn't.

"Eaten anything?"

He shrugged. "No."

"Yeah, me too."

June soon brightened things up for us, though. She appeared on deck rubbing her arm.

"You wouldn't believe it," she said. "I was in the toilet, and as I stood up the boat lurched and I got my elbow jammed behind the towel rail and couldn't move. I felt so stupid."

She was feeling slightly better, and certainly as long as she was in the cockpit, she was OK. She could manage brief excursions to the galley, too, because it was alongside the main companionway and she could poke her head up into the cockpit every now and then.

When I think of true sailors like Marcel Bardiaux and Miles Smeeton I am almost ashamed to say that none of us felt well enough at this stage to make written entries in the ship's log after each watch. The mere act of sitting down in the swaying cabin to write at the chart table seemed to bring on an immediate attack of seasickness that could only be fended off by lying down quickly or getting back into the cockpit. I remembered that my friend Bernard Moitessier was sick and ate nothing for three days after he left Durban in *Marie-Thérèse II* but I was neither comforted nor cheered by that thought.

I did manage to keep an abbreviated ship's log in a small pocket notebook though, mainly so I could chronicle the fluctuations of the barometer, but also to tick off the landmarks and the lighthouses we passed every thirty or forty miles. I navigated by dead reckoning, that fine-sounding nautical term for informed guesswork.

The Ship's Welfare Officer had revived enough to become concerned about the rest of us. She knew how important food was. She tried to get us to eat, even though she herself wasn't eating yet.

She cut the precooked chicken breasts into dainty little chunks and offered them to us in the cockpit. Kevin and I glared at her savagely. But she kept at it, and after a lot of friendly nagging we ate some to keep her quiet.

"This is forced feeding," Kevin protested.

"I'm not accepting complaints today," June told him briskly. "Just try to eat some."

So we pecked po-faced at a few chunks of chicken—and by some miracle we kept them down. We continued to glare at her and complain loudly every time she appeared with more tempting morsels, but through sheer persistence she eventually got us to eat some Pro-Vita biscuits (crisp whole-wheat crackers) spread with Marmite, a strange yeast extract that Britons learn to love at an early age, and which the rest of the world can't abide at any age. We also condescended to swallow a few wedges of cheese, but only when she was not looking. We didn't want to give her any satisfaction. And those few pieces of savory food were all we could bring ourselves to eat for the first two days.

Later that second morning, a northeasterly wind filled in from astern, parallel to the coast, and rapidly built up to gale force. We ran *Freelance* before it at full speed under a double-reefed mainsail and our working jib, shouldering aside wedges of white foam that streamed behind us and rose high on the following swells. She surged down the whited-capped crests while her mast traced wild arcs through the sky from side to side.

I watched her very carefully and was relieved at how easily she handled the seas, and how quickly she responded to the helm. A lot of small yachts become pig-headed and hard to handle when the wind blows strongly from astern. But *Freelance* was plowing along nicely with her tiller responding to the Aries wind vane as if some invisible helmsman were steering.

I loved the Aries. I had spent many hours working on it because *Freelance's* previous owners had neglected it. I laboriously cut away the corroded aluminum parts, replaced them with new spares, and oiled and adjusted everything until it was working perfectly.

The Aries was the brainchild of a British sailor called Nick Franklin, who set up shop in Cowes, Isle of Wight, after the first singlehanded transatlantic races established the need for a steering gear that would keep a boat sailing while the skipper rested below. He sold more than eight thousand of them.

The theory was simple. A large plywood wind vane turned an oar descending vertically down into the water behind the boat. The oar was hinged at the top, and, as it turned, the passing water made it swing from side to side. Lines from the oar were attached to the boat's tiller by a series of strategically placed blocks. Thus, if the boat wandered off course, the change in wind direction would turn the vane, which turned the oar, which tugged at the tiller, which turned the rudder, which got the boat back on course immediately. It was pure magic. It was the equivalent of an extra crewmember, one who never complained about working nonstop all day and night and never ate the last piece of chocolate in the candy locker.

It was wonderful to see how buoyant *Freelance* was, how quickly her transom rose to meet the froth-capped waves pouncing on her from astern, despite the heavy load she was carrying. We had enough canned food on board for three people for twelve months, and she was more than two inches down on her design waterline.

Conditions were far from comfortable, but to my inexperienced eye we seemed pretty safe. I couldn't really tell how hard the wind was blowing. We had no instruments for that. And when you're running downwind it is notoriously difficult to estimate the strength of the wind. Nevertheless, I noted it in my little pocket logbook as twenty-five to thirty knots, and it was certainly more than sufficient for us at that learning stage of our voyage.

We all stayed on watch in the cockpit that afternoon, wary and on edge. We had reached the Wild Coast, the last resting place of the *Waratah,* the area where the *Edinburgh Castle* had plunged into the abyss. This was the notorious area of freak waves. Many ships other than the *Waratah* and the *Edinburgh Castle* had been lost or damaged here, of course. In his book *The Perfect Storm,* Sebastian Junger describes the Wild Coast as "home to a disproportionate number" of monster waves.

"The four-knot Agulhas Current runs along the continental shelf a few miles offshore and plays havoc with swells arriving from Antarctic gales," he writes. "In 1973 the 12,000-ton cargo ship *Bencruachan* was cracked by an enormous wave off Durban and had to be towed into port, barely afloat. Several weeks later, the 12,000-ton *Neptune Sapphire* broke in half on her maiden voyage after encountering a freak sea in the same area."

I knew of many more similar incidents, and wrote about some of them when I was a cub reporter on the *Daily News,* playing second lieutenant to Steve Harper, the shipping reporter.

Durban's newspapers devoted considerable space to the workings of the port, and all junior reporters were required to cover the shipping beat as part of their formal training. For some it was a boring job, trudging the hot docks, wheedling your way aboard foreign tramp steamers, finding the tight-lipped master or mate, and trying to pry out of them the interesting things that had happened on their latest voyage. But I loved it. I felt very much at home in the docks. Indeed, it was my interest in yachts arriving in Durban that got me my first job on the *Daily News.*

After matriculating from high school I had no idea what I wanted to do for a living. For eighteen months I worked in the downtown offices of the New Zealand Insurance Company as a fire reinsurance clerk. The work was easy but boring. One day, for no good reason, I gave notice, and at the end of the month I went to live on a small yacht called *Vagabond,* owned by my friend Ray Cruickshank. She was berthed near Point Yacht. I used to spear and eat the fish that hovered in the shade of the boat, and when I got sick of that I used to go home for a decent meal occasionally. I earned gas money for my little motorcycle by freelancing—taking pictures of round-the-world sailboats and selling the stories to the *Daily News.* I tried for a full-time reporter's job at the paper, but there was never a vacancy.

One day an Australian yacht called *Active* arrived in Durban. Her skipper, Jack Tomkin, was looking for crew to continue the voyage to England, and I was chosen, along with Oscar Tamsen, a reporter from the *Daily News.* But Tomkin owed taxes in Australia and his debts caught up with him in Durban. A legal writ was nailed to the mast, and the boat was sold at auction. The cruise was off.

Tamsen, still clutching farewell presents from his *Daily News* colleagues, didn't have the heart to ask for his old job back, so I hurried up Field Street to the newspaper offices and cornered Ronnie Tungay, the city editor.

"I know you have a vacancy now," I said. "I really need the job."

And Ronnie, bless his heart, took me on. "You'll do all the shipping reporter's footwork," he warned gruffly.

I beamed at him. "Yes, sir," I said. "I'll do my best."

I soon learned a lot from Steve Harper about the monster seas off the Wild Coast and in later years June and I got to know the Wild Coast quite well from the land side, too.

We motored along its dusty, rutted roads many times on business and vacation trips, and a few years previously we had walked down the coast on a week-long backpacking trip from Port St. John's to Hole-in-the-Wall. The latter, incidentally, is named for an enormous boulder, visible from seaward, through which the heavy surf has pounded a large hole. Waves rush through it with a deep rumbling sound, so that the local Africans called it *esikhaleni*, meaning "the place of the sound." The tribe living in the area is known as the Abelunga, or European people—a reference to the earlier presence of shipwrecked sailors.

The Wild Coast is breathtakingly lovely, achingly lovely, the sort of countryside Alan Paton describes in *Cry, the Beloved Country* as being "lovely beyond any singing of it." Indeed, the countryside Paton was talking about was not far inland.

I well remembered the last time I saw Paton. My immediate boss, Roy Rudden, who thought my daily column could use a little more social news, brought Paton to my office one day, hoping I would find something to write about him. He was his usually grumpy, grizzled old self. With his leathery skin and beady eyes, he looked like an enraged turtle. For my boss's Rudden's sake, we said polite things to each other, but he didn't ask for publicity and I didn't offer him any. We understood each other very well. We were just ships passing in the night, he on his way to fame and fortune, and me on my way to obscurity and insecurity.

Three floral kingdoms converge on the Wild Coast: the subtropical flora extends south from Durban and meets the northernmost limit of the southern Cape temperate flora. And along the margins of precipitous gorges and plateaux there are examples of montane flora. Many of the plants found on this coast, such as the Pondoland palm tree *(Jubaeopsis caffra)*, grow nowhere else in the world, according to the Wildlife Society of Southern Africa. Everywhere the hills glow with Red-Hot Pokers *(Kniphofia uvaria)* and the Dwarf Kaffirboom *(Eryhthrina).* Orchids, lilies, ferns, proteas, cycads, heaths, and euphorbias all make their homes in the coastal grasslands and forests or the valley bushveld.

There is no road running along most of this coastline, precisely because it is so wild and underpopulated. The few roads that exist run at right angles to the shoreline, following the courses of rivers flowing into the sea. A hundred miles of rock pools and soft sandy beaches strewn with rare shells line the shore, with its profusion of wild bananas, soft grasses, and bright orange aloes growing on steep hillsides. African kraals dot the hills, groups of mud huts set close together for safety and convenience, and narrow paths beaten flat by generations of bare Xhosa feet lead from the hilltops through valley bushveld to the rivers down below. Steep cliffs and huge brown boulders interrupt the terrain in some places, and now and then a rushing waterfall cleaves a bed for itself through rock glistening with specks of shiny minerals.

When we hiked down this coast we found it tough going, and June and I fell far behind our hiking companions, a doctor and his family, until I taught her how to climb the steep parts with tiny steps, never losing the natural rhythm of her walking, but simply shortening the length of her stride. After that, she got on much better. Each night, June, Kevin, and I squeezed into a pup tent made for two, but during the day Kevin preferred to get away from us, and skipped on ahead with the doctor's kids while June I slogged along at the back.

And now Kevin was with us on the seaward side of the Wild Coast, without a hope of getting away from us.

I didn't think we'd find any freak waves or troughs today, because the wind was blowing with the current, not against it, but we had to be on guard, just in case. Southwesterly busters don't give much warning of their approach. The barometer seems to be ignorant of these small but intense coastal lows until a few minutes before they arrive. If you're lucky, the weather forecast will contain a report from a lighthouse keeper many miles to the south of you, reporting a buster blowing at fifty knots. That gives you time to prepare.

We had an emergency plan, in case we did run into a buster on this stretch of coast, where there is no harbor to shelter in, no bay or headland affording any kind of anchorage, for more than two hundred and fifty miles, until you reach East London.

The continental shelf south of Durban stretches between five and ten miles offshore, at which point the water is about one hundred fathoms or six hundred feet deep. From there, the sea bottom suddenly plunges to the abyss, one thousand fathoms deep and more, forming a huge underwater cliff face parallel to the distant shore. This cliff face forms the right bank of the fast-flowing sea river we knew as the Agulhas Current. The current flows fastest along this edge, and that's where things become most dangerous when a buster blows against it.

Inshore of the one hundred-fathom line, the current is slowed by friction against the sea bottom and by projecting underwater spurs of land, which also cause it to break up into huge swirls. The closer you get to land, the weaker the current and the more likelihood that you will even find a localized countercurrent flowing northward.

Local coasting freighters making toward Durban from ports to the south navigate within a mile of the coast. The daring few stay even closer, only a stone's throw from the surfline, because while this coast offers no shelter, it compensates by having no off-lying reefs or other dangers.

So the standing instructions for small sailboats are to get inshore fast if a southwesterly gale starts blowing. The seas are then much smaller and less dangerous than they are on the one hundred-fathom line, and if the buster brings winds of moderate strength, you might still be able to make way to weather against them. If you happen to stumble upon a north-going countercurrent, you will notice it immediately, because the seas will be flatter, farther apart, and more manageable. You won't make much progress toward the south, but at least you will be in the calmest, safest water.

If the buster brings really vicious winds, as they often do, you may have to get as close to the surfline as you dare, and either heave to or run under bare poles back north toward Durban.

Sailing close to the shore at night or in bad visibility brings its own problems, of course, and many yachts and even ships have been wrecked on the Wild Coast in southwesterly storms. The early Portuguese, following in the steps of Da Gama after he had opened the route from Europe to India, lost several merchantmen here. One of the earliest was the *Santo Alberta,* which was wrecked in 1593 while reputedly carrying a vast treasure. To this day, people search for that treasure, but it has never been found.

Sailboats participating in races between Durban and East London have discovered that while the surf temperature in midwinter is about 68°F, the temperature of the faster-flowing core current offshore is about 80°F. Their crews therefore constantly measure the water temperature to ensure they are getting the most help from the current. When they are confronted by a buster, they tack inshore until the sea temperature drops markedly—which usually happens about one and a half miles offshore—and then they tack out again to a point roughly five miles offshore to get all the help they can from the current until the seas become too big and steep. Effectively, then, those who can make way to windward against a buster do so in a corridor about three and a half miles wide.

The colder water inshore is often the color of green jade, whereas the warmer, faster-flowing current beyond the one hundred-fathom line is an indigo blue. If you're heading south from Durban, blue is fast and green is slow.

Our apprehension faded hour by hour as the coastline sped by on the hazy horizon ten miles away. *Freelance* was averaging five knots through blue water and the current was adding another three or four to our progress, so that by the time the sun went down we felt we were well past the danger area.

"It makes you wonder why we were so afraid of it," I said to June.

"Touch wood," she said. "Be careful what you say or you might have to pay for it later."

How right she was.

When Kevin came on deck to take the watch from 1800 to 2200, the seas had built in height and length. He rubbed the sleep from his eyes and looked at the steep breaking crests astern. He plainly didn't like what he saw.

"Is it time to steer by hand?" he asked.

I shook my head. "The Aries seems to doing just fine. Nothing has come over the stern yet."

"Um, I'd like to steer by hand. OK?"

"Sure," I said, "just disconnect the tiller chain."

I suddenly realized what I was asking of this neophyte sailor, this seasick, inexperienced seventeen-year-old son of mine. I was putting him in charge of a small sailboat in a gale in some of the most dangerous waters on the globe. Night was falling fast and he would be alone in the cockpit with no one to consult and no one to share the blame if anything went wrong. He was totally responsible for the safety of the ship and the lives of three people. I could see why he was apprehensive.

I sat beside him for fifteen minutes while he steered *Freelance* as if she were the Mirror dinghy he knew so well. He would listen for a wave breaking astern, then heave on the tiller to weave her through the swells, out of its path.

"Don't pull off too far," I warned him. "She might jibe."

"Of course not," he said, "I always head up."

Of course not. What a worrywart of a father. He knew what he was doing better than any Aries could know. And so I left him to it.

By 0130 on Saturday, about thirty-six hours after leaving Durban, we were off the port of East London, 263 nautical miles away, and very relieved to have the dreaded Wild Coast behind us. We overheard another yacht making a ship-to-shore radio telephone call to East London Radio. She was the *Clyde,* a Miura-class thirty-footer, a lighter and faster boat that had left Durban about two and a half hours before us with a full crew. We had never caught a glimpse of her, so we were very pleased to learn that we'd kept up with her, and proud that we beginners had maintained a speed of more than seven knots, albeit with the aid of a swift current.

Port Elizabeth, the next harbor offering any shelter, was one hundred and thirty miles ahead. I decided to carry on without stopping at East London, since our northeasterly gale had now turned into a southeasterly gale, which was still a fair wind, and not to be wasted.

But the seas continued to build, and *Freelance* began to feel a little out of control as she ran down them. The crisp little seas that had rapped politely on the transom and then passed by unobtrusively had turned into large sloppy waves, thumping against the transom carelessly and rising to within inches of the top.

So we cautiously dropped the double-reefed mainsail and ran the rest of that night under a reefed foresail only, making six knots but rolling spectacularly from gunwale to gunwale.

Walking on deck was impossible because of the jerky motion. When we needed to go forward, we had to attach our safety harnesses, then sit on deck and scoot along on our bottoms, bracing ourselves against the lifelines. Now and then I wondered how the old-timers got on. Men like Moitessier and Bardiaux didn't bother with lifelines, safety harnesses, or tethers. Moitessier once told me: "You get too reliant on lifelines, and one day they will let you down. You have to learn to cling like a monkey. That's much safer."

Down below, the violent rolling tossed us out of our bunks if we forgot to fasten our canvas leecloths.

Then, to my dismay, the low barometer began to fall even more, slowly at first and then quite quickly. I presumed our gale was about to worsen. But by then I was confident of *Freelance's* ability to handle following seas, so I planned to carry on, under bare poles if necessary. We would bypass Port Elizabeth and head straight for Cape Town.

At the present rate of progress, we would be off Port Elizabeth about two and a half days after leaving Durban, and Port Elizabeth was halfway to Cape Town. A five-day passage from Durban to Cape Town was almost unheard of for a boat our size, but for a while it seemed possible.

That evening, when I tuned the radio for a weather forecast, we heard a warning. A gale was indeed approaching—but a new one, from the opposite direction.

4

WEATHERBOUND IN PORT ELIZABETH

I could hardly believe it at first. It felt so strange to be running hell for leather in a southeasterly gale and heading straight for a "buster," a violent southwesterly gale from ahead. It seemed bizarre, even for this violent coast. According to the meteorological forecast, the new gale was supposed to take over from the old gale at about midnight, by which time we'd be near Port Elizabeth. Suddenly there was no longer any question of bypassing the port. We needed shelter, and fast.

Sure enough, our old gale was dying out and the swell was calming down by the time we entered the large open bight of Algoa Bay at 8 p.m. In the calmer seas, June changed out of her two-day-old clothes into pink pajamas. Daylight faded too quickly for us to find the port, so we struck the jib about five miles offshore and, mindful of the old warning never to enter a strange port at night, lay drifting under bare poles to await dawn.

My first thought was that we'd be comparatively safe in Algoa Bay because the new gale would be blowing off the land, and we'd be sheltered from the biggest seas. Then, after a few hours, it struck me that the new wind might be strong enough to blow us *away* from the shelter of land, and back up the coast, the way we'd come. I had no idea how good *Freelance* would be at going to windward in a gale, but I did know that the new wind would be blowing contrary to the current, causing large, steep-sided seas with plunging crests. I didn't want to get blown back to the Wild Coast in a buster. I remembered that another acquaintance from my schoolboy days, Henry Wakelam, had been capsized in this area under similar circumstances in his twenty six-foot sloop *Wanda*. And before that, the American Tahiti ketch, *Adios,* owned by Tom Steele, had capsized here with my old friend Ray Cruickshank on board. *Adios* was knocked down several times, rolled over, and badly damaged. She lost her mizzen mast, the main boom, the dinghy, and her rudder. Steele eventually managed to get the auxiliary engine going, and they motored to Port Elizabeth, though on the way they were struck again by an eighty-mile-an-hour gale that kicked up mountainous seas.

Although it was now pitch dark, I suddenly felt a desperate need to find the port and get in before the buster struck. We were all fatigued from lack of sleep and food. I didn't think we were fit enough to fight another gale.

My dead reckoning put us within a few miles of the Port Elizabeth harbor entrance, but we couldn't see it against the bright lights of the city. I had never entered Port Elizabeth harbor in a yacht before, even in daylight. We approached slowly under engine for about an hour, consulting the chart for clues, but still could get no idea of where the harbor lay. There were no navigation lights that we could identify positively, nothing except the blinding glare of a city strung out along the coast for miles. But we kept looking.

By midnight the wind had fallen dead calm, as it often does before a buster bursts through. My anxiety increased. In our fatigued states, we were likely to make silly mistakes. All three of us peered through the night, trying to spot the little red and green lights that marked the entrance channel, without luck.

Finally, I called Port Elizabeth Port Control on the VHF radio and confessed I was lost. I could just imagine them rolling their eyes and sighing at the landlubber who couldn't find his way into port.

Whatever they thought, they acted like professionals. The duty officer asked me what I could see.

"Two anchored ships," I told him.

"Keep coming north," he said, "and in twenty minutes I'll shine our searchlight in the sky. You should see it."

We crept forward, straining our eyes for buoys or small craft on moorings, but it felt as if we were still far away from land. Then, ahead and to the left, above the glare of the city, a ray of light stabbed into the black sky and waggled back and forth for a few moments. I quickly took a compass bearing on it.

The radio said: "Yacht *Freelance*, did you see it?"

"Yes," I said, limp with relief. "Thank you very much."

"Watch for the berthing gang," said the voice. "They'll guide you in."

As we rounded the breakwater, a flashlight blinked at us from a jetty ahead; and when we arrived at that spot, the light was flashing farther down, next to some moored tugs. Several yachts were tied up there, and we made fast alongside a Japanese one called *Pink Maru Maru*.

The chief of the three-man berthing gang called softly from the quay: "You all right, bossie?"

"Fine," I said, "thanks for your help."

The black faces disappeared quietly into the night.

As they left, the buster arrived. *Freelance* heeled over from the force of its onslaught against her bare mast, and Kevin doubled up our mooring lines. June and I hugged in the cockpit, and June laughed.

"What?" I said.

"My pajamas," she said. "We've just arrived safely at our first port in our own yacht. And I'm wearing pink pajamas and an orange anorak. So chic."

I hardly took in her words. I was still feeling very chastened and incompetent as a navigator and skipper. At the same time, I was vastly relieved that we weren't out at sea in this screaming southwesterly wind. It was 3 a.m. and we all fell into our bunks, exhausted.

It seemed too good to be true. In just two and a half days we had completed the most dangerous part of the voyage from Durban to Cape Town, the half with the least shelter for small boats. And it was too good to be true. The strong southwesterly wind continued, keeping *Freelance* weather bound in Port Elizabeth for fifteen days.

Perhaps we were lucky. The record, we learned later, was seventy-two days of strong westerlies, nonstop. Nevertheless, our frustration at being halted in our tracks so close to home was almost unbearable. Every day I would phone the local meteorological office for a weather forecast, and always the message was the same: "If you sail now, you'll run into a coastal low followed by a cold front. The high-pressure system you need should be formed in a couple of days." And after we had waited with increasing impatience for two days, the forecaster would blithely inform me with no apparent feeling of shame that more strong south-westerlies, cold and blustery, were heading our way from Antarctica.

Port Elizabethans called their city "The Friendly City." Everybody else in South Africa called it the "The Windy City." We wouldn't have minded the wind strength so much if it had been blowing in the right direction. In summer, the prevailing winds were supposed to be southeasterlies, which would have sent us speeding on our way, but something had obviously gone wrong with the weather.

We were in good company, though. The Hiscocks had been weatherbound here for ten days on their first circumnavigation in *Wanderer III* while strong to gale-force westerly winds blew. "We had fourteen fathoms of chain out to a wooden dolphin ahead," Eric Hiscock wrote, "at times the gust were so strong that the full length of the chain leapt out of the water to become bar taut with a clang that could be heard at the far end of the jetty, and we had to send a weight along it to act as a spring."

Half a dozen round-the-world yachts were now holed up in Port Elizabeth with us, all enjoying the hospitality of the Algoa Bay Yacht Club, but chafing to get away. Besides *Pink Maru Maru* (which was, in fact, bright red) there was *Ipi Tombi, Albroc, Starrynight, Lapwing,* and *Aqua Viva.* The latter was a Montevideo 43 owned by a Cape Town lawyer, Pieter de Klerk, and she was on the last lap of a four-year circumnavigation that would end in Cape Town. We had met Pieter when he called at Durban, and his pet cat Pepe had introduced himself to us there by walking down the jetty and inspecting our boat. Pepe became quite a celebrity at Point Yacht Club when it become known that he used *Aqua Viva's* toilet instead of a sand box. We all wanted to see him perching on the rim, doing his thing, but Pieter didn't encourage visitors bent on violating Pepe's privacy.

All seven of us were anxious to move on from Port Elizabeth because it was time to catch the southeast trades that would blow us north into the Atlantic Ocean. The trades started a couple of hundred miles north of Cape Town at that time of the year, but their southern limit was moving farther north every day. The longer we were delayed, the more contrary winds we'd have to fight before we found the trades and were swept north to St. Helena.

Meanwhile, June, Kevin, and I got to know Port Elizabeth well. It was a very English-looking city of more than a million people, and was well furnished with Victorian architecture, the centerpiece of which was the beautiful colonial city hall on Market Square, which had been designated a national monument. It was built between 1858 and 1862, and the attractive clock tower was added in 1883.

But the history of this part of the world goes back a lot farther than most people imagine. On March 12, 1488, the Portuguese navigator and explorer Bartholomeu Dias became the first recorded European to visit the sweeping bay, where there was freshwater to be found. The black Khoisan tribes were already established there, of course, but there is no record of any contact between them and Dias, who was more concerned with finding the sea route to India than fraternizing with the natives.

When Manuel de Mesquita Perestrello came along in 1576 he gave the bay a name: Bahia de Lagoa, or Bay of the Lagoon, a reference to the lagoon at the mouth of the Baakens River.

In 1690, a Dutch captain called Pieter Timmerman who was sent to survey the area was barely able to conceal his contempt when he reported that it was "nothing better than an exposed bight." He was right, as a matter of fact, for there was no shelter for a ship of any size. The present harbor at Port Elizabeth is totally man-made.

In 1772, the Dutch farmers who later became known as the Boers, started occupying the land around the bay, but when the British took over the Cape in 1799 they built a stone fort overlooking the Baakens River, not only to control the pesky Dutch who didn't want any form of British rule imposed upon them, but also to intimidate the local black tribes who were busy making war on each other. While they were at it, the British also managed to mangle the name of the bay, and instead of Bahia de Lagoa it became Algoa Bay.

It was in 1820 that four thousand settlers were sent out from Britain to form a permanent colony, and they landed through the surf in small boats. The first small jetty of what was to become the harbor was built with money contributed by local merchants in 1837.

Those were exciting times (to say the least) for raw settlers straight out of Britain, of course. In addition to the Dutch, the French were also making aggressive moves, and in the dry hinterland where many settlers had been given land, elephants roamed wild in the same areas the Bantu tribes were squabbling over.

One of the first things I did in Port Elizabeth was write a letter to the local newspaper, thanking the port authorities for their help in guiding us into port that night. I don't think it was ever published—certainly not in the two weeks we were there, anyway—but I felt better about having tried.

Aboard *Freelance* there was plenty of work to keep me busy. I found a space down below for the new inflatable dinghy we had bought in Durban, a nine-foot orange Metzler. It had been lashed down to the cabintop, where the sun could perish it, but I discovered I could make it fit on the starboard V-berth in the forepeak if it was fully deflated. The dinghy was one of several costly items we had invested in as a way of getting money out of South Africa. We figured that we could either sell them with the boat, when the time came, or separately, to raise cash. We also had a brand-new, five-horsepower outboard motor and—our pride and joy—a satellite navigation set, still in its box. The SatNav was the forerunner of today's GPS receivers, but in the Southern Hemisphere the satellite passes were few and far between, so in our tests at home we were able to get position fixes only once every couple of hours or so.

Nevertheless, thinking about it in the calm of Port Elizabeth harbor, it seemed silly to have a SatNav in a box, ready for sale in America, when we might never reach America if we didn't use the SatNav.

I set to work and pulled everything out of the box. I fixed the antenna to the stern rail, screwed the receiver in place in the navigation station, and wired everything up. I didn't want to depend on it entirely, though—it was just for emergencies, I told myself, like getting into Port Elizabeth harbor in the dark. I was teaching myself how to use the sextant again, and I didn't want to lose that skill. So I devised a compromise. I handed over the working of the SatNav to Kevin, who had been familiar with computers and electronic gear from the age of nine.

"You keep track of where we're going," I said, "but don't tell me unless you think we're heading into danger." I would use what few pilotage skills I possessed to fix our position on the coast, and my knowledge of celestial navigation to fix our position at sea. I would mark our course lines and positions on the chart, and Kevin was to keep a separate note somewhere and not let me see it unless I asked. And so it was arranged.

I noticed a smirk on Kevin's face.

"What are you smiling at?" I asked.

"You realize this gives me certain power, Dad?"

"Um, well, yes—what are you getting at?"

"What will you give me for the information I gather?"

"I'll decide at the time," I said. "What do you think it's worth?"

"Could be quite a lot under certain circumstances. I'm thinking in terms of an extra chocolate ration, of course. And maybe biltong."

Biltong was South African game jerky, a particular favorite with all of us.

I presumed he was joking, as usual, but I couldn't be sure. He was growing up fast.

"I'll have to think about it," I said. "Meanwhile, you think about the penalty for mutiny."

Meanwhile, I stole an idea from a book by Lin and Larry Pardey to make it easier for one person to handle our spinnaker pole, which we used to pole out the jib when we were running dead before the wind. We stored the pole vertically up the mast on a car attached to a long track, and I organized a halyard, some line, and some blocks so that the pole would take itself out overboard as it was lowered in the track. It meant we never had to handle the weight of the pole, and it was always attached in at least two places.

I stayed with the boat while June and Kevin explored ashore, not only because there was the usual never-ending list of jobs to be done, but also because I felt uneasy if *Freelance* was left unattended. Everything we owned in the world was on board, with the exception of a few sticks of furniture we had sent over to June's sister Carol in Idaho to keep for us, and nothing was insured. It was my responsibility to get it all to the United States, and I'm afraid I bore it heavily.

We knew people in Port Elizabeth but made no attempt to contact them. I didn't want to be accused of taking the chicken run again. Several months previously, one of June's coworkers had accused her of abdicating her responsibility as a white person in South Africa and taking the easy way out of the inevitable racial conflict ahead. June was indignant but replied calmly. "I'm not taking the chicken run," she said. "You might want to reconsider that. Going to sea in a thirty one-foot boat is not taking the chicken run."

I avoided contact with the Port Elizabeth's locals as much as possible, too, because we didn't deserve the sort of lavish hospitality South Africans traditionally dish out to foreign small-boat sailors. We were, after all, just a few miles from home. Only we didn't have a home any longer, except *Freelance,* and that made me feel very strange. Port Elizabeth at that time wasn't the happiest place for any of us.

From time to time, I would temporarily get over my obsession with keeping guard on *Freelance,* and join June and Kevin on the dreary twenty-minute trek across the docks and along the road to the city center. There wasn't a lot to do there, and we didn't want to spend any more money than we had to. We inspected the old lighthouse and the 1820 Settlers' Memorial, the Campanile, which celebrated the arrival of the British immigrants. We climbed the 204 steps of the Campanile to the observation room, and marveled at the view, but we saw only with our eyes, not our hearts, because what we really wanted to see was Port Elizabeth disappearing into the distance behind us.

We admired the shops and bought a few fresh provisions, which we lugged back to the harbor on foot against that incessant southwesterly wind. Every day we were trapped there we felt more desperate.

One evening, in the bar of the Algoa Bay yacht Club, June and I sat alongside the owner of the boat we were moored next to. He was Yukio Hasebe, a Japanese singlehander, and his boat was the twenty-nine-foot Yamaha sloop *Pink Maru Maru*. This wiry, smiling fifty-year-old was quite famous among the cruising fraternity.

"We should sail," he said, when we complained once more about the contrary winds. "Thirty knots is not so bad when you're out there. Always it seems worse in port." And he laughed and added in his halting English: "Of course, I am not good example sailor."

He was referring to his ordeal of a few years before when he'd nearly lost his life. His deep-sea career had led him on a meandering course around the world for eleven years, leaving a wake forty thousand miles long. But two little mistakes very nearly ended it.

The former advertising executive told us it happened in the South Pacific in 1979, when he was approaching the eastern coast of Australia in heavy weather in a previous boat.

She was being steered by a wind vane while Hasebe worked on deck. He was harnessed, as usual, but a sudden lurch hurled him back against the lifeline, which parted.

Hasebe fell overboard to weather and was trailed alongside, halfway along the boat. The harness was attached at chest height, which kept his head above water, but he couldn't get back on board.

The boat was heeled too far over and the slippery hull presented nothing for him to grasp. The drag of the water prevented his pulling himself up the harness tether to deck level. The windvane steered the boat inexorably on course.

"I just lay there, bashing against the hull and being towed and trying to breathe," Hasebe said. "The boat sailed on and on for maybe two hours, maybe much more, I don't know. I was bleeding from barnacle scrapes and getting exhausted."

Suddenly there was a splintering, shuddering crash as the yacht hit a reef off Queensland at full speed. Within minutes the swells had pounded her to pieces.

Hasebe was able to scramble over the reef to safety. The boat was wrecked, but his life was saved.

Hasebe said his first mistake was that his harness tether was too long. "It should have been much shorter, to stop me going overboard," he said.

His second mistake was that he didn't have a floating line trailing astern to deactivate the self-steering gear.

"If a line had been there, I could have cut my tether and grabbed the trailing line as it came past. Then the boat would have rounded up and waited for me."

Hasebe was married, and his wife lived in Japan, but they had no children. He told us that he had had a wonderful time in Durban.

"Point Yacht Club makes the best pies in the world," he said, licking his lips.

He was referring to the gravy-smothered beefsteak pies that the yacht club's Zulu chef was famous for. Each one was a meal in itself.

"I wrote home to my wife to tell her about the Point Yacht Club pie," he said, "but I told her that they cost two rands each and I can afford only one a week.

"She wrote back and said: 'Don't worry, I have work now and I will send you money, so you can have a PYC pie every day.'"

At that time, the South African rand was worth about thirty-nine cents U.S.

But Hasebe didn't head out into the southwesterlies pounding Port Elizabeth day and night, any more than we did. Like the rest of us, he gritted his teeth, waited impatiently, and dreamed of PYC pies.

Pieter de Klerk, anxious to get home and complete his circumnavigation, just couldn't accept the delay any longer. He decided to sail directly to Cape Town, having calculated that his forty-three-foot boat would probably make at least some progress against the southwester still blowing.

We were envious, but next morning I came back from the public telephone with yet another adverse weather forecast. At that moment, though, the sun was shining brightly and there wasn't a cloud in the sky. June was sitting in the cockpit, looking slim and relaxed in her pretty floppy white hat. A woman in the city had admired that hat and asked June where she had bought it.

"In Durban," said June.

"Oh, that explains it," said the woman. "We never get any nice hats around here."

I wasn't surprised when June told me about it. For 99 percent of the time, the wind was blowing too hard for hats in Port Elizabeth.

Kevin was sitting forlornly on the foredeck, plucking at the strings of a guitar. At least, he was plucking at the strings of a guitar handle, because there wasn't room for a guitar on our small boat, and I had removed the body of the guitar, leaving just the strings and the frets for him to practice on. He was at the stage where he greatly admired the rogue pop singers. It was oddly touching to see him plucking at a handle with strings that didn't make any noise; but Kevin didn't care. It was a small, comforting reminder of home, and it did the same job that a pacifier does for an infant.

He was a gifted child, suddenly starved of the intellectual stimulation he'd been used to. I felt sad that he wasn't able to bask in the glory he'd earned at his former high school, the boarding school Kearsney College. He'd won prizes there for academic achievement and come top in the school in the Matric, the national university entrance exam. We heard that he was the first pupil ever to score 100 percent in the Matric exam for an English essay. And for the first time, the Matriculation Board refused to release the winning essay for publication in the newspapers.

"The examiner probably didn't have much choice with my essay marks," he said. "They had to be either 100 percent or zero." He had written a well-reasoned but searingly critical analysis of the whole school system, with no holds barred.

When Kevin first started school, we had been warned that he was likely to run into trouble later on if he wasn't kept mentally stimulated with outside interests. So, when he was nine, we bought him his first computer. He was so quick at learning that he never needed to do homework to keep up with his classmates. He passed every exam with flying colors without an hour of study. But when he graduated to Durban High School he ran into a brick wall.

DHS was Durban's oldest and most prestigious high school. I myself had failed to gain entrance because of a poor academic record and had to be content with a lesser school, but Kevin's two elder brothers, Trent and Terry, had both gone to DHS. It was for boys only, of course, in the South African fashion, and it was run along the lines of a typical English public school—which is, of course, not a public school at all, but a private one.

Despite the subtropical heat and humidity of a Durban summer, DHS pupils wore the uniform of long gray trousers, long-sleeved white shirt, necktie, and black blazer. The senior classes, called forms, also wore a distinctive head-gear—the Eton boater, a flat-topped white straw hat.

From the beginning, Kevin chafed against the senseless application of authority by his masters and prefects. Prefects were senior pupils with special privileges and powers to discipline other boys. Although the headmaster and staff would never officially admit it, they often turned a blind eye when prefects resorted to caning and other physical punishment. Kevin rebelled. He refused to join sports teams, and was despised for it it. He refused to do homework, and was caned for it. And yet he managed to pass all his exams with high marks. Some days, unknown to us, he refused to go to school at all, and simply sat in the public park near our home. At the end of the term, he altered his school reports, and he forged them so expertly that neither June nor I noticed anything wrong.

But one day his form master, who taught sports, called us in to his office. "He won't cooperate," he complained. "I've tried everything. I cane him and he just cringes. He doesn't change. He's like a little hamster. I think he's schizophrenic. You must take him to a psychiatrist."

June and I were appalled, first, at the insensitivity and brutality of this so-called teacher; second, at the suggestion that we had failed to provide urgent psychiatric treatment for our son; and third, at the picture of a desperate child forging reports, running helpless to the park, being caned mercilessly, and hiding his misery from us. We had no idea he was being caned.

We secured an interview with a well-respected psychiatrist called Una Brunton-Warner who had a lot of experience with the Natal provincial school system. Kevin came with us, ashen-faced but unrepentant, and we handed him over to her.

We sat tensely in the waiting room while she examined him. Half an hour later, Kevin came out smiling. Ms. Brunton-Warner was smiling, too.

"There's nothing wrong with him," she announced. "Just get him out of Durban High School as fast as you can."

The two premier private boys' boarding schools in Natal were Hilton College and Michaelhouse College, neither of which we could afford. But close behind them in academic standards, cheaper and closer to home, was Kearsney College, at Botha's Hill.

The school year had finished when I went to Kearsney College to beg the headmaster, Colin Silcock, to accept Kevin. The school was already fully booked for the next year. Silcock and his deputy listened patiently and read the psychiatrist's report. They looked very dubious about making an exception for Kevin, and I had to admit that it didn't appear that he'd be a credit to Kearsney in any way, especially in the sporting arena, which was very important to the school. I was very frank, and told them all about his transgressions and deceit. I thought it might offer them a challenge.

Eventually the headmaster and his deputy looked at each other and shrugged. "Another academic pupil," said Silcock. "Well, perhaps . . . room for just one more . . ."

I left Kearsney greatly relieved. June, brought up in the American system, was not happy about sending our young son to a boarding school and seeing him only a few times a term, but she knew that Kearsney had a wonderful reputation for excellent teaching and character building.

So we bought him a full Kearsney uniform kit of formal, casual, and sports clothes, and with great trepidation we drove him the twenty-five miles to Kearsney College and abandoned him there.

To say he thrived there would be an understatement. With liberal-minded, understanding teachers, he blossomed. He couldn't work hard enough for them. He started playing rugby and tennis and he participated in cross-country runs. Very soon he was intensely involved in academic competition with the best minds in the school. He won the English prize, and the Afrikaans prize, and he was not far behind in math and science. He took major roles in stage productions and discovered, to his great joy, a whole room full of personal computers to play with. He was in his element and we were very proud of him.

It was astonishing to see how quickly he matured physically and emotionally. This was a time of great social upheaval in South Africa, and June and I sometimes wondered what would happen if a black uprising cut us off from Kevin.

With no prompting at all, he called us one day after police and soldiers had savagely put down a large black protest near the school and said: "Don't worry about me. If anything happens I'll meet you at the boat."

His crowning success was his last examination at school, the Matriculation or university entrance exam. He scored more points than anyone else in the school, finally triumphing over all his rivals.

But seventeen-year-old Kevin had been snatched away by his parents, and instead of sharing the joy of his accomplishments with his friends in Durban and Kearsney, he was sitting bored and lonely on *Freelance*'s foredeck in Port Elizabeth.

It was particularly awkward that our escape from South Africa had been so hampered. We had wanted a clean break, not this messy departure. We were just wasting time and spending money here.

June and Kevin seemed to take our enforced stay better than I did, though. At least, they were more philosophical about it, and saw no sense in trying to sail against gale-force winds. Kevin played his truncated guitar, and June read books and restowed her provisions to make them rattleproof at sea.

But the day finally came, the day when the wind went around to the north, and at 8 a.m. on Monday, January 26, 1987, a stream of yachts poured out of Port Elizabeth like salt out of a shaker.

Yukio Hasebe left immediately after us, overtook us to leeward, and soon streaked ahead. He had a light boat, a fin-keeler with a large foresail. We waved good-bye. We learned later that he had sprinted straight to Cape Town without nearing land, experiencing mostly contrary winds for eleven days. He had obviously followed his own advice about fighting those thirty-knot winds at sea, rather than avoiding them in port.

Our trip to Cape Town was to be longer than his, with several stops and the sternest test yet of our courage.

5

PORT ELIZABETH TO MOSSEL BAY

Like racehorses released from the starting gate, six storm-bound cruising yachts bolted out of Port Elizabeth early on Monday, January 26. For the first time in more than two weeks, the gale-force southwesterly wind had died away, and we were able to continue our voyages toward Cape Town.

Some racehorses are faster than others, of course, and *Pink Maru Maru* soon disappeared ahead of us, along with *Starrynight* and *Lapwing*. But we held our own against *Albroc,* while *Ipi Tombi,* an unhandy, amateur-built boat with far too little sail area, faded out astern.

We didn't mind that we weren't winning the race. We were just overjoyed to be released from Port Elizabeth at last.

The wind, as it turned out, was still against us, but not directly in our teeth. It was a light northwesterly, which meant we could make good progress in calm seas and a moderate swell from the southwest.

Later that morning, the breeze went around the southeast at ten knots so that we had it behind us. We eased the main boom out almost until it touched the lee shrouds and watched happily as *Freelance* waltzed down the gentle faces of blue waves at five knots. Virgin-white foam from the bow wave hissed loudly along the hull, exploding into millions of tiny white bubbles. Each bursting bubble scented the air with the kind of tingling freshness a thunderstorm leaves in its wake, and we could taste it on our lips.

When you leave Port Elizabeth going westward, the one hundred-fathom line moves out from the land and forms a great shallow area known as the Agulhas Bank. Here the mighty Agulhas Current spreads out, slows down, breaks up into large swirls, changes direction, and mixes with cold water coming up from the Roaring Forties. This is not good news for small boats.

The British Admiralty chart we were using made special mention of this "remarkable and interesting feature" because, in all the length of the seashore we were traversing, which the old Portuguese explorers dubbed The Cape of Storms, this was the area—between Cape St. Francis and Mossel Bay—with the most gales.

The warning on the chart cautioned gravely: "The greatest number of gales are experienced between the meridians of 22° and 24° E and the parallels of 35° and 37° S, or where the Agulhas Current is deflected to the Southward by the eastern margin of the Agulhas Bank, and the struggle takes place between the cold and warm currents of the sea, and the cold and warm currents of the air, which go as it were hand in hand."

I saw Kevin reading it on the chart table, and put my finger to my lips.

"Don't tell Mum," I whispered. "No need to alarm . . ."

He laughed. *"She* pointed it out to *me,"* he said.

The Agulhas Bank hangs from the bottom of Africa in a huge triangle measuring two hundred and seventy miles from east to west and one hundred and twenty miles from north to south. It's not so shallow as to create a grounding hazard for yachts or even ships. It's mostly three hundred to four hundred feet deep, and only shallow in comparison with the depths outside, which quickly plunge to over six thousand feet, or more than a mile.

The real hazard for shipping is the bank's ability to create localized storms. It's a giant bad-weather factory. In addition, the swift currents that scour its surface are quite unpredictable in force and direction. You simply never know where the current is going to take you, or at what speed. Mostly, however, the trend of the current near the land is toward the east. A little farther out to sea—but nobody can ever say with any certainty how far—the current usually sets toward the west or northwest. On the far southern edges of the bank, off Cape Agulhas, the current sets west and joins the main set that runs toward Australia in the Roaring Forties. As if this weren't confusing enough, the current often sets strongly toward land. The chart was sprinkled with waggly lines representing current flows, and warnings such as: "After S.E. gale, a strong current reported to set into Struys Bay." Some of the currents were said to reach two to two and a half knots, a dangerously high speed for a sailboat like *Freelance,* whose top speed was just over six knots.

Just in case navigators weren't taking all this seriously enough, their Lordships of the Admiralty had sought to instill more fear by adding to the chart details of icebergs that had been spotted on or near the Agulhas Bank in years gone past. "Small Iceberg seen in January 1850" said a note only thirty-two miles from the Cape of Good Hope. "Numerous Icebergs seen here in April 1853," said another directly south of Cape Agulhas." And, off to the southwest in deeper water: "Five Icebergs about 250 ft. high seen here in April 1828."

I hadn't heard of icebergs in these waters in modern times, and even allowing for the fact that the Southern Hemisphere is much colder than the Northern hemisphere, latitude for latitude, it seemed extraordinary for 'bergs to put in an appearance only thirty-five degrees from the equator. That's the equivalent of Cape Hatteras or the Mediterranean in the Northern Hemisphere. Nevertheless, presumably it was still possible.

We didn't have much choice, though. We had to cross the bank unless we were prepared to sail one hundred and twenty miles out to sea to skirt around it. But at least we now had a working satellite navigation receiver that would not only give us accurate position fixes, but also tell us what the current was doing to us. I could find that out by comparing each SatNav fix with the corresponding dead-reckoning position.

There was just one problem. Kevin was in charge of the SatNav and I had made him promise not to divulge its reckonings to me.

"Um, there's been a change of plan," I told him when we met in the cockpit at the change of watches. "I need regular SatNav fixes after all."

He wasn't quite awake yet. "Oh," he said.

I waited a minute or two for him to respond, but he added nothing. Then, gradually, a canny smile appeared on his face. "Chocolate or biltong?" he asked.

I sighed. "Chocolate, I suppose. We're running low on biltong."

And so the Ship's Welfare Officer slipped an extra four squares of Cadbury's fruit-and-nut milk chocolate into Kevin's nightly comfort bag. The comfort bags were small cloth bags of treats June prepared for each of us to nibble on during the long night watches. We reached eagerly for these bags, tucked in under the forward edge of the canvas dodger, as soon as we came on watch. There was usually a piece of biltong, a quarter slab of chocolate, a cookie or two, hard candies, and an apple or orange. The hardest thing, when we weren't feeling seasick, was not to eat *everything* in the first ten minutes of a lone four-hour watch.

It was wonderful to be able to fix our position with great accuracy every couple of hours or so, when a convenient set of satellites flew overhead. Kevin began to plot our progress on the chart while I confirmed the SatNav positions as best I could the old-fashioned way, with occasional compass bearings on lighthouses or landmarks I could identify from the chart. We didn't keep the SatNav running all the time because it used electricity from our meager supply. We had two twelve-volt batteries, a big one and a small one. The small one was about the size of a car battery, and the big one was a little bigger. We used the big one for everything except starting the engine. The small one was reserved for that. But we had no way to charge the batteries except by running the engine, which had a small thirty-amp alternator built into the flywheel.

The boats we had left Port Elizabeth with faded out of view over the horizon and we were once again alone on the westward edge of the Indian Ocean. We made good progress that afternoon and evening, but the wind dropped after dark and progress slowed.

We were all gradually getting over seasickness. None of us felt completely better, but the symptoms were slowly fading, particularly in the calmer seas. After leaving Port Elizabeth we managed to keep a proper ship's log, writing up details of our course, the weather, and ship's business at the end of every watch. What with our improved health, better navigation, and more seamanlike bookkeeping, I felt we were making good progress. I was proud of my ship and her neophyte crew.

At night we usually sailed without navigation lights in order to preserve battery power, but that night I was forced to switch the lights on when a trawler came up from astern at 10 p.m. We just barely had steerageway, and from the moment she appeared over the horizon I could see that she was heading straight for us. When you think about how much space there is on the open ocean, you would be forgiven for imagining that the chances of one boat accidentally running into another are infinitesimal. But you'd be wrong. There seems to be some unexplained force that attracts vessels to each other, just as straws cling to each other in a saucer of water.

I switched on our lights when the trawler was still a couple of miles away, but she plowed on inexorably, not heading to miss us close to port or starboard, but aiming straight for our transom. I was about to start our engine and motor out of her way when she finally veered off and passed us two hundred yards to windward.

That was about the extent of the excitement that night, except that fine on the starboard bow we could see Seal Point light at Cape St. Francis, made famous by the cult surfing movie, *Endless Summer,* for having the world's most perfect breaking waves. We were entering the area where the maximum number of gales occurred. But there were certainly no gales around that night. At 2 a.m. when he went off watch, Kevin noted in log: "Vessel barely maintaining steerage way." In fact, we were becalmed most of rest of night, making only two miles along our course. We were now nearly abeam of Cape St. Francis and about three miles offshore.

It was in this area, along the southernmost coast of the continent of Africa, that Vasco da Gama saw lights flickering ashore in 1497, presumably from manmade fires. Da Gama had recently met some of the people inhabiting South Africa at that time, of course.

There had always been heated discussion in South Africa about who occupied the country first, the blacks or the whites. We were taught in school that the Bantu tribes had arrived from the north at roughly the same time as European whites had set up colonies in the south, but what nobody bothered to explain was that the land was already occupied before either of those groups arrived. Almost all of the original inhabitants—the cattle-rich Hottentots, the hunter-gathers called Bushmen, and the Strandlopers (literally "beachwalkers") who built large shell middens along the coast, were killed, died from European diseases, or intermarried.

Da Gama, running ten years behind his fellow Portuguese explorer Bartholomeu Dias, was trying to find the sea route to India, and having better luck than Christopher Columbus. He did in fact find the way, and revolutionized trade between Europe and the East, making Portugal overnight one of the wealthiest nations in the world.

On his way from Portugal in his flagship, *San Gabriel,* Da Gama landed in St. Helena Bay, north of present-day Cape Town, to make repairs and get water and wood. There he met Hottentots.

"The inhabitants of this country are tawny-colored," noted an anonymous diarist, believed to be Da Gama himself. "Their food is confined to the flesh of seals, whales, and gazelles, and the roots of herbs."

Da Gama was much intrigued by their manner of dress. "They are dressed in skins, and wear sheaths over their virile members," he noted. Da Gama personally swapped one copper coin for one of these sheaths, but whether he kept it as a souvenir or applied it to his own virile member is not revealed.

What Da Gama couldn't have known was that the Hottentots, like the Bushmen, had an unusual physical characteristic—their penises were never less than semirigid. Hence, perhaps, his fascination with their "virility."

On the day after they arrived in St. Helena Bay, Da Gama's men captured a native who had been "gathering honey in the sandy waste" and forcibly took him aboard the *San Gabriel.*

"And being placed at table, he ate well of all we ate," Da Gama recorded. "On the following day, the captain major (that is, Da Gama, referring to himself in the third person) had him well dressed and sent ashore."

Inevitably, however, there was a skirmish during this first contact—perhaps the first recorded fight between whites and blacks in South Africa, but the forerunner of many, many more.

In their moving book about the vanishing tribes, *Testament to the Bushmen*, Laurens van der Post and Jane Taylor explain what happened. The Hottentots had been so friendly that a Portuguese sailor called Fernando Veloso had gone with them to their dwellings, to find out more about them and the way they lived.

But he was apparently suddenly overcome with panic that they might be cannibals, and so he ran back to the ship, pursued by the puzzled Hottentots. He was shouting and screaming by the time he reached the beach, so that his shipmates presumed he was being attacked by the Hottentots. Da Gama's men are said to have fired on the Hottentots with crossbows. It seems fairly certain that the Hottentots threw their assegais, and wounded Da Gama and three or four others. But we shall never know what really happened that day. It must certainly have been an unfortunate misunderstanding, for few people who have met them would call Bushmen or Hottentots ferocious or warlike people.

The Bushmen I met deep in the Kalahari Desert in 1959, when I was the photographer on an expedition to Ngamiland led by the legendary mercenary commander Mike Hoare, were without exception friendly, courteous, and reserved. They trod very lightly upon the earth. They asked for nothing and expected nothing. They were gentle, spiritual people who were literally being wiped off the face of the earth by encroaching "civilization."

On watch that night from 2 a.m. to 6 a.m. I sat in the cockpit nursing the tiller and coaxing every bit of power I could out of the light breezes. There were scattered lights on the pitch-dark shore, too, five hundred years after Da Gama passed that way, but not from native fires, just from scattered farmhouses and vacation homes. The light that attracted most attention was the single powerful flash of the lighthouse at Seal Point, just south of nearby Cape St. Francis, which held me almost hypnotized for hours.

The summer sun was already hot on my back when June came to relieve me at 6 a.m. Kevin was asleep in the quarter-berth below. June touched me gently on the arm and said: "Are you OK?"

"I'm fine," I said briskly.

"You seem a little tense."

"I'm OK."

"We hardly see each other any more," she said softly. "We just pass in the companionway; and after that you're either asleep or navigating."

I shrugged. What was I supposed to say? I was a new captain and I took my job seriously. The ship came first. The ship always came first, because if you saved the ship you saved the people. The ship took all my attention. Surely she could see that? Just as she had a job, I had a job, too, and mine was to look after the ship.

I almost said: "This isn't the Love Boat, for goodness' sake," but luckily I didn't, and just then the gannets started diving into the sea a hundred yards away. Thank goodness for the gannets.

If you've never seen Cape Gannets diving, you've missed one of nature's great sea spectacles. They're large, handsome birds, blinding white with deep, black, trailing edges to their wings, and pale yellow heads.

Hundreds of them now filled the sky over to starboard, attracted by a large school of surface fish. While some hovered with their heads at an angle, peering intensely into the water below, others were already flying down at full speed. Soon, hundreds of white arrows were shooting into the sea, sending plumes of white water leaping skyward. Some came straight down with the speed of bullets, folding their wings in a W shape as they approached the water and then, at the very last millisecond, folding them flat against their bodies. Others came in at angles, crossing each other as they darted into the sea

In the reddish morning sun, this savage scene of slaughter was drenched in color and vibrant movement—a seething battlefield in which the frenzied blue-and-white sea surface was stained red in patches with bloody froth and foam.

June and I watched in awed silence, her awkward queries forgotten. I patted her on the hand and went below to sleep.

By 9 a.m. the wind had gone to the northwest at ten knots, and we were able to hold our course along the coast toward Plettenberg Bay, beating on one long tack in calm seas. But by noon, when I came on watch again, the wind was back to its old tricks, blowing from the west again at twelve to fifteen knots, and gradually increasing all afternoon until by 4 p.m. it was howling at twenty to twenty-five knots under cloudless skies. Kevin and I reefed the mainsail and the working jib, and, thinking about Yukio Hasebe's advice that it was preferable to be at sea in thirty-knot winds if you wanted to make progress, I decided to stick it out rather than to run back to Cape St. Francis where we could find shelter.

The seas, riding on the backs of the ever-present southwesterly swells, quickly became short and choppy, making *Freelance* rear and plunge, and knocking her speed back to four knots. As her bows pitched into an oncoming wave she would stop almost dead, as if she had run into a brick wall. Solid jets of spray would rocket up from the weather side of the bow and land thirty feet aft in the cockpit.

To keep her going, we had to adjust the Aries wind vane so that she sailed farther off the wind, but that meant less progress along our course. This was our first experience of sailing her to windward in heavy weather and it was not a gratifying one. She was certainly nothing like as weatherly as our old C&C twenty-eight-footer, *Trapper*. But then, I told myself, *Trapper* was a light racing boat, designed for a different purpose.

The clouds came scurrying in from the horizon, low and menacing. The seas began to build up, so that by 10 p.m. we had given up trying to get to windward, and for the sake of comfort and safety we were hove to under a double-reefed mainsail only.

With the tiller lashed down to leeward, she lay at an angle of about forty-five degrees to the onrushing seas, and although a large wave would push her head down to leeward now and then, she rode with a positive, buoyant action that quelled much of my nervousness.

We stayed that way all the rest of the night in atrocious weather—wind, rain, and an increasingly troublesome swell. It was the very weather we had so carefully avoided in Port Elizabeth.

In the morning, spirits were low. We found we had actually lost ground through current and leeway. Kevin and I were feeling sick again, and June wasn't eating, just in case.

There seemed to be no sign of a break in the wind, so I decided to run back to Cape St. Francis for shelter after all. This news was well received by the crew, but I felt cross with myself, not only for letting a little gale get the better of us, but also for being cowardly and indecisive.

Kevin and I crawled along the sidedeck to the foredeck, where we raised the reefed jib, and we pulled off downwind. The difference in motion and noise was unbelievable. Suddenly *Freelance* came alive, dancing confidently among the white-crested waves. It was that wonderful feeling of running again, and we made splendid progress. This is what *Freelance* was made for, running in the trade winds of the deep oceans, not beating along shallow coastal waters.

Within hours we were anchored in Kromme Bay in the lee of Cape St. Francis, in thirty feet of crystal-clear water. It was 1 p.m. and the wind was still blowing from the southwest at more than twenty knots, but it was sunny and reasonably calm in the roadstead.

We ate well and rested that afternoon, but I insisted that we keep an anchor watch all night in case the wind changed and put us on a lee shore. There was nothing for the watchkeeper to do except sit there in the cockpit for four hours and watch for any sign of the anchor dragging or the wind changing. But neither of those things happened.

It was a long, boring watch. I looked at the distant white beach dimming and brightening as ragged bunches of fast-moving clouds each obscured the moonlight in turn. This was the very spot where Bernard Moitessier had anchored in *Marie-Thérèse II* when he was confronted by a gale warning just as we were.

He was afraid to heave to, as we had done, because he felt that his boat was too heavy and solid to recoil from the blows of the seas. He was right. Dear happy-go-lucky Bernard, in an effort to make his boat more stable, had filled her bilges in Durban with a mixture of concrete and old steel bolts. And in his usual way he had overdone it, so that she was down on her marks and wallowed badly. This was the man who would one day be revered as one of the greatest bluewater sailors of the twentieth century.

Like me, he had wondered about the sense of taking shelter here. "It seemed absurd to retrace (my steps) with the wind after a course I had so much trouble to make good in the other direction," he wrote in his best seller, *Sailing to the Reefs*. On the other hand, he noted, "the *Sailing Directions* . . . spoke of a violent westerly which, a few years ago, had lasted without a break for seventy-two days." So he also came to the conclusion eventually that it made more sense to anchor in calm water than to be blown backward in atrocious conditions outside.

Of course, when he did anchor here he suffered a loss he could ill afford. His chain parted because it was too thin, and he left his expensive anchor, a CQR, lying on the ocean floor. That was no joke, he admitted, but at least he had saved the chain. With a little ingenuity and work, you could make an anchor, he maintained, if you could find a forge on shore or if you had a friend who did arc-welding. To make a chain, however, was quite another matter.

I'm sure that saving a worthless, rusty chain while losing a perfectly good anchor never occurred to him as being the triumph of justification over logic.

By the time we departed from Cape St. Francis at 6:30 a.m. the next day, the southwesterly wind had died away. We set off well fed and well rested, and found a fair wind outside blowing at eight knots from the east-northeast. It was too good to last, of course. It went light and boxed the compass, so we motored for three hours from noon to 3 p.m. Then, to my dismay, the southwester came back, light at first but gradually increasing in strength.

But we were getting better at this. We reefed down again and plugged along on the beat at two and a half knots toward the next possible anchorage at Plettenberg Bay about seventy miles west of Cape St. Francis. All the rest of that day, and all night, we tacked inshore to within a couple of miles of the beach, and then back out to sea, where we hoped to find a favorable current.

When we were within striking distance of Plettenberg Bay, the classic dilemma connected with the Agulhas Bank presented itself: the wind speed was dropping and the barometer was fairly high, but the weather forecast from Cape Town Radio was for more strong southwesterlies.

Should we seek shelter in the bay, or carry on in the hope that the forecast was wrong? We were making good progress, and I knew it was a crime to waste a good wind. But caution and timidity won the day. The wind died away completely, and after four hours of motoring in a flat calm we dropped anchor near the bluff of the huge open bay and waited for the expected southwesterly gale to hit us.

It didn't, of course, and we began to wonder seriously about the accuracy of the South African government weather reports. Meanwhile, however, we took the opportunity to top up our diesel fuel tank. It was a small one, good only for about eight hours' running in calm water. It was situated beneath the floorboards in the galley and it was awkward to fill from our spare jerry cans, even when the boat was still. At sea, it was next to impossible.

We had a much bigger fuel tank built into the stern compartment, but it was unusable. Because *Freelance*'s previous owners hadn't added a biocide to the tank, it had become fouled with plant life, those hardy microorganisms that thrive on diesel fuel when a little fresh water is present. They breed so quickly that they form dense rafts in the fuel, and their sludge blocks the filters as the fuel makes its way to the engine. Even the mightiest diesel is hostage to these pesky critters. We didn't have time to clean out the main tank before we left Durban, so we emptied it and abandoned it, opting instead for a small "temporary" tank in the bilge, which I thought was quite adequate since I didn't intend to do much motoring.

Like most Durban sailors, I was still under the influence of the Spartan British school of yachting, which held that sailboats should be sailed, not motored. Anyone who motored, when sailing was even remotely possible, was regarded as a blackguard and a cheat, a scoundrel of the first water.

Thus, even when we ran the motor at sea to charge our batteries, we ran it in neutral. We knew the Hiscocks would have been proud of us. Those British stalwarts had sailed right around the world in the heavy-displacement *Wanderer III* with only a puny little four-horsepower Stuart-Turner two-stroke engine and a couple of gallons of gasoline. They might as well have had a couple of gerbils running in a cage attached to the propeller shaft. Nobody could accuse them of cheating. They had really *sailed* around the world.

Americans, we discovered, had a far different philosophy about motoring at sea. Strangely, they felt no shame, and shockingly, they installed enormous engines of twenty horsepower or more. When *Starrybright* and *Lapwing* had pulled out ahead of us after leaving Port Elizabeth, we had looked at each other and sniffed. Although their sails were set, we knew their dirty secret. Their very large engines were running. In gear. And they weren't even trying to hide it.

There was an uncomfortable swell rolling into the anchorage at Plettenberg Bay, which wasn't as pretty as Cape St. Francis, so we stayed only five hours. We heard on the radio that the weather forecast had been changed and that the expected southwesterly had apparently been delayed. So we weighed anchor at 5:20 p.m. and motored offshore for two hours—it was dead calm, I hasten to add for the benefit of purists; no chance of sailing—to avoid the inshore countercurrent.

Kevin's plottings of the SatNav fixes showed that we had found a favorable current so we stayed with it all night and made good twenty-four miles toward Cape Agulhas in teasingly light airs. We were so pleased with the SatNav's precise positions that we named it Prince Henry. After the venerable Navigator, of course.

At dawn, when a little land breeze sprang up, June spotted a ketch to starboard about ten miles inshore of us. We couldn't identify her, but we suspected she was American because her superior speed strongly suggested that she was under power as well as sail.

"Why's she battling the countercurrent so close inshore?" June asked.

"She has probably come out of Knysna," I said.

We, too, would have put into Knysna, just eighteen miles west of Plettenberg Bay, if we hadn't been delayed so long in Port Elizabeth. It was an enchanting little town, our favorite vacation spot, and we had many happy memories of wonderful trips there with the children.

Knysna (pronounced NIZE-nuh) is the gem of South Africa's Garden Route. It's surrounded by serried ranges of the Outeniqua Mountains and, closer in, by indigenous old-growth forests of exotic hardwoods such as the six-hundred-year old Outeniqua yellowwoods. Elephants still roam in this forest. On the southern side of the town lies a stunningly beautiful turquoise lagoon fringed with white-powder beaches, with access to the ocean through a cleft in high cliffs known as the Knysna Heads. That strange and rare creature the sea horse (*Hippocampus capenensis*) breeds in this estuary.

"Remember the Royal Hotel?" I said.

June laughed. "How could I forget? Cold Castle Lager and iced oysters on the half shell."

All during the hot, long, spectacular drive through the mountains in our VW camper on the way to Knysna, I'd be thinking of the cool arbored beer garden at the Royal Hotel in Queen Street. No matter where we were staying, we always stopped at the Royal first.

"Phantom Pass," said June. "Annie Veldkornet, the illegal crab catcher. Gwen Devenish's dairy farm, where we camped on the river and you forced Trent to jump off a tree down a slide you made from the dinghy's anchor line and a mainsheet block. Captain Jim and Jackie Jooris's caravan park where they bandaged the tree branches . . ."

And as we chanted our most precious memories to each other in a liturgy of retrospection, we bade good-bye to another happy part of our lives in the country we loved so deeply.

Later that morning, the wind went to the southeast and, delighted with our luck, we ran west for nearly forty miles until the breeze died and left our sails slatting in an uneasy swell. At 6 p.m. we were almost abeam of the small fishing harbor of Mossel Bay, and I was again feeling the pressure of captaincy. It was all about taking intelligent decisions based on knowledge and experience, and whereas I had some knowledge, I had only a few days' experience.

It was the usual problem, naturally. The radio weather forecast was promising that the delayed southwesterly gale was now about to burst upon us.

But what if it didn't blow as hard as they were forecasting? I now knew that *Freelance* would go to windward, albeit slowly, in winds of twenty knots in reasonable sea conditions. I also knew that if we ran for shelter like a frightened rabbit, we could be stuck in Mossel Bay for many days, perhaps weeks, suffering from port paralysis.

On the other hand, we were on a dangerous section of the Agulhas Bank, and we had been warned about it. In February 1966, my old acquaintance Jean Gau had capsized near here in his thirty-foot Tahiti ketch, *Atom*. He was on his second circumnavigation at the time, one of the most experienced small-boat seamen in the world. He had already survived a battering from Hurricane Carrie six hundred miles southwest of the Azores, which sank the four-masted bark *Pamir* with thirty-five seamen and fifty-one cadets. He had weathered the hurricane hove to.

But when Gau was rounding the Cape of Storms, the vicious waves of the Agulhas Bank did what the Atlantic hurricane couldn't. They capsized *Atom,* rolled her over, and dismasted her. Gau set out to cut away the loose wreckage before it could stove in *Atom's* hull, but his wire cutters dropped overboard and he was forced to part the stainless-steel shrouds and stays with a hacksaw blade that he held in his hand. After pumping out her flooded bilges, he managed to get his auxiliary engine going, and he put into Mossel Bay harbor for repairs.

Atom was broader and heavier than *Freelance,* but I figured their chances of survival in a bad storm would be very similar, and that it would be experience and seamanship that counted most. If Jean Gau was unable to prevent a capsize, I certainly wouldn't be.

"We're going to Mossel Bay," I announced finally.

"Good plan," said Kevin and June enthusiastically. I was very thankful for their support.

It was dark when we approached the little fishing port, and we seemed to be much closer to the rock-strewn coastline that we ought to have been. I don't know whether it was due to a stray current or plain incompetence on my part.

"Are we OK on this course?" June asked diplomatically. She was at the helm, and feeling nervous.

"We're fine," I said, shamelessly, not really knowing whether we were too close or not, since we didn't have a large-scale chart of the harbor entrance. "Things always seem closer at night," I added, but my heart was pounding hard.

We were moving fast and the seas were building up behind us. But before my apprehension could grow into panic, the red and green lights of the harbor piers suddenly came into view, and I told June to swung the tiller over. I started the engine, and Kevin struck the sails.

When we entered the little man-made harbor, I was vastly relieved to find a whole lot of frightened rabbits inside. *Aqua Viva* was there, to our surprise, as was *Starrynight* and *Lapwing*. *Albroc* was there, too, having motored nonstop for two whole days, as we found out later. Two other cruisers we didn't know were *Amore II* and *Ev-a-Dene,* a Hartley Tahitian from our home port of Durban. No sign of our friend Yukio Hasebe in *Pink Maru Maru,* though.

But even as we rafted up alongside *Aqua Viva* in the crowded little port, and Pepe jumped aboard *Freelance* to make friends again and have his head scratched, I had premonitions of our stay being a repeat of our experience in Port Elizabeth.

"How long, Pepe?" I asked, since cats are all-knowing. But if he knew, he didn't tell. Which was just as well.

6

MOSSEL BAY TO CAPE TOWN

The threatened gale materialized as forecast, sending increasingly large swells through Mossel Bay's harbor entrance. We put extra fenders between ourselves and *Aqua Viva,* whose crew put extra fenders between her and the concrete wharf, but we spent an uneasy night being jerked back and forth.

Next morning, a fishing boat moved from the wharf to be hauled out at the marine railway, and we moved to her spot alongside the concrete quay, to which huge old tires had been lashed, some of them doubled up. It was an improvement, but it was still a very uncomfortable berth as the surge running into the harbor mouth flung us backward and forward.

Kevin got it in perspective, though: "It's better than being out at sea, wet through, frightened, and freezing cold, going backward, and feeling seasick," he said. Who could argue?

The coldness was something we hadn't expected. It was, after all, the height of summer. But on his night watches at sea, Kevin had been wearing all the sweaters he could muster, plus several pairs of socks, one on top of the other, on his feet.

We tended our lines and fenders for seven whole days in Mossel Bay while another series of southwesterly depressions came rampaging up from the Roaring Forties. After a couple of days, an Australian yacht called *Swaggie,* tired of fighting gale-force headwinds, came into port to join our restless band. We learned from the cruisers' grapevine that our undercanvassed friend *Ipi Tombi* had apparently been forced back to Port Elizabeth by the southwest gale we had weathered. There was no word of plucky Yukio Hasebe and his *Pink Maru Maru.*

Mossel Bay (The Bay of Mussels) has a special standing in South Africa's history. The Portuguese explorer Bartholomeu Dias stumbled upon it in 1488, while he was seeking the sea route to India. Dias had come creeping down the west coast of Africa with two caravelles and a storeship, but north of present-day Cape Town he had encountered a violent storm that lasted thirteen days and his little fleet was driven far to the south. When he was able to turn east again, he found no land, a fact that caused some concern among his men. After a while, Dias turned his caravelle north, and finally they come to the African continent again in the vicinity of what is now called Mossel Bay. They had unwittingly rounded the bottom of Africa without sighting it.

He found Hottentots living there, and tried to procure some of their cattle to replenish his provisions, but the contact was not friendly, and Dias decided to carry on eastward. That decision was not popular with his crew, either, and by the time the expedition reached the Great Fish River, a little east of present-day Port Elizabeth, the men were in full revolt, seriously fearful of falling off the edge of the world. They threatened to cut Dias's throat if he didn't turn back.

All was not lost, because Dias had got farther than anyone before him, and proved that there was an end to the continent of Africa. On the return voyage he discovered and named Cape Agulhas as well as another cape to the west, which, for reasons not hard to guess, he called Cabo Tormentoso—the Cape of Storms. It was King John of Portugal who proposed a new name for it in view of the possibilities Dias's expedition's had opened up with regard to trade with India—the Cape of Good Hope.

About nine years later, in 1497, Vasco da Gama also called at Mossel Bay and got on so well with the Hottentots that the place became an important port of call for the many Portuguese ships that were to follow. Here they could take on fresh water and provisions. Dutch seafarers later named it after the large numbers of mussels they found there.

We in our turn called it Morsel Bay, because there wasn't much of it, and there wasn't an awful lot to do there either, except perhaps practice your Afrikaans on the natives. We did locate a good source of fish-and-chip suppers, however, and we dropped in at the offices of the local newspaper for a chat.

Perhaps I do it an injustice though, because Mossel Bay is a popular holiday resort with fine beaches and spectacular scenery. It too is part of South Africa's Garden Route, a highway that runs along an enchanting stretch of coast with lakes, mountains, golden beaches, cliffs, and dense indigenous forests backed by serried ranks of mountains growing ever more purple with distance and height. The trouble was, we were biased. We resented being there. We wanted to be in the South Atlantic, on our way to America, past the hurdle of Cape Town, where we would have to smuggle our Krugerrands through the customs inspection.

Every day we monitored the weather forecasts for shipping, and every day we learned of more southwesterly gales on the way, with their low, gray nimbus clouds racing overhead, and showers pelting down. The locals said the weather was extraordinary. This was the season for southeasters, not southwesters. This kind of thing had never happened before. But, of course, that's what the locals everywhere always tell the long-faced tourists.

Amore II had a weatherfax receiver on board and her crew, René, produced gloomy charts every day. We were invited aboard *Ev-a-Dene* and we met the owner of the American sloop *Lapwing*, a Westsail 32. He was Jeff Oakes, and he was sailing around the world singlehanded. I bought some stainless-steel fittings and a foghorn from him. Oakes came from Tampa, Florida, and said he had earned enough working as an aircraft mechanic in three years in Saudi Arabia to pay cash for the boat and cruise for six years. *Some wages,* I thought.

The yacht club in Mossel Bay was new, bright, and friendly. It had a wonderful view over the bay, and full bar facilities, but no food yet. That didn't matter to us, though, because our wonderful fish-and-chip shop provided us with really fresh local fish and French fries almost every evening.

To work off the calories we went for walks, but only two of us at a time since *Freelance*'s lines needed constant tending. June and I had a memorable trek along a cliff path above the lighthouse, surrounded by very rugged scenery. Huge caves and inclined rock strata dominated the cliff. Below us, seagulls turned and twisted on the inshore current, being lifted by the headland of Cape St. Blaize, and below them lay a boiling cauldron of sea.

In a high cliff face like this, not far from Mossel Bay, at Blombos Cave, human beings were living more than seventy thousand years previously. Scientists who examined the ancient dwelling place in 1993 were astonished. They concluded that homo sapiens came out of Africa not only with fully modern anatomies, but also with at least thirty thousand years of experience in modern behavior. It was a finding that stood current theories on their heads.

But for us, that day, the endless beauty and fascination of South Africa were obscured by our great feeling of sadness at having to leave them. This was turning out to be the most drawn-out, most harrowing farewell we had ever experienced. To cheer ourselves up we bought some ice cream in town on the way back, which undoubtedly added more calories than the walking had lost, but we didn't care. We took some ice cream back for Kevin, too, and he was very glad to see us for once.

A yacht called *Timabel* left port while we were on the cliffs. She was slightly smaller than *Freelance,* and bound for Portugal with a tiller for a caravelle being built there to celebrate Dias's discovery of Mossel Bay.

Timabel had been given an official farewell by the Mayor, the Town Council, a brass band, the works. But she sneaked back after dark when a gale-force headwind sprang up and apparently laid her flat on her side.

Next day, to our amazement, *Timabel* sailed again, this time into a strong southwesterly. We admired their spirit, for the forecast was for continued strong southwesterlies, and we knew she would make little or no progress.

The cruisers' grapevine revealed that Yukio Hasebe and *Pink Maru Maru* had made it to Cape Town after eleven days of nonstop beating from Port Elizabeth. We envied him.

And then, next morning we woke up and the southwesterly gales had stopped. Saturday, February 7, was fine and clear. Better still, it was blowing fifteen knots from the southeast. Sanity had returned to the weather at long last.

By 6:30 a.m. we had cleared harbor. We romped along splashily toward the most southerly tip of Africa, Cape Agulhas, in a sea lumpy from leftover southwesterly swells, making our top speed of six knots under all plain sail.

The world's first solo circumnavigator, Joshua Slocum, had sailed the thirty-eight-foot *Spray* around Cape Agulhas about ninety years before.

In his book, *Sailing Alone Around the World*, he says:

"Gales of wind sweeping the cape even now were frequent enough, one occurring on an average, every thirty-six hours; but one gale was much the same as another, with no more serious result than to blow the *Spray* along on her course when it was fair, or to blow her back somewhat when it was ahead.

"On Christmas, 1897, I came to the pitch of the cape. On this day the *Spray* was trying to stand on her head, and she gave me every reason to believe that she would accomplish the feat before night. She began very early in the morning to pitch and toss about in a most unusual manner, and I have to record that, while I was at the end of the bowsprit reefing the jib, she ducked me under water three times for a Christmas box. I got wet and did not like it a bit: never in any other sea was I put under more than once in the same short space of time, say three minutes. A large English steamer passing ran up the signal, 'Wishing you a Merry Christmas.' I think the captain was a humorist; his own ship was throwing her propeller out of the water."

Two days later, Slocum passed Cape Agulhas with a fair wind, but was forced into Simon's Bay by another gale, presumably from the northwest. From there he made it to Cape Town without trouble.

It soon became clear that our nice southeaster had ambitions to grow into a full gale, and by noon we were running under a working jib only. By 6:30 p.m. the barometer had dropped nine points, an ominous sign, and we reefed the jib. It was blowing a steady thirty knots, but this was a favorable gale, so we were not too concerned. It was helping us along, even if it was more boisterous than we would have wished for, and we were still making top speed downwind, surfing briefly down the faces of steep swells topped with spilling breakers.

As the sun set among the fleeing ragged clouds ahead of us, June handed out mugs of steaming soup and slices of buttered bread in the cockpit. Only someone who has tried to produce the simplest meal in a small boat bucking and rearing in a storm at sea will know just how much work that entailed, and what cunning strategies were involved in such simple tasks as pouring from pot to mug, or setting down a loaf of bread, or a knife, on a surface that kept hurling them off.

Eric Hiscock rightly said that almost anyone could learn to sail a boat, and anyone with an elementary knowledge of arithmetic could learn to navigate. But cooking a meal in the confined space of a small yacht's violently lurching galley was the most difficult of all the arts concerned with cruising under sail.

And, knowing that, I'm ashamed to say that Kevin and I showed no gratitude to our brave and clever cook. We glared at her again, accepted our mugs grudgingly, and sipped from them with great hesitation after long intervals. We were feeling seasick again. Not enough to retch, or to prevent our taking a watch on deck, but just enough to make us feel like death warmed up at the first mention of food. June, in charge of our welfare and morale, understood the need for hot food to ward off the fatigue that leads to mistakes. She watched intently while we sipped our soup, knowing that we were quite likely to tip it over the side the moment she turned her back.

After midnight on that first night out of Mossel Bay the wind began to abate. By 2 a.m., when *Freelance* was sliding along nicely in a ten-knot southeaster, the situation seemed to have improved greatly—except for two things. The first was that the barometer was, incredibly, still dropping. It had got down to 1007 millibars. The second was that Cape Town Radio was forecasting a southwesterly gale.

We looked at each other in astonishment to see if we'd heard it right. Another one? Another southwesterly gale? Kevin shrugged. "It's getting to sound pretty normal," he said.

One every thirty-six hours, I thought. *Slocum was right.*

We were nearly fifteen miles offshore at that time, still on the Agulhas Bank, and some fifty miles east of Cape Agulhas.

I marked our position on the chart. "If we can make it to Cape Agulhas in time, we can anchor there," I said. "It sticks out and it will shelter us from the southwest."

"How do you mean, 'if we can make it?'" June asked.

"I mean before the southwesterly gale arrives. We have to get there and anchor before the wind comes up, otherwise it will just blow us backward, back to Mossel Bay."

"The forecast didn't say exactly when the gale would start," Kevin pointed out.

"They never do," I said. "They just don't know."

"How long to Cape Agulhas?" Kevin asked.

"Say twelve hours at four knots."

"What do you think?"

"Let's go for it," I said.

It made sense to me to ride out the coming gale at anchor in the lee of the great cape that, true to its Portuguese name, stuck out like a giant needle from the very bottom of the African continent, rather than lose hard-earned ground by running back. If the gale arrived before we got to Cape Agulhas, we could always run with it as a last resort, back to Sebastion Bay, behind Cape Infanta, or even as far as Mossel Bay, if need be. *Freelance* was good at running before gales. But then, she was getting a lot of practice.

So we changed course in the dying wind, heading inshore toward Struis Bay, a large bight just north of the cape. When the wind died altogether in the early hours of the morning we started up our little BMW diesel and *Freelance* kept going west, sliding easily at four knots over massive long swells left over from the southeasterly gale, so that by daybreak we found ourselves feeling our way blindly in dense coastal mist a few miles from Cape Agulhas.

The mist cleared as the sun came up. And just in time. There, not half a mile ahead of us, was breaking white water. I took one horrified look and, by sheer instinct, swung the helm over and reversed our track. I yelled for Kevin to come up from his bunk, and we stood staring unbelievingly at the breaking waves.

"The water's thirty feet deep there at least," I said. "What's going on?"

"It's a full lee shore. These huge swells left over from the southeasterly gale are just toppling over and breaking."

"There's white water everywhere," I said. "We can't anchor in there. Let's get out of here."

"Where can we go?"

"We'll have to take our chances at sea," I said. It was the book knowledge in me talking, the only knowledge I had at the time. Time after time I had read that the safest place for a small boat in a storm was out at sea, far from land.

And so, in the calm that preceded the southwesterly gale, we motored due south from Cape Agulhas, heading for Antarctica, to put as much distance as we could between ourselves and the land.

We didn't get far, however. Two hours later, when we were about ten miles south of the cape, the gale hit us with a fifty-knot punch. It came without warning, just like the southwesterly busters that hit Durban every summer. One minute it was dead calm. The next, it was blowing a full gale.

We snatched down the sails, lashed them securely, and lay ahull, that is, we drifted broadside on to the wind and waves and left *Freelance* to look after herself. I took the first watch, while Kevin and June lay in their bunks down below, secured in place by their canvas leeboards. There wasn't much for me to do, except hold the kicking tiller to absorb the shocks of waves breaking against the rudder, and watch for traffic approaching in the shipping lane. Luckily, the wind was blowing us away from the land at a slight angle.

The seas built up rapidly. First there was simply a carpet of small, closely packed white horses filling the horizon all around us and kicking up a layer of spray that blew downwind like smoke. Then, in a matter of minutes, bigger waves formed and jostled with each other for room. Within the hour, large waves were riding on the backs of fast-moving swells, and at the front of each wave was a plunging white breaker several feet high.

The wind screamed through the rigging, a high-pitched banshee wail that made my stomach contract with fear, and the mast trembled so hugely that it shook the whole boat as a terrier shakes a rat.

As the hours drew on, the waves grew bigger but farther apart. As we rose on swells twenty feet high, I could see waves topped by seething waterfalls at intervals all around us. But it wasn't until almost the end of my watch that the first of these isolated monsters bore down on us from the port side.

Like a deer trapped in the headlights of a car, I watched the inevitable happen. I felt the cold fear of helplessness as the breaking crest of the wave towered overhead and roared down its own face toward us.

I crouched down in the cockpit, terrified, still clinging hard to the tiller, and flinched as the solid water crashed against *Freelance*'s hull with a sledgehammer blow that made her shudder from stem to stern.

In a second, we were knocked down. Her mast was almost flat on the water, and her leeward decks were buried in surging foam up to the level of the portlights on the cabin side.

I started to fall against the cockpit coaming, but already she was staggering back onto her feet, and as she straightened up she was bodily thrown sideways a few yards. Then her deep long keel got a grip on the water and she held herself back while the wave passed on in majestic fury.

I scrambled up from the cockpit floor and looked around, white and shaking. There were other waves like that one around us, but none directly in line with us.

It was some time before I realized that there was no damage. June opened the sliding hatch and peered out anxiously to see if I was still there, and asked if everything was OK. I looked around, and nothing seemed out of place. "Yes," I said, "we're fine." She slid the hatch closed again.

It takes a lot of experience to know how your boat will respond in a storm, and how much of a battering she can take. Perhaps I had previously underestimated the effect of large waves. I hadn't expected the solidity of the blow. It was like being struck by wet concrete. But since we had sustained no damage I reasoned we'd be safe enough lying ahull like this—that is, lying sideways on to the wind and swells without any sail up—until the waves got so big that they started picking us up bodily and flinging us to far leeward. Then we'd have to run off before them, choosing the safest path between them; but meanwhile our wide keel was dragging sideways through the water, slowing down our rate of drift so we wouldn't lose any more ground than we could help.

Crouching in the cockpit with my back to the seas, holding on tightly to the winch barrel, I thought bitterly about the people who had accused us of taking the chicken run. This didn't seem to me to be a particularly easy way out.

For eighteen hours we sat and took our punishment while it blew fifty to fifty-five knots. On our watches down below, it was impossible to sleep because of the violent movement, the noise, and our anxiety. The best we could hope for was some respite from the physical assault and drenchings in the steeply canted cockpit. Everything below was dripping wet and cold. We couldn't change our clothes because of the violent motion in the heaving cabin, so when we weren't on watch in the cockpit we fastened our lee-cloths to keep us in our bunks and lay there in our wet oilskins, shivering with our eyes open, praying for the wind to drop.

Interestingly, the raw fear I had felt on deck at the approach of that first big wave gradually dissipated, and was replaced by lower-grade anxiety. There is, apparently, only so much fear the human mind can put up with. After several hours on watch in these conditions, the unimaginable becomes the normal, and the fact that you haven't been drowned yet gives you every hope that you will live a little longer.

I had often heard that storms were just a normal part of a sailor's life at sea, as indeed they are, but during all those years when I dreamed of crossing an ocean I had never had any confidence in my ability to handle bad weather. My secret fears were twofold: first, that I would not know how best to position the boat in the seas, and second, that I would not physically be able to reef the sails or raise a storm jib on a heaving foredeck.

But now I felt there was hope. I could already see how *Freelance* would best handle a bad storm, and I knew I was capable of controlling her. It was not exactly a feeling of happiness that swept over me as I lay in my bunk, wet and shivering, but rather a feeling of deep relief. I had laid a ghost. We were facing a real storm, and we were doing fine. I had a lot to learn still, but my anxiety was waning, and I felt a lot better about our prospects.

Eric Hiscock once wrote, poignantly: "Fortunate indeed is the man who, early in his sailing career, encounters and successfully weathers a hard blow." Hiscock himself was not so fortunate. This world-famous circumnavigator lived for many years with the private fear that really bad weather would overtake *Wanderer III,* his little wooden sloop, and that he would prove inadequate. Well, eventually he did have to face a real storm, of course—and to his great relief both he and his vessel coped splendidly.

As we drifted eastward we picked up an electrifying radio call for help. It was a Mayday from Jeff Oakes on *Lapwing.*

Like us, Jeff had closed with the shore at Cape Agulhas, expecting to find shelter from the coming gale, but he'd suddenly found himself trapped in the thundering surf we had seen. He had been forced to drop anchor in a spot that now exposed him to the danger of being blown ashore by the southwesterly. His anchor line was bar-taut, so he couldn't raise the anchor on his own to run out to sea, as we had done, and he couldn't slip the cable without fear of being swept ashore immediately.

We listened intently to the drama that unfolded. *Lapwing* wasn't much more than fifteen miles away, but there was no chance of our even seeing her through the wind-driven spume, let alone doing anything for her.

Cape Town Radio, monitoring the marine frequencies, replied to his call, and a South African Air Force helicopter was dispatched with a crew who managed to board the yacht, raise the anchor, and shift her to a calmer anchorage behind a reef. It was a remarkable rescue job.

We took turns at keeping watch in the cockpit through that wet, cold, frightening day and night, looking out for large ships coming our way, but the few lights we spotted while we were at the tops of large swells seemed to be much farther out to sea. The professional sailors were obviously giving Cape Agulhas and the Agulhas Bank a wide berth, for which I was very grateful.

Our westerly gale died away gradually to a steady twenty knots early next morning, and we were able to beat against it with a double-reefed mainsail and storm jib. We zigged and zagged, in toward Cape Agulhas and out to sea again, until, shortly after dawn, we could truly say that we had weathered it. The cape looked surprisingly low and insignificant in the watery morning light, and we were glad to see the last of it. We were battered and short of sleep, but we had rounded the bottom of Africa, and, thankfully, suffered only minor damage from the storm—a fitting on the Aries self-steering gear had been wrenched off by a giant wave. But now, even if we had to steer by hand, we could turn north again and lay our course to Cape Point, at the end of Dias's Cape of Good Hope. It was eighty miles away, and we could lay it on one tack.

But it wasn't that easy, of course. It never is. Shortly after dusk we were set in toward land by an errant current at Danger Point, near the notorious Birkenhead Rock, upon which the British troop ship *Birkenhead* foundered in 1852 with the loss of 454 of the 638 men on board. There were ghosts lurking all along the Cape of Storms.

I switched on our navigation lights because there were usually fishing boats in this area, and we went about on to the starboard tack to gain westing against the choppy seas still being driven by that twenty-knot southwesterly. We hadn't been on our new course five minutes when there was a hail from astern, and to our great surprise *Lapwing* appeared out of the pitch darkness. Jeff Oakes, looking none the worse for his adventure at Cape Agulhas, shouted that he had been motor-sailing all the way. But he too had been set inshore—close enough to see breaking surf, he claimed—and like us, he was heading out to sea again. With his big diesel roaring, he pulled ahead and was soon out of sight.

By midnight we were well clear of Danger Point, so I set a course directly for Cape Point, about forty miles distant. It lies at the foot of the peninsula headed by Table Mountain and Cape Town. *Freelance* plunged on toward the northwest at a steady four knots, tucking her shoulder down deep into the warm Indian Ocean for the last time. When we reached the lighthouse at Cape Point we would enter the Atlantic Ocean and the sea temperature would drop fifteen degrees.

Just before dawn we spotted the triple beam of the Cape Point light cartwheeling on the starboard bow, right where it should be. It was the brightest lighthouse in the Southern Hemisphere, with nineteen million candlepower. June smiled and Kevin clapped me on the back. "Good navigating," he said. But I knew what he really meant was: "Thank goodness the worst is behind us."

Famous last words. Needless to say it wasn't all over yet. We rounded the Cape of Good Hope, the craggy tip of the Cape Peninsula, and ran north toward Cape Town along a mountainous coast of unsurpassed beauty. We simply couldn't take our eyes off it. When Sir Francis Drake, the English pirate turned explorer, came across this cape in 1580, he described it thus: "The most stately thing and the fairest Cape we saw in the whole circumference of the world." We didn't doubt it.

The Hiscocks were impressed, too, when they came past on their first circumnavigation. "The panorama was magnificent, as the rising sun bathed the mountains of the peninsula and Cape Hangklip in a hazy, golden light," Eric Hiscock wrote in *Around the World in Wanderer III*.

"We had seen no finer piece of coastal scenery than this. Bold and lofty stood the Twelve Apostles, and presently, as we made our way to the north, out from behind them peeped the flat top of Table Mountain and the steep cone of Lion's Head."

As we, too, were swept north amid all this beauty I couldn't help thinking of the two happiest years of my childhood, which were spent just a few miles from here, in Simonstown on the other side of the narrow peninsula. It was there, at the age of fourteen, that I was introduced to the sea and went for my first sail.

But I didn't have much time for rumination on the past. The wind was backing to the southeast and freshening. Off the fishing village of Hout Bay we spotted the well-known South African ocean racing yacht, *Voortrekker,* speeding north well inshore of us, and I called her on the VHF radio. Her home port was Cape Town, a few miles north, and I wanted to know what weather we could expect when we got there. I had been alerted by scurrying white clouds ahead, pouring through gaps in the high-peaked Twelve Apostles. We were in the lee of the mountains at the time, but we'd be exposed to the full blast of the south-easter when we turned the corner near Cape Town.

But *Voortrekker* obviously wasn't monitoring the radio, and she sped on her way unheeding. Adding to my worries was the fact that I had no large-scale chart of the approaches to Cape Town, or the harbor itself. I remembered, from having sailed into the port once before, that there were no hidden dangers to worry about; that if you followed the coastline at a respectful distance, you wouldn't get into trouble. But I couldn't remember the way to the Royal Cape Yacht Club, which lay deep inside the labyrinth of man-made docks, piers, and jetties, and so I dug out an old street map of Cape Town. It wasn't exactly explicit, but it gave me an idea of the general direction to head in, and made me feel less uneasy.

In fair weather, none of this would have mattered much, since we could have pottered along gently and found our way at our leisure, but I had a feeling that we were in for a dusting once we rounded the top end of the peninsula. Accordingly, we double-reefed the mainsail and changed the working foresail for the storm jib.

As we approached the harbor entrance at 6 p.m. my worst fears materialized. The wind suddenly blasted through at fifty knots and laid us over almost flat in the water. I started the engine, then went to help Kevin take the mainsail down. But the twelve-horsepower BMW was no match for this wind, and we made no progress at all even though it was running at full power. So we raised the mainsail again while June took the tiller, and then we beat back and forth in the tight confines of Table Bay docks under sail and motor, looking anxiously for a gap that would lead us into the Duncan Dock.

With our sidedecks under water, we made slow progress against the screaming wind, which whipped the lapels of our spray jackets against our faces until they stung. Then, more by chance than judgment, I found the right gap and we were making short tacks in the even closer confines of the Duncan Dock, going about every couple of minutes with a deafening crackle of flogging mainsail. The water, thank goodness, was flat, but smoking with white spindrift. The large ships and fishing boats alongside the wharves jerked at their mooring lines, squeezing them thin until water ran out and flew downwind in clouds of spray.

We came eventually to the head of the dock and could see, through another gap, the floats in the Royal Cape Yacht Club marina. But the slips all appeared to be full, and we were fearful of going through the narrow entrance because there was no room to maneuver under sail inside the marina.

Luckily, I remembered the panic buoy. It was a large mooring buoy placed near the entrance to the marina for occasions such as this. Vessels could sail up to it, make fast, and lie there until conditions calmed down enough for them to enter the marina.

I sent June and Kevin up to the foredeck with the boathook, to grab the line on the buoy as we motor-sailed up to it. It was a difficult maneuver, because as soon as we lost way, the sheer power of the wind spun the boat around sideways on, and we started to drift off to leeward.

Twice, after I had placed the bows alongside the buoy, June and Kevin failed to grab the line. It was a thick hawser, obviously meant for a large ship, and simply wouldn't fit in the crook of the boathook. Worse, it was badly twisted, and had no loose end that could be raised to the foredeck. I cursed the members of the Royal Cape Yacht Club for not maintaining their panic buoy so that a yacht could use it, and we tried again, because we had no option. On the third attempt, June and Kevin managed to hook the buoy itself, and Kevin leaned over and grabbed the rope hawser. By the time I had raced up to the foredeck to help him, he was stretched taut over the stainless-steel pulpit. The three of us clung to the hawser like grim death and managed to hold *Freelance* against the gale. When we'd got half a turn around the leg of the pulpit I sent Kevin back to get a line, and we made both ends of it fast to the hawser before dropping back clear of the buoy.

We tamed the flapping mainsail with tiers, and sank back exhausted in the cockpit, almost too tired to talk but glad, wonderfully, wonderfully glad, to be safely tied up in harbor in this killer wind that they called a black southeaster.

We lay at the buoy all night while the wind shrieked and plucked at our rigging. We didn't care. We had rounded the Cape. We passed out, exhausted.

Next morning, while the gale was whipping gray cloud low around the base of Table Mountain, a powerful harbor launch hove to alongside us. A white-uniformed customs or immigration official asked where we had come from, where we were registered, and where we were bound for. We told him the yacht was South African, registered in Durban, and bound for the USA.

"See you before you leave, then," he yelled. "Have a nice stay in Cape Town."

Our hearts sank. See us? Would they search the boat before we left? If they caught us trying to smuggle Krugerrands out of the country they had the power to confiscate the boat, too. Almost everything we owned in the world was aboard *Freelance*.

June and I had discussed hiding the Krugerrands somewhere on the boat. It would have been easy to cement them into the bilge, for instance, and fiberglass over the concrete. But we decided that if they suspected us at all, they wouldn't hesitate to pull the yacht apart. They would know where to look.

Many years earlier, I had been aboard a seventeen-foot sloop that was pulled apart by British customs officials. In calm weather, I had accepted a tow across the English Channel from France by a motor cruiser that, unknown to me, was suspected of being involved in the robbery of a large collection of jewels. The customs slit open my fenders and emptied the gas tank of the outboard engine. They drilled holes in the mast and they emptied my jerry jugs of water. Even my smelly kitbag, stuffed with dirty socks and underpants from a three-month trip, was carefully searched.

So in the end, June and I agreed to play innocent. We decided to leave our Krugerrands virtually out in the open, hoping that such naïveté, such obvious lack of criminal intent, would mitigate any punishment. We hoped that if they did discover our gold coins (God forbid) and confiscate them, they might at least let us keep our boat.

So we shoved the coins into an open cubbyhole, alongside our six-month supply of teabags, above the V-berth in the fo'c'sle. In their transparent plastic sleeves, they were in plain sight of anyone sitting in the main cabin and looking forward, so we could hardly be accused of deliberately hiding them. We knew we were taking a big chance, but we were damned if we were going to act like criminals when this was our own money.

We could only hope for the best.

7

JOY AND TEARS IN CAPE TOWN

South Africa has three official capitals: Pretoria, Bloemfontein, and Cape Town. Pretoria is the administrative capital. It's self-important and Calvinistic. Bloemfontein is the judicial capital, home of the Supreme Court. It's drab and quietly standoffish. Cape Town, the Mother City, is the legislative capital, the seat of Parliament. It's older, more mature, staggeringly beautiful, friendly, and cosmopolitan. It makes up for the others.

The climate is Mediterranean, hot and dry in summer, wet and mild in winter. Capetonians are more outward-looking than most South Africans, more tolerant, and friendlier to outsiders. The main nonwhite population consists of Coloureds, Malays, and the vestiges of Bushmen and Hottentots.

Cape Town is a lively city of more than two million, dominated by Table Mountain, a flat-topped nature reserve thirty-five hundred feet high, whose twenty-three square miles of granite, shale, and sandstone erupted from the sea bed some two hundred million years ago. When the southeaster blows, the mountain wears a cap of white cloud that the locals call the tablecloth. And their name for the predominant summer southeaster is the Cape Doctor, because it blows away all ills. In truth, it blows away everything that isn't nailed down.

To the northwest, Lion's Head and Signal Hill look out over Table Bay, where large fleets of sailing ships anchored a century ago. On the far side of the city, behind sunny seaside coves with beaches of soft white sand, the Twelve Apostles line the scenic cliffside road to Chapman's Peak and the Cape of Good Hope, some thirty miles south.

To the east lie the world-famous botanical gardens at Kirstenbosch, known for it collection of *fynbos,* an Afrikaans word that translates, literally, as fine, or delicate, bush. These are the native plants growing north and east of Cape Town, made up of eighty-five hundred species, about five thousand of which are unique to the area. Many are tiny and fragile, but others are hardy and well established. The best known outside South Africa is the protea, of course, but the fynbos vegetation around the Cape Peninsula is so rare and unusual that it actually forms one of the world's six discrete plant kingdoms.

Cape Town really is something special, and not only in the botanical sense. It's a throbbing modern city, but its edges are softened everywhere by timeless old buildings, many of them architectural gems—and even a castle with cells and torture chambers dating from 1666—that bespeak three and a half centuries of sea contact with Europe. It was in 1652 that Jan van Riebeeck established a supply post here for the Dutch East India Company's ships plying Da Gama's old route to India.

Once again, I must admit to bias, of course, because June and I knew the city quite well. I spent part of my childhood nearby, and later attended the Argus Company's school of journalism there as a young cub reporter. June had visited the city many times on business trips when she was editor of South Africa's largest parenting magazine. But, bias or nor, I believe that anyone with an ounce of sense would agree that it is an entrancing city.

The morning after we tied up to the panic buoy at the entrance to the Royal Cape Yacht Club's marina, the wind dropped sufficiently for us to motor in and moor in an empty slip next to *Lapwing.* Jeff Oakes had arrived half a day ahead of us, and had slipped into the marina before the wind changed into high gear.

The club secretary gave us honorary membership, as was the custom for all visiting yachts, and we quickly took advantage of the showers and dining room.

That evening, we were sitting having drinks in the waterfront lounge when a cat fight started up outside.

A room full of people stared out of the tall glass windows.

"Isn't that Pepe?" said June, pointing to the smaller of the two balls of flying fur.

"From *Aqua Viva?*" I asked.

"Yes, it looks like him."

Without thinking I ran outside. It was Pepe all right. The bullying club tomcat had cornered him.

With the club members gazing on, I leaped into the fray and tried to grab Pepe, but he backed off onto a nearby boat, followed swiftly by the club cat. I climbed aboard and managed to chase the club cat off. Then, after a short chase, I was able to grab Pepe by the collar and march with him down the dock to where *Aqua Viva* was moored. I deposited him safely on board, but he wasn't the least grateful for this help from a seafaring friend.

From the looks I got when I returned to the club lounge, most of the spectators who witnessed my lightning raid were on the side of the club cat. No matter, I still figured a seagoing cat deserved to be helped. Besides, as I've said, this was no ordinary cat. This was not even an ordinary sea cat. This was one who could use a human toilet. He couldn't flush it, of course, but his delighted owner had said it was far easier than having to deal with messy, smelly, cat litter while crossing an ocean.

In any case, the members of this club were quite used to odd characters from boats. When Bernard Moitessier arrived here in *Marie-Thérèse II,* he and his great buddy Henry Wakelam, aboard *Wanda,* used to shoot cormorants for the pot with a catapult and ball bearings. Moitessier himself, needing to top up his water tanks, borrowed a dinghy, filled it with fresh water from the club hosepipe, towed it alongside his boat, and bailed the water aboard with a bucket. Even Wakelam, not exactly the most fastidious of men, was aghast at that.

"Bloody Frenchman," he said, shaking his head. They routinely insulted each other.

Moitessier protested that he had cleaned the cormorant guano out of the dinghy before he started. But Wakelam wasn't convinced.

Moitessier was moved to remark: "A dog-biscuit stuffer like you needn't be so fussy."

That was the pot calling the kettle black, of course, for they were both living on a basic diet of rice, lentils, dog biscuits, and curried cormorant.

I had known Wakelam for many years in my schoolboy days in Durban. It was hard not to be aware of him around Point Yacht Club, if only because he rarely wore anything other than an abbreviated pair of canvas shorts he had made for himself from a tarpaulin he claimed had fallen off a passing railroad car. You may have heard of shorts that will stand up on their own. I can vouch for the truth of that. I had seen Henry's famous shorts standing by the side of the shower in the PYC locker room, waiting patiently for their master to step into them.

While Moitessier described himself as a vagabond, Wakelam, clad in those shorts, barefoot, tall, lean, tanned, and grinning through his black beard, was definitely a pirate. We junior members of the club admired him greatly because there was hardly a rule he wouldn't break. He especially hated officialdom and took great delight in deflating pompous egos. He loved to shock people, and was very successful at it. He was also very scathing of people who wouldn't take chances.

He was almost beside himself with glee one day when I saw him returning to the locker room with two cans of paint, one black, one white. He noticed my quizzical look.

"Go have a look at *Urda,*" he said, grinning wickedly.

Urda was an old powerboat out in the line of moorings, presumably named after the three goddesses from Norse mythology. Some might have called *Urda* stately, in an Edwardian kind of way. Her cabin was simply a large box with windows running from the roof to the deck all round. She looked rather like a floating railroad car with heavily draped curtains.

The name *Urda* was painted boldly on both sides at the bow. But Wakelam had whited out the final "a" and painted a black capital "T" in front of her name.

When Moitessier arrived in Durban with *Marie-Thérèse II* he noticed two local yachts built to the same design, although they looked quite different. The first, called *Vagabond,* belonged to my friend Ray Cruickshank, who secured for Moitessier the job with Louw and Halvorsen. The second, called *Wanda,* belonged to Wakelam, who subsequently became Moitessier's great friend, and about whom he writes extensively in his book *Sailing to the Reefs.*

They were an unlikely fit. Wakelam was practical, a detail man, always busy, a good engineer. Moitessier was a typical colonial, a spoiled dreamer. He never did any more than he absolutely had to. But he was suave, charming, intelligent, and persuasive. Perhaps Wakelam wittingly or unwittingly sought some social redemption by aiding this seemingly helpless waif of the seas.

South Africa has always been the breeding ground of self-sufficient, larger-than-life characters, and both Wakelam and Cruickshank had built their boats from a book they found in the Durban city library. Each, quite separately, had taken out *Cruising Yachts: Design and Performance,* T. Harrison Butler's exposition of his metacentric shelf theory. Harrison Butler was a British eye surgeon, but he was also a practical sailor and an accomplished amateur naval architect. Among the selection of designs in his book was a pretty little double-ender, a heavy-displacement twenty-four-footer with a beam of seven feet. She was called *Thuella,* and both Cruickshank and Wakelam fell in love with her.

All of her lines, the sheer plan, the half-breadth plan, and the body plan, were squeezed onto a book page five and a half inches wide by eight and a half inches deep. It should be impossible to build a boat from plans as small as these, of course, but that didn't stop either one of them. They had the page copied and enlarged, and enlarged again and again, until they could shape the full-sized sections from it.

Wakelam built his boat in the bush, under a tree, in every minute he could spare. He even cut natural crooks from tough, indigenous African trees with close grain and natural resistance to borers. His full-time job was that of a calculator-machine mechanic. In those days, office calculators were large electro-mechanical machines with rows of whirring digits. It was a high-tech job, and he was good at it.

Although *Thuella's* scantlings were given in the book, Wakelam took no chances. He figured out what he thought was reasonable for the thickness of a beam or a plank, and then added a substantial amount for safety. *Wanda* ended up very strong indeed, but very heavy, slow, and unstable. She did eventually capsize on the way to Cape Town, as previously noted. Much of her instability came from the huge, solid wooden telegraph pole of a mast he installed, which made her top-heavy.

Even he was worried about that after he'd finished it, and the Durban newspapers carried pictures of *Wanda* being hove down in the yacht basin so that her mast was level with the jetty and her sidedecks were under water. He wanted to know if she'd recover on her own from a capsize. In his famous canvas shorts, he stepped from the jetty on to the mast top and cut the lines holding the mast down. *Wanda* did, in fact, slowly struggle upright, even with him on top of the mast, but you could see she was reluctant. And you just knew she would roll her guts out, wobbling from side to side like a metronome, in a following wind. As a final touch, he fitted her out with heavy *black* sails that he had made himself— from more railroad tarpaulins, we suspected. And yes, we were all shocked, which must have gratified him greatly.

Cruickshank, on the other hand, was an expert woodworker and shipwright. He had a better idea of how strong the individual components of a wooden yacht ought to be. He knew that over-heavy timbers did not necessarily make a strong boat. Strength came from properly sized timbers strongly fastened together. He made sure *Vagabond* was strongly fastened, and on occasion I used to help him fasten the planking with square copper nails and large rooves.

Vagabond turned out to be a beautiful boat. Moitessier described her as "an adorable little sloop . . . small but really good; it would sail like a dream in any wind and reach!"

When she was finished, Cruickshank asked me to help him sail her to Lourenço Marques, now Maputo, several hundred miles up the coast in what was then Portuguese East Africa, now Mozambique. He asked me because he had seen me sailing the Point Yacht Club dinghy, so he knew I could sail. He couldn't. He'd never been to sea on a sailboat.

I couldn't navigate, though, and neither could he. But that didn't stop us. We spent a week getting seasick and fighting headwinds, the current, and a storm, and getting lost, and then found our way back to Durban. We were naive, but *Vagabond* looked after us well.

Moitessier was always grateful to Cruickshank for finding him a job at Louw and Halvorsen's shipyard, but it was Wakelam that he bonded with. "Henry had a real brain," he wrote in *Sailing to the Reefs*. "I have never met a man so clever at doing any job that may crop up, with practically non-existent materials. He was the very personification of resourcefulness and practical intelligence. The friendship that was to unite us for a number of years was to be a real enrichment to me."

Wakelam possessed another rare quality, said Moitessier. He had a heart of gold and an unselfishness that could make him forget everything else to help a friend or even a complete stranger in difficulty.

No doubt the owner of *Urda* would have had difficulty believing that, but in my own experience Wakelam was always willing to help someone like Moitessier, someone with real ambitions to go deep-sea cruising.

By the time they got to Cape Town, these two had formed a formidable team. Both arrived at the Royal Cape Yacht Club with next to no money, and had to find work almost immediately. Wakelam was soon employed building a wooden boat. Moitessier found work with a fellow Frenchman as a maintenance engineer in a factory—something he knew almost nothing about, of course, but hoped to learn in a hurry.

In their spare time they made their own sheets and halyards from nylon hawsers discarded by whaling ships. They also fashioned their own self-steering gear from scrap material, much of it rescued from the RCYC's "rubbish heap."

Moitessier startled club members for ten days by taking a hammer and chisel and pounding away at the inside of his cabin. He was chipping out the excess concrete and steel nuts and bolts that he had poured into the bilges in Durban in an attempt to stiffen up *Marie-Thérèse II*. It was painfully slow work, but he managed to lighten her considerably.

Then Wakelam accused Moitessier of being fastidious and "a spoilt bourgeois" because he would not eat dog biscuits for breakfast, as Wakelam did.

Moitessier finally agreed that it was perhaps time to revise his opinion of those dog biscuits, since they hadn't managed to kill Wakelam. But he had no intention of paying full price for them, cheap as they were. Instead, he wrote a letter to the manufacturer, saying (untruthfully) that he had bought dog biscuits by mistake in Durban, but had tried them and found them delicious, especially the yellow ones. He asked the manufacturer for forty pounds at factory prices.

The answer came back quickly. The biscuits weren't intended for human consumption, but exclusively for dogs. The manufacturer would take no responsibility if Moitessier insisted on dining upon them.

Other South African companies were more understanding, and soon both Wakelam and Moitessier were finding cases of canned food in the hallways of the club, supplied totally free, with little notes wishing them good luck on their voyaging. After a year of scavenging in Cape Town, the vagabond and the pirate were stocked up for their next voyage to the West Indies.

Moitessier's girlfriend, whom he simply refers to in his book as Joyce, had cooked for him and worked on board for the best part of his stay in Cape Town. She wanted desperately to sail with him, but Moitessier wasn't ready for a permanent partner then, and never would be. His boat was his mistress. *Wanda* and *Marie-Thérèse II* (named after a fiancée Moitessier had jilted) sailed for the West Indies with just one man aboard each.

Saying good-bye to Cape Town was a quietly distressing business for us. This was our final port in South Africa. We not only knew Cape Town and loved it, but we had family and very dear friends here.

June, Kevin, and I took the cable car to the top of Table Mountain. It was beautiful up there and the crystal-clear air was redolent of the Mediterranean, filled with the warm, tangy, resinous smell of the fynbos. We sat on an outcrop of rock and looked northwest over the dark-blue Atlantic. Twelve hundred miles over the horizon lay a tiny island called St. Helena. It was our next stop.

"Think you can find it?" Kevin asked mischievously. He meant without his help, of course. It was me and my sextant versus him and Prince Henry.

"I hope so," I said. "It would be a great pity to miss it."

"Plenty of ships have," said Kevin.

He was right. In the days of sail, any ship that missed the little island had a hard time beating back to it against the trade winds. For some of the unhandier vessels it was quite impossible. To be certain of finding St. Helena in those times, when longitude was difficult to ascertain precisely, ship's masters would steer well east of the island until they were on its exact latitude. Latitude was relatively easy to find with a sextant alone—no chronometer was needed. Then they would run due west along the line of latitude until the high peaks of St. Helena hove in sight dead ahead. If my navigational skills didn't prove adequate for finding longitude, we might have to follow their example. But for the moment I wasn't going to worry about it. My plate was full enough already.

As our gaze fell on little Robben Island, a penal colony a few miles north of the city, our minds filled with thoughts of Nelson Mandela, who had spent twenty-three years incarcerated there. He was a "banned" person, one of many thousands, and we expected him to die there. Newspapers, radio stations, and television stations were forbidden by the Afrikaner government to mention his name, or report anything he said. They could not use a picture of him or disclose his whereabouts. The relatively small number of whites who knew anything about him at all regarded him as a terrorist.

Just a few months before we left Durban, prime minister P. W. Botha, leader of the minority white government, had declared a national state of emergency, the latest crackdown against black dissidents protesting the apartheid system of legalized racial discrimination.

What followed was a total news blackout. Thousands of black protesters were arrested by paramilitary police and detained without trial, suffering torture and abuse on an unprecedented scale. Anyone criticizing apartheid rule was automatically labeled a terrorist, and state funds were secretly diverted into "antiterrorist" projects. The army began its biggest campaign ever of invading and interfering with the politics of neighboring countries that supported antiapartheid movements such as Mandela's African National Congress, and approved assassination as a means of "political persuasion." With

Draconian laws to back them up, the security forces wielded vast, unaccountable power.

The state of emergency was the latest battle in a war between South Africa's black and whites that had started more than twenty years previously. In July 1963, military commanders of the African National Congress, a communist-backed black freedom movement, gathered in secret at Lilliesleaf farm, Rivonia, near the city of Johannesburg, to discuss their antiapartheid plans.

But they had been betrayed. Wind of their meeting had reached the South African Police, who arrested the sixteen black leaders and charged them with sabotage and attempting to overthrow the white government. Nelson Mandela, a lawyer, was among them.

There was no doubt that the ANC sponsored armed insurrection, nor that its fighters were funded and trained by Libya, Somalia, Cuba, the USSR, and other nations whose policies were anathema to South Africa's ruling whites. There was also no doubt that the ANC killed people with explosives and land mines. They deliberately conducted a war of terror.

But white South Africans were a tough target. The Afrikaners, in particular, having been persecuted by the British in earlier years, and having been defeated by them in the Boer War, were not easily panicked by acts of terror.

Many of us English-speakers had grown up with violence, too. One of my earliest memories, from the time I was five years old, was of dead soldiers with their limbs jutting out at odd angles, tangled up in overhead telephone wires, with red leaping flames and billowing smoke in the background. That was in Birkenhead, England, during World War II, after the Germans had bombed a nearby military barracks.

I was wounded in that attack, and for years proudly showed school friends the tiny scar on my face where a shard of glass had entered. I don't recall being frightened. It was what you expected if you were at war. And in any case, we had been bombed out of our house before, in Plymouth, when the roof was blown off. My mother and I were luckily in the little Andersen shelter that my father had built in the backyard. It was no big deal if you were a kid and it was what you were used to.

In later years, when I became a journalist in Durban, I saw many scenes of violence and grew to know the revoltingly delicious smell of human flesh roasted in a mud-and-wattle hut deliberately set on fire during faction fighting.

As a new press photographer, I was sent into Cato Manor, one of Durban's black shantytowns, when white police were dispatched to quell an antiapartheid protest that turned into a riot. I still remember the smell of sweat, the dust, police batons flashing in the hot sun and crunching on soft flesh, the screams and grunts, black women with babies on their backs, running clumsily, lopsidedly, in silhouette against a swirling background of light dust.

Many black people were beaten senseless that day, and one of the photographers working for a competing newspaper, Laurie Bloomfield, of the *Daily News,* shot a picture that circled the world. It showed a uniformed South African policeman with his baton held high above a cringing Zulu man, both silhouetted against the dust, and behind them hundreds of frightened black people running for their lives. Unfortunately, none of my pictures managed to capture the pain and drama of that day in the same evocative way.

Thus, in later years in South Africa, we whites shrugged when another ANC landmine went off, and we simply determined to be more cautious about where we shopped when they blew up a crowded supermarket. June was different, though. She had grown up in the peaceful rural wilds of Utah and Idaho with a cowboy for a father. She had never before been exposed to this constant, low-level form of violence, and she never got over her feeling of unease. She was ready to leave South Africa long before I was.

Neither Mandela nor his coconspirators regarded themselves as terrorists, of course. They called themselves freedom fighters. And their excuse for the terror they were causing in South Africa was a valid one: there was no other way to get the white government to listen to them. Blacks were in the majority by far, but they had no vote. They couldn't live where they wanted, work where they wanted, or even fall in love with whom they wanted. Interracial marriage was illegal. Even interracial sex was illegal, under the so-called Immorality Act. They were about as oppressed, under South Africa's apartheid laws, as any nation ever has been. They were downtrodden by whites in every way.

If they protested publicly they were beaten and thrown in jail. Or worse. In 1976, the minister of justice and police, Jimmy Kruger, reacting to an outbreak of black student riots, recommended that black demonstrators be killed, as a way of crushing widespread antiapartheid protests. At least six hundred black demonstrators are believed to have been killed by police during several months of rioting in 1976, perhaps many more, after the Afrikaner government tried to force black Africans to use only the Afrikaans language in school.

It was a pattern that was to continue unabated. And it was this monstrous evil that Mandela and his fellow terrorist leaders were trying to eradicate. They were fighting for the freedom of South Africa's oppressed blacks, and hoping that the world would see the righteousness of their cause.

It was the constant threat of all-out civil war that prompted me, along with all of my white friends, to fit bars over our windows at home, and build six-foot brick walls around my property. Every white home was a fortress. June and I, like many English-speaking South Africans, felt particularly irrelevant in this fractured society. As part of the English-speaking minority among the whites, we had no hope of forcing any changes to the Afrikaner government's apartheid policies through the ballot box. We had worked for years for anti-apartheid newspapers, and even they seemed to make no difference.

Simply by remaining in South Africa and supporting an opposition party in Parliament, we lent legitimacy and the appearance of fairness and democracy to a system deliberately designed to strip blacks of their human rights.

And, as I've said, when I found ANC graffiti in my backyard it was the last straw, the final irony. I could see no peaceful future for South Africa, only prolonged bloodshed. South Africa needed a new start. And so did we.

In Cape Town we hired a car for a day and drove south down the Cape Peninsula toward the Cape of Good Hope, a beautiful nature reserve. On the way we stopped off to have a farewell lunch with my uncle and aunt, Walter and Laura Wynne, in the coastal town of Fish Hoek (hoek meaning corner, or bay, in Afrikaans) where my aunt had been town clerk.

"I can't believe you're all going to America on a thirty-foot yacht," said Uncle Walter, shaking his head. "You need something bigger."

"*Freelance* does just fine," said Kevin defensively.

"With any luck, the worst part is over," I added. "From Durban to Cape Town is the hard part. The Cape of Storms. The rest is a piece of cake."

Even as I said it, the three of us knocked on wood.

"And do you have jobs in America?" Uncle Walter wanted to know.

"No," said June, "but we'll find some."

"Where?"

"We don't know yet."

Uncle Walter sighed and shook his head again. He was a successful builder and developer who had lived in the same town all his life. He didn't understand us at all.

"Well, I wish you lots of luck," he said. "I think you'll need it."

A few miles farther on, the winding road ran along the coast of False Bay, squeezed between tall mountains on the right and a mile-long beach of white sand, on the left. Creamy breakers broke abruptly in the surf line, and a south-easter whipped foam off warm, turquoise seas. And so we came to the village of Simonstown, birthplace of my mother, and the scene of the two happiest years of my childhood.

The British had built a large, strategically important naval base at Simonstown, quarrying stone for its construction from the lofty Simonsberg immediately behind it. It was now owned by South Africa, and run by the South African Navy, but its connections with Britain ran strong and deep.

My father, a petty officer in the Royal Navy, had served aboard one of His Majesty's ships that called at Simonstown before World War II, and there he had met and married my mother. She went to live in England, where my sister, Sandra, and I were born, but after the war, when my father left the navy, we all escaped the drabness and privation of battered Britain by emigrating to South Africa.

I was just thirteen then, and ready to start a new life. Now here I was again, aged fifty, starting yet another one.

I drove slowly down Church Street, past the Dutch Reformed Church, and past the Laquelene Boarding House where we had lived for two years, and those wonderful childhood memories came flooding back.

There was the tree I had climbed to smoke my first cigarette, and nearly fallen out of with my head spinning madly. There was the storeroom I had sneaked into, where I had rummaged through trunks belonging to—of all people—the chief of the local police, who was also staying at the boarding house. Among his stuff I had found an illustrated book on love and sex. It was by far the most exciting book I'd ever read and I spent a lot of time in the storeroom when nobody was around.

And there was the white sandy beach, fringing the little cove almost under our kitchen window, where the dinghies and fishing boats were drawn up. It was a tiny natural harbor, private and mostly deserted, guarded on the False Bay side by a long flat rock.

One summer afternoon, after school, I was standing on the rock when a sailing dinghy came along. It was a fourteen-foot Redwing, with tan sails. A young man was sailing it. He beat up close to the rock and yelled: "Want to come for a sail?"

When I said yes, he pulled in close and I scrambled aboard. We headed out into the open seas of False Bay and he showed me how to work the jib and change places from side to side when we tacked. The warm seas splashed in, and I bailed the bilges dry from time to time with a thing that looked like a soup ladle. We surfed down the backs of waves with the sails billowing and I could feel the whole boat thrumming in the wind. It was wonderful. It was marvelous, better even than searching the police chief's trunks, because they couldn't arrest you for sailing. I didn't realize it when he finally landed me back on my rock and waved good-bye, but I was hooked on sailing for life.

Very soon I was sailing on the big yachts that came around from the Royal Cape Yacht Club in summer. They left their dinghies on our beach, and I looked after them. I sailed with Fred Smithers on the Knud Riemers-designed *Viking,* and at the age of fourteen I was piloting *Makoti,* a thirty-five-foot sportfishing boat, in the tuna grounds off the Cape of Good Hope. She was owned then by Harry Pegram, a Constantia wine farmer. During the week I would return home from school, row the dinghy out to *Makoti,* and start up her twin Universal engines to keep the batteries charged. Occasionally, when the mackerel were biting, I would take a hand-line, half fill the dinghy with their wriggling bodies, and row them to the fish market downtown, where I would try to sell them—always without success, because when the mackerel were biting, everybody had mackerel.

It was a wonderful life, but it didn't leave much time for homework. I was caned many times for that reason by my Latin teacher and my Afrikaans teacher, who, like many Afrikaners, had supported the Nazis during the war. He hated my Englishness and my inability to speak Afrikaans. Once he actually lifted me off the floor by my ears before a class shocked into silence. But it turned out that I was good at languages, and after two years I caught up with my fellow students who had learned Afrikaans from their first days at school. The caning and public humiliation stopped, but the sarcasm never did.

It didn't worry me much. I had discovered how to turn a rowing dinghy into a sailing dinghy with a spare oar and an old blanket.

I left Simonstown still deep in thought and drove on down to the Cape of Good Hope, or Cape Point, as we called it, and we gazed down in awe at the rugged end of the peninsula, where the Indian Ocean met the Atlantic. Gulls wheeled and screamed below us and the restless ocean cast up its swells in loud crashes against the craggy dark rock, swamping the coast in fine mist.

"Somehow it looks more fearsome from here than it does from the sea," June said.

"Yeah—I would never have gone to sea if I'd seen this first," said Kevin.

"It's why we stay away from land," I said. "It's safer at sea."

"We hope," said June.

We looked at each other and grinned.

"Yes, we hope," I said. *It's what the books say, anyway,* I thought.

So far, we had done nothing more than creep slowly around the coast, taking shelter many times on the way. After this, we would be heading out into the middle of a large ocean. There was no shelter out there, nowhere to hide from a storm.

Two baboons scampered away from our car as we made our way back, chattering angrily at having been disturbed. I laughed, remembering how they used to bark and throw stones at me when, as a kid, I explored the old quarry above Simonstown. I was in no danger. They weren't at all accurate. And if I threw a stone back, they would lope off, disappearing rapidly among the sunwarmed outcrops and scrubby bushes.

Back at the Royal Cape Yacht Club we said good-bye to our cruising friends, including Yukio Hasebe, and made *Freelance* ready for sea. After ten days in port, we were ready to leave Cape Town.

But first I had to attend to the paperwork. The customs and immigration clearance procedures seemed endless. I trekked from one government office to another and stood in long lines, armed with passports and ship's papers. In the end, I was issued with a ship's clearance certificate embellished with a large red wax seal.

"That's it?" I asked.

"Ja, meneer," said the official. "Yes, sir. You're free to go."

It was a long walk back to the yacht club on a hot and dusty road, but I didn't mind. Free to go, the man had said.

Krugerrands and all, I thought. I whistled nonchalantly and clutched my little bag filled with stamped passports and legally sealed ship's papers.

Next morning, Saturday, February 21, we were getting ready to leave after breakfast when I heard my name called on the yacht club's paging system. In the foyer of the club I met the white-uniformed official who had hailed us at the panic buoy on the day after our arrival in Cape Town.

"Hello again," he said. "They tell me you're ready to leave."

"Yes," I said, my heart sinking.

Oh God, not now. Don't inspect the boat now.

"All set, then? Passports in order? Received your clearance?"

"Yes."

Please don't ask to come on board. Please, God.

"Good." He smiled. "Tot siens. Good-bye. And safe voyage."

"Thank you," I said.

And thank you, God. Thank you, thank you.

We cast off and called Cape Town Harbor Radio on the VHF radio, requesting permission to leave port, bound for St. Helena.

There was a pause while they checked the list of yachts that had received formal clearance. I ground my teeth impatiently. Finally, they came back: "Ja, OK *Freelance*, you're clear."

We motored out slowly, packing and stowing for sea, passing through the artificial basins where large ships were berthed.

On the final stretch to the open water of Table Bay we came close abeam of a jetty. From behind it, a large harbor tug, foaming at the bow, came heading straight for us.

My heart skipped several beats. Was this the search party? Was this how they did it? Did they have to catch you under way to prove you were smuggling?

At the last moment the tug veered off around our stern. I waved a weak salute of thanks to the helmsman standing up high behind the sloping bridge windows and someone waved back.

I set a course to clip by the eastern side of nearby Robben Island, Nelson Mandela's island, and late that afternoon we watched Table Mountain, now wearing a heartbreakingly beautiful tablecloth of brilliant white cloud, slide under the horizon.

Our African life was behind us. Only now did I really believe we were free to go. We were on our way to a new life in the New World, Krugerrands and all.

Our first miracle had been granted. We'd got the Kruggerrands out of South Africa. Now we needed only Miracle Number Two to transmute them into U.S. dollars.

Meanwhile, watching Africa drop astern, we felt no joy. We felt nothing but deep sadness, too deep for tears or even words.

8

CAPE TOWN TO ST. HELENA

My "kidnapped" crew, June and Kevin, had become skilled and valuable crewmembers, as I knew they would. They trusted my judgment and never complained. No skipper could have asked for more.

But the tensions that had plagued us even before we left Durban followed us as *Freelance* drove westward and northward through the vast expanse of the South Atlantic Ocean toward St. Helena.

June and I both felt the need for reassurance. In this lengthy, worrisome business of selling up our home, leaving our country, and setting sail on a little yacht toward an uncertain future, we had been pushed to the borders of our individual braveness. We needed to comfort each other.

But the business of sailing the boat twenty-four hours a day left us very little time to get together. We met at the change of watches, passing in the hatchway. And the intimacy we sought was unattainable with Kevin on board.

I became withdrawn and obsessed with the task of delivering this boat and these people safely to the United States. I badly needed to relax, to start enjoying myself. But I couldn't. Everything I owned, and more than half my family, was on this little boat. *Freelance* wasn't insured to cross an ocean. Insurance was prohibitively expensive, so we carried none. If I lost her I lost everything. The responsibility weighed very heavily. I was not sparkling company.

And besides, where were we actually going? It hadn't been possible to organize jobs in America. We had nothing lined up, no contacts, nowhere to live. We'd heard that journalism was so different in the States, and so difficult for a foreigner to break into, that we didn't even know if we could earn a living there. Quite often, sitting alone in the cockpit in the middle of the night, I wondered what madness had seized us.

For the first day and night out of Cape Town, a southwesterly wind sped us on our way, but on the second day it headed us, and we could no longer lay our course. With a double reef in the mainsail we sailed hard on the wind, edging in toward land again. That was worrisome because I didn't want to find myself blown onto a lee shore in this area.

I asked Kevin, who was on watch, for the best course we could make, and I plotted it on the chart. *Freelance*'s bow was pointing straight toward another fascinating part of Southern Africa—the Skeleton Coast.

In his book *Skeleton Coast,* John H. Marsh says mariners dread it. "Treasure seekers know it as 'the Coast of Diamonds and Death.' Maps mark it merely as the Kaokoveld, which, freely translated, is Herero for 'Coast of Loneliness.'"

The desert of the Kaokoveld stretches five hundred miles north and south, and two hundred miles into the interior. It's nearly the size of Britain in area, but it's almost uninhabited for the simple reason that most of it cannot be inhabited by humans. Along the coast there are only sand dunes and salt pans. There is no sign of vegetation for hundreds of miles.

Tantalizingly, the soil of the Skeleton Coast is diamondiferous. In the 1940s, the South African government had to declare the whole zone a prohibited area to prevent people picking up diamonds in the sand and flooding the world market.

Marsh maintains that there is no more treacherous coast in the world than this, and mariners have good cause to fear it. The fact is that the shore is alive. It grows. Because the swift north-setting Benguella Current carries and deposits sand, the shore moves westward, farther and farther out to sea, so that wrecks of old ships now are high and dry inland. The German liner *Eduard Bohlen,* which went aground there in 1909, was well over half a mile inland forty years later.

According to Marsh, prospectors looking for diamonds once dug into a sandhill hundreds of yards from the beach, and found an ancient galleon. She must have been there for centuries. The growing coastline makes nonsense of nautical charts, of course.

The white sands of the arid coast hide the skeletons of many men as well as ships. Only a handful of the crews and passengers of ships that went aground there before World War II survived the long torture of death from thirst and exposure. And the coast has claimed many victims because, like the Agulhas Current farther south, the Benguella Current runs at speeds of up to four knots, and often sets strongly onshore.

We definitely didn't want to end up there. If we went about onto the other tack, we'd be heading almost straight out to sea, away from the coast, but we wouldn't be making any northing, which meant we wouldn't be getting any closer to the start of the southeast trade winds.

While I dithered about what to do, the wind solved the problem for me. It gradually died away until we were left sitting in a dead calm one hundred miles off the coast. A choppy swell was running, so we handed the foresail and strapped the mainsail in tight to lessen the constant slatting that was driving us mad.

The batteries needed to be charged, so I told Kevin to start the engine and run it for an hour.

"In gear?" he asked.

"Why not?" I said. "Let's be daring. There's no one to see us. If you don't tell, I won't, either."

So we motored with the swell on our beam for an hour, steering three hundred and thirty degrees magnetic, the course to St. Helena. And lo! it was just the nudge *Freelance* needed. It tipped her over the invisible edge of the tradewind belt, and a weak breeze filled in from astern after Kevin turned the motor off. It was a shy little zephyr, not too sure of itself at first, and it went to the south-southwest for a while, but by midnight it was well established in a southeasterly direction and blowing a respectable ten knots. We were in the heel of the southeast trades at last, on course for St. Helena, and pulling steadily away from the dreaded Skeleton Coast.

The next morning, under a blue sky and puffy white cumulus clouds, Kevin and I raised our twin foresails, a special rig for running in the trade winds. *Freelance*'s original owners, the two Swedish sea captains, had designed them. They were striped bright yellow and blue, the colors of the Swedish flag. But the captains had never got as far as the trade winds, and as far as I could tell, the sails had never been used.

Trade wind work involves running dead before the wind for days and weeks on end. The fore-and-aft rig used by all modern sailboats is tricky to handle on the run. The area of the mainsail is well aft, so that the wind keeps trying to push the stern around, and that can be dangerous if it results in a broach in heavy weather. That's why we so often lowered *Freelance*'s mainsail and ran before the wind under jib only when we were rounding the Cape.

Another problem with the fore-and-aft rig is chafe. If the mainsail is to be at all efficient, you have to let the boom go forward so that the sail is squared off, and then it presses against the lee shrouds supporting the mast. As the boom moves up and down with each puff of wind, the sail wears against the rigging. Twenty-four hours of that, and you've got a hole in your sail.

Consequently, many different rigs have evolved for running in the trades. Large yachts often still carry an old-fashioned squaresail on a fixed yard. That's probably the most efficient and most convenient downwind sail of all, but we couldn't carry one on a boat as small as *Freelance*.

Twin jibs, one set to port and the other to starboard, are popular, because they fly forward of the mast where they can't chafe against any rigging. They may be set from a single stay, or from two stays specially set up a little forward of the mast, and they are usually held out with wooden or aluminum booms hinged at the mast.

Lack of chafe is not the only advantage of twin jibs, though. They also move the sail area's center of effort forward, so that the boat is being pulled by the nose instead of being pushed by the backside. This makes for much easier steering downwind, and boat balanced in this way is much less likely to broach sideways and roll over after running down a swell with a big breaking wave.

No matter how you rig your sails, however, the bane of the trade winds is rolling. Almost all sailboats roll extravagantly when the wind is behind them and the swells are large. There is simply nothing to stop the sideways movement of the mast, and the boat quickly develops a maddening, vicious roll from gunwale to gunwale that even such stalwarts as the Hiscocks were moved to complain about.

"The centrifugal action was considerable," Eric Hiscock says in *Around the World in Wanderer III,* describing his boat's action in the trade winds, "and anything which was not securely lashed or chocked off, including ourselves, was thrown violently across the cabin. It is said that the human body will in time accustom itself to anything, but I fancy the motion of a small yacht at sea must be one exception."

I thought I had found the answer to that, though. Many years before, I had read an article in the British *Yachting World* magazine about the invention of a sailor and marine engineer called Hugh Barkla. He had worked out a way to keep twin jibs spread forward on each side at an angle of forty-five degrees to the boat, so that together they formed a deep-V shape. He did this with a special twin-staysail (twistle) yard, hinged in the middle and supported by its own halyard. It occurred to me that if the sails were angled forward in a deep-V, they would steady the boat if she tried to roll. It seemed worth trying, anyhow.

I cut out the article and filed it away in a big box with a hundred other clippings that might come in useful some day, but years later, before we left Durban, I dug it out and designed some stainless-steel fittings for the twistle yard. A local metal shop made them for me.

In all the fuss of leaving South Africa, we had never had a chance to try the twistle yard, so it was like the first day at school on *Freelance's* foredeck that morning as Kevin and I tried to sort out the acres of crackly cloth and get them attached to the right fittings.

When all was ready, I hauled up the sails and tightened the halyard of the twistle yard. Four hundred square feet of blue and yellow stripes bulged with power momentarily, then suddenly flapped out of control when a snap shackle broke under the strain. I quickly replaced it with an ordinary shackle and we trimmed the jibs again.

What a difference. A delightful difference. *Freelance* took off with a whoosh of power that transformed the misery of wild rolling into an exhilarating surge of speed and stability.

The greatest problem with the twistle yard is trying to explain it to anyone who hasn't seen it in action. It seems extraordinarily difficult to grasp the concept of a pair of aluminum poles joined to each other with a hinge, floating free six feet above the foredeck and swinging around the forestay as a solid unit with the twin staysails. In the end, we simply handed out photocopies of Hugh Barkla's original article and waited for the penny to drop.

I had been right about the twistle yard's effect on rolling. The difference in *Freelance*'s stability was quite amazing. Not only was the frequency of rolling sharply reduced, but so was the speed and angle of the roll. Best of all, the snap-jerk at the end of each roll quite disappeared.

We all loved the new motion, but June, in particular, was ecstatic. "You won't believe how much easier it is to work in the galley," she said.

Freelance was fast for a traditional, full-keeled boat of only twenty-five feet on the waterline. Under the twin jibs, with the Aries vane gear steering, she often notched up more than 130 miles a day and once she did 142.

Meanwhile, the sea we found ourselves in now was very different from what we'd grown accustomed to. It was cold, for a start, part of the green, frigid Benguella Current from the Antarctic that licked Africa's west coast. It was also nearly three and a half miles deep, though we were heading toward the Walvis Ridge, an underwater range of mountains running almost due north and south. After we'd crossed the mountains, the water would be miles deep again until we reached St. Helena.

The fact that the water was so deep occasionally haunted me in the still of a night watch in the lonely cockpit. It felt weird to be suspended at the interface of the sea and the atmosphere, more than three miles above solid ground, and not to know what was going on in those three miles of water beneath, what unfriendly creatures might be lurking there. I felt at one with William Beebe, the naturalist and explorer, who remarked in *The Arcturus Adventure* that "I came to have the feeling that far down beyond where my eyes could penetrate were uncounted hosts of little eyes peering upward . . ."

It's a reflection on the difficulty of underwater exploration that we humans know infinitely more about the back side of the moon than we do about the bottom of the earth's oceans and the things that live there. We do know some things, of course. We know, for instance, that the southwest coast of Africa is one of those places in the world where upwellings of mineral-rich cold water occur. The minerals provide abundant food for plankton, which is the collective name for minute organisms of plants and animal life floating in the sea. The vegetable plankton multiply quickly in the bright sunshine and fertile water of the South Atlantic. They are the lowest order of life in the sea and almost all sea animals depend on them. They, in turn, are eaten by the animal plankton. Together, they appear as nothing more than a slight cloudiness in the water, but they form sustenance for thousands of different kinds of fish. Beebe described plankton as "myriad, myriad motes—more like aquatic dust than individual organisms, which filled the water from the very surface to as deep as any eye could penetrate."

You can live on plankton. It was Beebe's contention that shipwrecked men need never starve if they could manage to drag on old shirt through the water at night, like a net. "The great percentage of crustaceans makes plankton a rich, nourishing food, even raw," he wrote.

Dr. Alain Bombard, a French scientist, tested Beebe's theory in 1952, when he drifted all the way across the Atlantic from Casablanca in a rubber life raft, existing solely on fish and plankton he caught in a fine net.

It's worth noting, should you ever be tempted to emulate Bombard, or find yourself in need of food on the ocean, that animal plankton, the best sort for humans to eat, almost totally disappear during the day, when they sink into the depths of the ocean to get away from the light. This habit of theirs, the rising and falling according to the position of the sun, is what gave them their name. In Greek, plankton means wandering.

One of the greatest wonders of the sea is the sheer amount of life it sustains, almost all of which is hidden from our eyes as we sail over it. Beebe once set himself to counting the number of plankton he caught in a net about three feet in diameter. On a dark, moonless evening, he dragged it through the sea at a speed of two knots for one hour.

After many hours of eye-straining work at the microscope, he conservatively estimated that his catch consisted of 40,662,000 individuals, mainly crustaceans, snails, and shrimps. From this it is apparent that the fecundity of the world's oceans is quite beyond human comprehension—so much hidden life, and so much death, too, of course. Countless myriads of dead plankton drift down through the water every minute of every day, forming a thick layer on the ocean floors.

Incidentally, Beebe repeated his experiment in full daylight, and caught only about one thousand plankton creatures, instead of forty million. "Plankton will have nothing of the sun, or even of moonlight," he concluded, "and remain well below the reach of the stronger rays."

While the deep cold water we found ourselves in was wonderful for plankton and the beginnings of sea life, it was very lonely out at sea for human beings, with no land in sight for the first time during our trip. I knew small-boat sailors who loved getting out to sea, away from the dangers of land, but I was always on edge, always slightly wary of what could happen if the weather got really bad and there was no shelter at hand. I hid this anxiety from June and Kevin, but I often wondered if they felt that way themselves.

I wished I could be like John Muir, the naturalist and founder of the Sierra Club, who felt so at home in the high mountains, and who understood the habitat so well that he could wander where he liked without the slightest fear of being stranded without food, water, or shelter. I thought perhaps Bernard Moitessier had the same kind of fearlessness at sea, too, though I am almost ashamed to say I suspected that he felt at home on the ocean because he really didn't understand the dangers as well as I did.

I looked at the long swells rolling ceaselessly toward us from the southwest, refugees from the Roaring Forties, and tried to love them; but my intellect rebelled. It would have been so much nicer and safer without them. While I found beauty and even sense in the little tradewind clouds that passed overhead like puffs of white cotton against the deep blue sky, I would inevitably find my gaze wandering to the far windward horizon, searching for the first signs of gray that foretold an approaching squall.

But my dear *Freelance* protected me from the dangers of the sea. Almost every day I checked all the important fittings I could see from deck level—the terminals of shrouds and stays, the shackles, the running rigging, and so forth. Down below, lying in my bunk at night, even when I was half asleep, I could sense from her movements when she was carrying too much sail, or needed more. When she was doing well, I would stretch out a hand and pat her fiber-glass side by way of encouragement. On deck, I would disconnect the Aries wind vane and steer by hand for an hour at a time, just for the joy of it. I was becoming deeply attached to my last little bit of South Africa.

Five days out of Cape Town, we celebrated June's fiftieth birthday.

"I would never have dreamed I'd spend this birthday on a tiny yacht in the middle of the South Atlantic," she said. "Who could have guessed?"

"Most Idaho girls don't even know where the South Atlantic is," said Kevin. June laughed. "I've come a long, long way," she said.

She made the day memorable by baking us a loaf of bread. As *Freelance* had no oven, she baked it in our pressure cooker (without its valve) on the kerosene stove. To our jaded palates it was quite delicious, a rare treat. The loaf was cooked in the afternoon and had its picture taken in the cockpit with its proud cook. Then, before it could get cool, we slathered butter on thick slices and wolfed them down. Sadly (but not surprisingly) the birthday loaf failed to survive Kevin's early evening watch.

That day was notable for another reason, too. I took my first sextant sight of the voyage. I had last handled a sextant sixteen years previously, when I was the navigator aboard a lightweight wooden thirty-three-foot racing sloop called *Diana K.* It belonged to my old school friend, Dave Cox, and I'd helped him build it in his mother's backyard in Durban North. Four of us raced her from Africa to South America in the first Cape-to-Rio race.

A few months before we were due to set sail, Dave took me aside. "I haven't got time to learn to navigate," he said. "There's too much still to do. You'd better start learning."

We didn't have a chronometer, so June bought me a self-winding Rolex wristwatch that was accurate to within five seconds or so a day. I taught myself celestial navigation from a little book written by Mary Blewitt and practiced taking sun sights from the end of Durban's North Breakwater, with shark anglers all around me. When we set off for Rio in *Diana K,* I had never taken a sextant sight at sea. But Mary Blewitt was a good teacher, and I not only found the finish line off the Brazilian coast but also taught Dave how to navigate so he could bring the boat back.

Bernard Moitessier had given me a copy of a French navigation manual in Durban, but he must have overestimated my ability to read French, for I understood very little of it. It was *La Navigation sans Logarithmes,* by S. de Neufville. I didn't feel too bad about it, though because Moitessier himself couldn't understand most of it, only the part that allowed him to get the simplest sun sights around noon. We discovered that Marcel Bardiaux also had failed to grasp the nuances of de Neufville's method, and had thrown it out.

On *Freelance,* as on *Diana K,* I was the only person who could navigate. The difference this time, however, was that we had a machine on board that could navigate.

At the same time, I didn't trust Prince Henry, the satellite navigator. Even now, electronics are notoriously unreliable on small yachts, which is hardly surprising, considering the atrociously damp and salty conditions under which they operate. So I wanted to navigate the old-fashioned way, and not have to risk my life on the ability of a box of electronic circuits to communicate with a similar box of tricks orbiting the earth.

Kevin and I therefore kept up the arrangement we had begun while rounding the Cape. I would navigate the old-fashioned way with my sextant, and he would keep an eye on me. I told him to get fixes as often as he liked, but he wasn't to leave on the chart any trace of the SatNav fix for me to see. He was to inform me only if it looked as if I was going to miss St. Helena completely.

Unlike the old sailing ships, I had accurate time from radio signals and a quartz-controlled calculator/clock that my sister Sandra had given me for a birthday several years previously, so I didn't need the Rolex any more, although it was still on my wrist. I combined a midmorning sight with a noon sight to give me both latitude and longitude daily.

But when I took that first sun sight on the day June baked her bread, nothing made sense. My plotted position was about nine hundred miles out. I went over the figures again and again, looking for an arithmetical error, but there was none. I checked the nautical almanac and the sight reduction tables, and I could find nothing there, either. Then it came to me. I'm not sure how it did, but I was very relieved that it did. Nine hundred miles equals fifteen degrees on the earth's surface, and under my pre-Copernican method of navigation, fifteen degrees was the distance the sun traveled in an hour. I was an hour out in my timing of the sight. And little wonder. "All the clocks on this ship show different times!" I wrote frustratedly in the log. I reworked the sight with the correct time, and it tallied with my dead reckoning plot on the chart to within a couple of miles. Good enough. The navigation department was in business again.

As the Southern Cross dipped lower in the sky each night, the sea became warmer and turned darker blue. *Freelance* bustled northwestward at full speed under her twin jibs, throwing up twin plumes of white at her bows. The noise of her passage through the water was unnerving, especially down below at night. I lay in my bunk, with Kevin on watch on the cockpit, knowing full well it was impossible to see anything floating in the water ahead. Except on a few occasions, when there was a bright moon and almost no wind, the darkness and the foaming streaks of waves conspired to hide everything in our path.

It was like driving down a highway at top speed, blindfolded. I wondered what would happen out here, hundreds of miles from the nearest land, if we crashed into a log, or a metal container lost overboard from a freighter. *Freelance* had a watertight bulkhead just forward of the forepeak, but what if she hit something farther aft, with her shoulder? On many nights I spent my watch below dozing uneasily, mentally planning how I'd wrap a sail around the hole, wondering whether our bilge pumps could cope with the inflow, assessing the chances of our life raft really inflating, as advertised, when we threw it overboard and pulled its cord.

But interspersed with the anxiety were moments of beauty, amazement, and delight. I was lying on the foredeck one afternoon, watching the cascading bow wave rise nearly to deck level, when a tiny flying fish darted forward out of it, a shimmering fairy of a thing no bigger than a locust, a little bubble of foam glistening and quivering in its short and desperate flight. It was the first of many flying fish we were to see (usually taking off in shoals) but I never again spotted one quite so small. A few nights later, Kevin noted curtly in the ship's log that a flying fish had crashed into him in the cockpit in the middle of the night. He didn't need to add that he nearly died of fright. He said *Freelance* had been surrounded by dozens of dolphins for about half an hour before the flying fish hit him.

At 10:30 p.m. on Friday, February 27, while I was alone on watch, a large shooting star lit the sea and sky brilliantly for a second. I was momentarily stunned, not knowing what it could be. It was behind us, to starboard, and in a split second it had separated into globules like white-hot molten iron. It could have been a meteorite I suppose, or a piece of space debris burning up, but for hours I was intrigued by the realization that I was probably the only person on earth to have witnessed its arrival.

A week out of Cape Town, and almost halfway to St. Helena, June and I stripped naked in the cockpit, delighted to feel the warmth of the sun on our bare flesh once more. We poured buckets of seawater over each other, while Kevin slept below. Afterward, we washed the salt off our bodies carefully, with face cloths dampened with a little of our precious fresh water supply. Then, smelling fresh and clean once again, we celebrated the halfway mark with some special chocolates June had put aside for the occasion.

They teach you in school that the trade winds are steady in force and direction, but it's not true. The so-called southeasterly trades that were blowing us from Cape Town to St. Helena varied in strength from five to twenty-five knots, and in direction from east to southwest. Nevertheless, at the beginning we reeled off runs of one hundred and thirty to one hundred and forty miles a day. Then something went wrong with the trades. The barometer dropped, and depressions worked their way violently through the weather system. Fierce squalls, with lightning and heavy showers, had us scrambling to reduce sail, especially at night when they seemed most frequent. We had to strike our twin jibs and run under a poled-out working jib while *Freelance* behaved abominably, rolling from side to side and dipping her gunwales with the precision of a metronome. It seemed almost as if we had accidentally slid into the doldrums, that miserable equatorial region of calms, rain squalls, and lightning storms. Perhaps we were a little late in the season, and the trades were changing.

Ten days out of Cape Town, a bad lightning storm came up astern at dusk. Our metal mast was the highest point around for hundreds of miles, so we dropped a long chain overboard from the backstay to act as a ground in case we were struck. We took down all sail, went below, sliding the hatch tightly shut behind us, and left *Freelance* to look after herself. The wind battered us at about fifty knots for half an hour, heeling *Freelance* over from the windage of the bare mast. Lightning struck all around us, close enough for the flashes and the ripping noises of thunder to be almost simultaneous, but we were not hit.

By 2 a.m. the wind had disappeared completely. It was dead calm and we bobbed and curtsied in a choppy leftover sea. A light drizzle set in shortly afterward. For twenty-four hours we suffered through alternating calms and squalls, raising sails, snatching them down, and cursing the pilot books that promised steady trade winds in this area. When the trade wind did finally recover its good humor it blew from the south and then gradually eased back into the southeast.

Moitessier, the vagabond, and Wakelam, his pirate friend, both had good weather most of the way from Cape Town to St. Helena, and Moitessier even found it a little boring. "In this part of the Atlantic, the sea is completely empty," he says in *Sailing to the Reefs*. "Life on board became almost suburban. It was a week since we had left Cape Town, a completely uneventful week, like a cruise arranged by a travel agency. Shortly after our sailing, the southeast trade wind had set in and it was blowing gently in nature's familiar rhythm."

Moitessier was wrong about the sea being dead, though. Our trailing lure caught two beautiful fish, a bonito, which we threw back, and a glistening dorado, which we ate. A dorado straight out of the water makes delicious eating at any time, but when you've been dining on canned food for nearly two weeks on a small boat at sea, it tastes like manna from heaven. June fried some mouth-watering steaks for supper, and we soaked more in lemon juice to make Fish Tahitienne for the next day.

Meanwhile, in *Freelance*'s navigation department the tension was mounting. The navigator's big test was coming up. I estimated that St. Helena would be in sight at dawn on Sunday, March 8, but at 6 a.m., at the end of my watch, there was nothing to be seen. Kevin, who knew exactly where we were, kept a poker face and gave me no comfort. I couldn't bring myself to go below to sleep. I fetched the binoculars and scanned the horizon ahead. Nothing. St. Helena was a high volcano, ten miles long and six miles wide. I should be able to see it. Frank Wightman, in *Wylo*, had sighted it thirty-five miles away. But no. Nothing. I bit my nails and stared ahead until I could see nothing but little dancing specks in my eyes.

June popped her head up through the hatch at 8:20 a.m. and suddenly yelled: "Look!" She pointed over the starboard bow. There it was, the dark rugged shape of the island, unexpectedly close, suddenly released from the sea haze that had been hiding it. Kevin grinned widely. "Congratulations, Mr. Navigator," he said. "I was just beginning to wonder if Prince Henry and I should tell you."

"We would have missed the island by about five miles on our present course," I noted ruefully.

"I know," Kevin said, "but it's usually visible for twenty miles or more in daylight, so I guessed you'd spot it."

Oh, how wonderful I felt. There are no words to describe adequately the ecstasy of a successful landfall made with the help of a sextant and a lot of worried calculating.

We changed course and ran toward the far eastern edge of the island. In a few hours we were getting a close-up look at the dark, forbidding cliffs of the wild natural fortress to which the defeated Emperor Napoléon Bonaparte was exiled by the British from 1815 to his death in 1821.

Freelance ran down the island in boisterous seas with two reefs in her mainsail, while we excitedly consulted the chart and pointed out the landmarks to each other: Gill Point, King and Queen Point, and Barn Long Point. The cliffs were dark brown, tall, and devoid of vegetation and beaches. The whole island was bleak and forbidding, a brooding prison fortress, and yet, in our exhilaration at finding it, we thought it looked wonderful.

There was no harbor on the island, so we anchored off the only town, Jamestown, a cluster of gray buildings shorehorned into a narrow green cleft whose mouth led to the sea. There, in the lee of island we dropped anchor among half a dozen other small yachts. But the only possible anchorage was crowded, and the holding poor, so we shifted to Rupert's Bay next door and, after several tries, we found a patch of sand that gave our thirty-five-pound CQR a firm grip in ninety feet of water.

We had taken fifteen days, five hours for the passage from Cape Town to St. Helena, a very respectable time for a boat of *Freelance*'s size, and we were well pleased with ourselves.

The Hiscocks, with their vast experience, had taken sixteen days, one hour in *Wanderer III*. Henry Wakelam had taken seventeen days and twelve hours in his little twenty-four-footer, *Wanda*. Bernard Moitessier, in the bigger *Marie-Thérèse II*, had taken eighteen days exactly, seventeen of which, he said, were of fine weather, completely trouble-free. Frank Wightman, in *Wylo*, had taken nineteen days.

We felt very proud of ourselves for averaging 112 miles a day on our first ocean voyage. But we didn't forget Hugh Barkla's contribution. His twistle yard had proved to be worth its weight in gold.

9

ST. HELENA ISLAND

Nothing seemed to have changed on St. Helena in a quarter century. I had been here once before, twenty-seven years previously, when I was working my passage from Durban to London as a greaser's steward on the Union-Castle liner *Warwick Castle.* The landing steps were still topped by a steel bar, from which thick ropes hung down at intervals. As you approach the landing from seaward, you begin to understand the purpose of those ropes. The Atlantic swells rise and fall five or six feet against the steps, sometimes as much as fifteen feet, ascending and descending like an elevator gone mad. As an incoming swell lifts you to the top of the steps, you grab a rope and swing yourself ashore before your boat starts to fall away rapidly and leaves you to step off into space. Landing at St. Helena is exciting, to say the least. The only thing more exciting is trying to get back into your boat from the steps.

But we managed quite well with our little inflatable dinghy. Only on one occasion did we send a frisson through the crowd of locals that regularly gathered at the steps like Cornish wreckers in search of a good cargo of laughs to plunder.

There is nowhere to moor a dinghy, so you have to take it ashore with you. The drill is to unload all your gear by hurling it ashore bit by bit onto the head of the steps as your boat rises to the top of each swell. Then you get your passengers ashore, one by one, at the top of each ascent, watching with your heart in your mouth as they cling like monkeys to the ropes and swing themselves over the void. Then, finally, you kill the engine, tilt it up, grab the dinghy painter, throw yourself onto the landing at exactly the right moment and, with the help of your crew, you try to wrestle the dinghy bodily ashore before it falls into the boiling sea six feet below. You must naturally do all this without overbalancing or falling off the landing. As you can imagine, there is some judgment required here in handling the dinghy and doing so many things in one split second. We did surprisingly well in our comings and goings, except for a small debacle one afternoon when I jumped into the dinghy after launching it from the landing, only to find it falling down faster than I was.

Gravity took me down to meet it eventually, but by the time I reached it I was over the outboard engine, which I hit with a nasty thud. I clung to it like a leech, and was able to drag myself back on board, wet only to the waist. The incident raised a few smirks in the crowd, but nobody laughed outright, so I didn't feel totally disgraced.

The village of Jamestown was crammed into the arid mouth of mile-long Chapel Valley a few hundred yards away, alongside the gateway of the castle, where an inscription dated 1645 told of a ship called the *Dolphin* that stopped to replenish her food and water supplies.

On the other side of the gateway stood the Grand Parade—but it was grand only in comparison with the narrow Main Street farther south, and the even narrower Napoleon Street and Market Street, which split off it.

On either side of the valley lay cottages and commercial buildings of a bygone age, most of them built in the eighteenth and nineteenth centuries, when the British-controlled island was used by the Royal Navy as a base from which to smash the slave trade between West Africa and America. Many of the ten thousand freed slaves who came to St. Helena in transit elected to stay on as laborers or domestic servants.

We were unused to being on dry land, and the cobbled streets of Jamestown rocked as we walked them. As we passed a hotel and bar, June lost her footing completely and fell down. Kevin and I, fearing that the gawking locals might misconstrue the reason for her fall outside a bar, quickly hauled her up and marched her off, one at each elbow.

We were delighted to find little old shops with ancient wooden counters where they still weighed out groceries on brass scales. The Consulate Hotel, with its snug, low-beamed pub, was built in the 1750s. There were no traffic lights, no television stations, no railroads, no airport, and only a few old cars and buses. Time seemed to have stopped in the 1800s in Jamestown.

We learned that there were six thousand inhabitants of this forty-seven-square-mile British Crown Colony, and they still spoke an old English dialect, substituting Ws for Vs, as Charles Dickens's characters often did. They talked of "wittles" for victuals, of "superwision" and "rewenge." We were told that a radio program recorded there for British listeners had to be abandoned after the resident veterinarian kept referring to himself as the island's official "wet." In Britain, that meant "wimp."

As you look south from Jamestown, up into the steep cleft of Chapel Valley, you catch a startling glimpse of green high up against the sky, and you begin to discover St. Helena's extraordinary secret—above the twelve hundred-foot contour line the moonlike landscape suddenly gives way to tropical vegetation and fertile green valleys. Everywhere there is wild flax, once grown for linseed oil, fabric, and cordage, but no longer needed in the age of synthetic materials.

When Charles Darwin visited St. Helena in the *Beagle* in 1836 he commented: "It is a curious little world within itself; the habitable part is surrounded by a broad band of black, desolate rocks, as if the wide barrier of the ocean was not sufficient to guard the precious spot." Even today its remoteness is emphasized by the lack of a harbor and an airfield. Nowhere is there a stretch of level ground big enough to accommodate an aircraft sufficiently large to cross the ocean.

Up in those rolling hills, two thousand feet above sea level, a few miles out of town, lay Plantation House, the Georgian residence of the British governor.

When the Hiscocks arrived in St. Helena on *Wanderer III,* His Excellency the governor sent his car for them with an invitation to lunch. Our reception was rather different. In the police station at the castle we were asked to hand over our passports, presumably to prevent our escaping from the island without

having paid our bills. We didn't like the idea, and thought it might even be illegal under international conventions, but there didn't seem to be much of an
alternative, except to accept the offer of free accommodation in the castle's dun-
geon prison.

With a group of fellow yachtsmen we hired a bus to see the governor's man-
sion and Napoléon's tomb. The bus, like most of the vehicles on the island, was
of ancient vintage, a twelve-seater, 1926 American Ford. It was a convertible
with a cloth top, a type they called a charabanc.

Plantation House dated from 1792 and had the shuttered windows and elegant proportions of the era. Its setting in impressive parkland lent it an air of
great grace and timeless dignity. But since the governor had declined to send his
limousine to bring us to lunch with him—despite our having made a better passage time than the Hiscocks, mind you—I elected to ignore him and say hello
to His Excellency's famous reptile instead. Jonathan, a giant Galapagos tortoise,
was reputed to be more than two hundred years old.

I had met him on my first visit to the island; but the creased and wrinkled
tortoise they pointed out to me now in a paddock in front of the governor's residence seemed smaller than the one I remembered. Yet the locals swore it was the
original Jonathan, the one who was landed by a visiting ship in 1882, when he
was already one hundred years old. In any case, he showed no flicker of recognition when I patted his ugly old shell as I had done a mere twenty-seven years
before. He offered us no hint of welcome to his lovely island. In fact, he evinced
an almost gubernatorial indifference to our presence, so we left him to chew his
lettuce and reminisce over times gone by. We headed off to Longwood Old
House, where Napoléon was kept prisoner, and where he died.

The French government has obviously never trusted the British to look after
Napoléon's artifacts on St. Helena; probably with good reason. Consequently, a
French vice-consul was stationed permanently at Longwood with a staff of eight
specifically to maintain the Old House, where a large tricolor flew defiantly from
a tall flagpost. All the rooms were preserved exactly as they had been when
Napoléon used them, and housed a fascinating collection of letters and important documents relating to French imperial business.

Napoléon was not a happy prisoner. His feelings of gloom when he first set eyes on his forbidding prison island from the deck of HMS *Northumberland* in 1815 were not alleviated by his incarceration in the mist-trapping heights of Longwood, where he learned to hate the gray overcast skies and copious rain. He died in 1821 surrounded by his aides. His body lay in state in the drawing room while hundreds of islanders, soldiers, sailors, and East India Company servants filed past.

An autopsy revealed that Napoléon had cancer of the stomach and a perforated ulcer. These two factors were agreed to be the cause of death, but there was a dispute among the eight doctors present about the state of the liver, and from that time to the present there has been speculation that he actually died of arsenic poisoning.

At the end of a tree-lined avenue nearby we found his large flat tomb surrounded by iron railings. It was a beautiful spot, quiet and dignified. Considering how much trouble Napoléon had caused them, I thought the British had reacted with great magnanimity in choosing a burial site really worthy of an emperor. Nevertheless, Napoléon's body was exhumed from this tomb in 1840 and returned to France in its lead-lined coffin.

But we hadn't been there more than a few minutes when two young members of our party, a man and a woman, clambered over the railing, laughing. The woman lay down on her back on the tomb, and spread her legs. The man lay face down on her, and they pretended to make love while their cheering friends took photographs.

June and I looked at each other, stunned and embarrassed. Like Kevin, the local bus driver turned his head away, pretending not to notice. The desecration didn't last longer than it took for a few flashguns to go off, but I felt an immediate surge of anger and disgust. That was soon modified by the thought that perhaps I had become old and conservative, and no longer related to the younger, fun-loving generation. But deep in my heart I knew that this was no way for strangers of any age to behave in a foreign land. If nothing more, it was extremely bad manners, and I was sad that one of the perpetrators was a South African.

* * *

No humans lived on the remote island when it was discovered in 1502 by Juan de Nova, the commodore of a Portuguese fleet returning from India along the route that Vasco da Gama had blazed. He landed there on St. Helen's day, May 21, and named the island after the saintly mother of Constantine the Great. For years, the Portuguese managed to keep its existence a secret while they used it as a revictualing station, supplying water and fresh fruit for their ships. They also turned goats loose on the island to provide meat—with the usual disastrous results for the island's vegetation.

The first person to live there permanently was an extraordinary character called Dom Fernando Lopez, a Portuguese military officer who had deserted to the enemy in Goa, on the west coast of India. Portuguese troops recaptured, him, however. As punishment they cut off his right hand, one finger of his left hand, his ears, and his nose.

In the spring of 1516, Lopez managed to stow away on a ship bound for Portugal, hoping to be reunited with his family. But when they reached St. Helena he was overcome by doubts and remorse, escaped from the ship, and disappeared on the island. Friendly companions who had helped him remain hidden on the ship searched for him in vain, and left some food and clothing for him.

Lopez lived his hermit's existence on St. Helena for thirty years. At first, he remained out of sight when ships called, but later he became well known. He planted fruit and vegetables, and raised goats and poultry, which he exchanged for clothing and other goods from passing ships.

But the burden of his old treachery still lay heavily upon him, so he eventually accepted an offer of a passage to Europe, where he received absolution from the Pope. With that weight off his mind, and the threat of eternal damnation removed, Lopez might well have spent his waning years in comfort with his family in Portugal, but he chose not to. He returned to the solitary hardships of St. Helena and the life he knew best, and there he stayed until his death.

* * *

The Union-Castle liners, which were the island's only regular link with Britain and South Africa, stopped running in the 1970s as air travel became the favored mode of international travel.

The Warwick Castle, a cargo-passenger liner on which I had made my first visit to St. Helena, had stayed only a few hours—just long enough for most of the greasers to go ashore and get blind drunk. My job on the ship was to play nursemaid to eight of them on the starboard watch. The greasers were the engine-room grunts, and I was their steward, or peggy. There was no lower form of life on the *Warwick Castle* than the greasers' peggy. But I didn't mind, because I was saving the cost of my fare to England. Better yet, I would actually be paid a peggy's wages when we got there.

I hated it when the greasers had shore leave, though. First I had to strip their bunks of linen and blankets in case they smuggled them ashore and sold them for drinking money. I had to hide the cutlery in their messroom for the same reason. And when they reembarked, I had to make up their bunks again and then spend half an hour cleaning the vomit from their mens' room.

Besides taking care of their bed linen, I had to fetch their meals from the tourist-class galley, serve them in their tiny messroom up by the bows, and wash up all their dishes and cutlery.

When I was still new at the job, a few nights out of Durban, my opposite number from the port watch wandered into the messroom after supper, when I was washing the dishes.

"Wotcher doin' then?" he asked.

I shrugged and held up a soapy plate.

"You don't 'ave to do that," he said, opening the large brass porthole above the galley sink. "This is what we do." He took the plate from my hands and threw it out of the porthole. "Throw 'em all out," he said. "That's what we do."

I was aghast. Thoughts of having to pay for eight plates, eight mugs, and eight saucers, ran through my mind. "What will they eat off?" I asked.

"I'll show you. Come with me."

He led me along the narrow passageways and stairways to the tourist class galley to a section I'd never seen before. Giant dishwashers belched and hissed. Steam fizzed through racks. He pointed to stacks of hot, newly washed plates and said: "Grab a handful any time you need 'em."

And that's what I did from then on. I never washed another plate or mug. When the greasers had finished eating, I threw the crockery out of the porthole.

It occurred to me that if the oceans were to dry up overnight, you'd be able to trace the path of every Union-Castle liner that ever sailed, from its trail of dirty but perfectly sound dishes.

I asked a steward why they were never missed. "Every time we get into a gale in the Bay of Biscay, we start to roll terribly," he explained with a wink. "Great stacks of newly washed dishes overbalance and get smashed. Seems to 'appen every voyage. Act of God, y'know."

I never threw the knives, forks, and spoons overboard because I had to account for them to the purser. The captain himself came around on official inspection one day when we were near the equator, and reprimanded me for putting wet cutlery away in the drawer. "Must put it away dry," he said. "Fearful health hazard, wet cutlery. Specially in this heat."

I tried to look contrite. I said: "Aye, aye, sir," in my best toady fashion and he disappeared aft with a couple of gold-braided officers in his wake. Little did he know what was happening to his crockery.

Years before, another Union-Castle liner, the *Braemar Castle,* had dropped anchor while the Eric and Susan Hiscock were visiting St. Helena. "Seeing *Wanderer* rolling in the roadstead, her master, Captain Cambridge, at once sent over a boat to bring us aboard for breakfast with him in his ship's air-conditioned dining saloon," Eric Hiscock says in *Around the World in Wanderer III.* "We much enjoyed the freshness of that meal in such cool civilized surroundings, and when we left we were richer by four pounds of butter, apples, Jaffa oranges, and up-to-date magazines."

I had always been heartened by the recognition Captain Cambridge accorded the Hiscocks. It was a salute from one master mariner to another, a gesture that demonstrated an understanding of the difficulties and hazards of small-boat voyaging. It takes many professionals to fetch a large ship across an ocean, each versed in a separate discipline—the stowage of cargo and liquids, provisioning, cooking, navigation, engineering, medicine, helmsmanship, meteorology, signals, security, seamanship, electronics, and so on. On a small sailboat, one or two amateurs do all that, and they face exactly the same oceans, the same gales, and the same hazards of the sea, in a much frailer vessel.

The luck that befell the Hiscocks did not visit us in *Freelance,* of course. The Union-Castle line was long out of business, and the only way to get to St. Helena while we were there—other than by private yacht—was aboard the Royal Mail Steamer *St. Helena,* a cargo-passenger ship that plied between Avonmouth, England, and Cape Town every two months. She called at Las Palmas, Ascension, and St. Helena along the way, carrying sixty-seven passengers. It was evident that St. Helena was now more cut off from the world than ever before, even more remote than its twelve hundred miles from the nearest African mainland would suggest. Up until 1869, when the Suez Canal opened, a thousand or more sailing ships called at Jamestown every year. Now, the harbormaster told us when we paid a courtesy visit, only about two hundred yachts a year dropped anchor in that deep and restless anchorage. It was one of the world's truly quiet spots.

Near the harbormaster's office was a quay with a crane used to transfer cargo to and from barges. This was where Bernard Moitessier had *Marie-Thérèse II* hauled out while he and Henry Wakelam spent a whole month replacing five planks that had gone rotten. Dear Bernard, who quite cheerfully agreed that he lacked some of the most elementary knowledge of boatbuilding, had built his boat without wood preservatives of any kind.

When he saw the extent of the damage, Wakelam was horrified. He wondered how Moitessier could have had the nerve to sail from Cape Town with five planks reduced to the strength of cardboard. Moitessier wondered that himself, too, but apparently didn't search very hard for an answer.

At this same spot, Frank Wightman had wanted to haul *Wylo* out to find and repair an annoying leak, but The Rollers set in for eleven days and made it impossible to use the crane. The Rollers (always referred to with capital letters) are giant swells that coming rolling in from the north—against the prevailing winds—and fling themselves against the cliffs and the seawall. Vertical walls of roiling water spurt thirty feet or more into the air, and the rebounding waves rush out to sea to meet the incoming ones, causing turmoil in the anchorage and stopping all boatwork. Nobody knows where The Rollers come from, or why. Sometimes they last only a few hours, but often they will go on for a week or more. In the end, Wightman and his crew, Graham Young, decided to sail on to Ascension Island, where there was said to be a fifteen-ton crane.

Wightman is almost unknown in comparison with such great names from the golden age of cruising as Moitessier, Bardiaux, and the Hiscocks, but he had as much influence on me they did. As a teenager I could almost recite by heart the opening paragraphs of his first book, *The Wind is Free:*

"In fancy I used to see her running in the big seas. Under a lowering sky and through a welter of angry water she fled, rising and falling, outlined in the whiteness of her speed, magical and swift.

"Sometimes she slept upon her own reflection off golden beaches, which palm trees barred with shadow. And in fancy I was always with her. This was my refuge from the long littleness of life.

"Sometimes, through shrouded nights bejewelled with stars, her charred shadow drifted down the silver pathway to the moon. And I was always with her. This was my escape from the platitude of existence."

I never met Wightman, a South African. He lived a reclusive life aboard *Wylo,* a near-replica of Harry Pigeon's thirty-four-foot yawl *Islander,* on a sea lagoon north of Cape Town.

Wightman was the epitome of the frustrated traveler. His dream, like that of so many of us, was to be free of the shackles of conventional suburban life, free to wander where the flying fish play and the coconut palms dance to the tune of the warm trade winds. He wanted to be master of his own destiny, accountable to no one and completely free of debt to society.

This, of course, is the driving urge that afflicts most red-blooded young men, and many women, too—to travel, to experience adventure, to see new people in new places, to prove yourself the equal of your peers, and to be self-sufficient. Such urges are usually smothered by the early need to find steady work to pay the rent or the car installment, and the later need to provide food, clothing, shelter, medical care, and an education for the family that your raging hormones have brought about. It is a trap from which few escape. The dreams gradually die, to be replaced with pretty pictures and cruising stories in the yachting magazines.

Wightman was as trapped as anybody; the difference was that he kept his dream alive through several decades of enforced drudgery and conformity. Then, finally, he did build his own boat and escape. He sailed *Wylo* from Cape Town in 1947, eventually ending the voyage in North America. It was a modest achievement compared with some of the small-boat voyages that followed, but it was considered very daring at the time. He was a true vagabond of the sea before Moitessier could even pronounce the word.

Before he built *Wylo,* in the long period of waiting, Wightman shipped aboard the square-rigger *Birkdale* from Cape Town to Australia. In *The Wind Is Free,* his description of the sailing ship fighting for her life in huge seas after broaching on a tremendous swell during a Southern Ocean storm, and her crew's labors to pull her head off before she capsized, stands comparison with the best of maritime literature.

I need hardly say that, unlike us, Wightman and Young were invited to visit the governor. On this occasion, however, His Excellency neglected to provide transport, and the pair had a long wearying walk, miles uphill, to Plantation House. Colonel and Mrs. Gilpin showed them the grounds and took them to meet the tennis players on the lawn, after which they went to say hello to our old friend Jonathan the tortoise. Governors come, and governors go, but Jonathan stays forever.

If the island of St. Helena was one of the earth's quiet spots, it was often far from silent at Anne's Place. Anne, a bustling woman of considerable charm and energy, ran a small indoor/outdoor restaurant and bar near the castle. It was the favorite watering hole of the visiting yacht crews. The sound level of conversation, always fairly high when sailors and beer find themselves in close proximity, would rise dramatically at Anne's Place when one of the handheld VHF radios carried by crewmembers announced that another boat was drifting out to sea. It happened quite regularly because the anchorage fell away steeply into deep water, and boats whose anchors dragged even a little would quickly find themselves adrift. People would gulp down their drinks and go flapping off into the dark night to wake up the man with the diesel-powered ferry boat who could take them chasing after their yachts.

Anne provided a special logbook in which many visiting cruising sailors pasted pictures of their boats and crews, wrote heroic descriptions of their voyages, and even left messages for friends they knew would be calling at St. Helena later. Something made me decline Anne's offer to add my sixpenn'orth to this illustrated "post office" book. I like to think it was good taste, but I fear it was more a combination of guilty conscience, a cubbyhole full of Krugerrands, and a desire not to leave tracks.

A few yards away from Anne's Place, just off the public gardens, was a plaque commemorating the visit of Captain Joshua Slocum in 1898, aboard the yacht *Spray*, out of Boston. The Canadian-born American was the first man to sail around the world singlehanded. He was received in St. Helena with great cordiality. He gave public lectures about his daring voyage. And—need I say it?—he was invited to stay with the governor at Plantation House. He was, in his own words, "entertained royally."

Despite the rather pointed lack of attention from the present governor, June and I loved the island and its shy, soft-spoken inhabitants. We decided that one day when we got rich, and when we were not burdened with the tensions that weighed us down on that voyage, we would go back there and stay for six months. Anything less wouldn't do it justice. I wasn't sure how much it appealed to Kevin, though. There was hardly anything to keep an intelligent seventeen-year-old occupied for long. He was too young to partake of the traditional sailor's pastimes of drinking and wenching, too old to be amused by swings and roundabouts. The local newspaper made him laugh, though. "They've had an automobile accident in Jamestown," he told us. "Some residents are calling for radical change: they're thinking of installing their first traffic light."

The weekly *St. Helena News* cost five pence and consisted of twelve small pages, typewritten and photocopied. The main lead was a message from Her Majesty the Queen about Commonwealth Day. A far more interesting inside page was labeled "Flashback." It featured ancient stories taken from the official *St. Helena Records* detailing past proceedings of the island court:

January 7th 1689: John Knipe complains of Bridget Coales refusing to marry and let him kiss her, that he asked her if he were not as good as the Butcher. Wherefore she called him "downe look dog" and compared him to an old dog of her father's. Bridget to pay $15 damages.

September 7th 1723: Dr. Wignall complains of Parson Gilles calling him "Rogue, Rascall and Villain" and threatening as soon as he was well to lead him up and down the valley by the nose.

January 4th 1725: Governor has been dangerously ill and owed his life to medicines supplied upon the accidental arrival of the *York* galley bound to the Coast of Guinea.

Dr. Wignall is always drunk and nearly killed the Governor by giving unsuitable medicines, his excuse being he had nothing else to give.

Dr. Wignall for drunken disorderly conduct placed in the stocks for one hour and he sung and swore the whole time.

* * *

Two days after we arrived at Jamestown, the Durban yacht *Ev-a-Dene* sailed into the anchorage. We had first met them in Mossel Bay, and they had sailed from Cape Town on the same day as us.

Dave hailed us a little ruefully. "How long have you been in?" he asked.

I told him.

"We thought we'd made good time—seventeen days only," he said.

I shrugged modestly, but felt very smug. *Ev-a-Dene* was a much bigger boat, crewed by four people. She probably should have beaten us, considering we'd had the same weather. I figured the governor definitely wouldn't be sending for *them*.

The next day we experienced the magic of modern technology. From *Freelance*'s own cabin, June made a radio telephone call to her sister Carol in America. It was possible because St. Helena was an outpost of Cable & Wireless Ltd., a company with underwater cable links to the island of Ascension to the north, thence to the West Indies and England. We simply contacted St. Helena Radio on our little short-range VHF radio, and they patched through a collect telephone call to Carol in Idaho. She would be joining us for a short cruise in the British Virgin Islands when we got there, and June wanted to let her know our updated schedule.

As we passed the old castle in our comings and goings, I noticed that the section of it that they quaintly called The Treasury was a place where you could officially exchange foreign currency. I was tempted to ask if they'd turn my gold Krugerrands into British pounds, but something stopped me. St. Helena had strong connections with Cape Town. They obviously knew, in The Treasury, that ordinary law-abiding South Africans didn't arrive in St. Helena with a fistful of Krugerrands. Maybe I'd be arrested and deported. My mind raced with possibilities that seemed fanciful on reflection, but which contained sufficient grains of truth to make me wary. I decided not to bother The Treasury after all.

Just before we left St. Helena, I attended to some personal business I'd been putting off. I paid a visit to the island's official dentist. I'd lost a filling from a tooth out at sea, somewhere between Cape Town and St. Helena.

The dentist was a contract man from Britain. When he'd finished repairing the damage, I scanned the government tariff board on the wall, and offered him the statutory twelve pounds sterling for his services—about seventeen American dollars.

"No, no," he said, smiling. "I'm a simple man. I like to work in small, round figures. Let's make it five pounds."

It's a memory of St. Helena I shall always cherish.

We tore ourselves away after a week's stay, and were surprised at how businesslike our departure seemed. By now we all knew our jobs on board, we knew what to expect when we got to sea, and we knew how the boat behaved in calm and gale.

As we motored out of the anchorage, we looked back at Jamestown, crammed higgledy-piggledy into its cleft between Rupert's Hill and High Knoll.

June said: "I can't believe we're doing this."

"How do you mean?"

"I mean doing it like this. Going to sea without any fuss. Just going, as if we were merely setting out for the corner store."

"No apprehension, you mean?"

"Yes. Does anyone realize we're heading into the South Atlantic, aiming at a tiny island thousands of miles away, on a thirty-one-foot yacht?"

The little BMW diesel thumped away energetically for a moment or two before Kevin replied: "Yes, I do. I realize there'll be no cold drinks, ice cream, or fresh bread for at least sixteen days."

I chuckled. "You've become excellent crewmembers," I said. "You've found confidence. And that makes me confident, too."

It sounded pompous, I knew, but it was true. At least some of my apprehension had been lifted. Unfortunately, there was still plenty left, and it wouldn't be erased until we'd arrived safely in America with dollars instead of Krugerrands, and found a car, two jobs, a home, and a university for Kevin to go to. I had to find out how to import *Freelance* legally, and then sell her, an act complicated by the American embargo on South African-made products. Maybe I couldn't import her. I didn't know, and couldn't find out. Maybe the immigration people wouldn't accept my outdated visa. Maybe I'd be thrown out of the States with my boat. There was still plenty to fret about. But first we had to get there.

I called the harbormaster on VHF Channel 16.

"This is the yacht *Freelance* clearing port, bound toward Fernando de Noronha."

"Roger *Freelance,* have a safe trip. Anything else we can do for you?"

"No thanks," I said, "we're all set . . . oh wait . . . you could do one thing. Please say good-bye to the governor for us."

10

ST. HELENA TO FERNANDO DE NORONHA

Calm weather plagued us for the first two days out of St. Helena, but on the third day the wind veered to the east-southeast and filled in at ten to twelve knots, sending *Freelance* bustling over low swells toward the tiny island of Fernando de Noronha, off the coast of Brazil, about eighteen hundred miles away.

We had decided to make a dogleg around Ascension Island, a dependency of St. Helena that lay seven hundred miles to the northwest. We didn't plan to stop there, for two reasons. First, we were running late because of the extra time it had taken us to round the Cape, and we wanted to be out of the Caribbean by the beginning of June, when the official hurricane season began. Second, a notice at the police station in St. Helena had warned yacht crews that they wouldn't be welcome in Ascension. Apparently visiting yachts had become a nuisance on the arid little island, which was short of water and lacking in provisions for outsiders.

What we could do, however, was contact Ascension by VHF radio when we got there, to report our position and have it officially recorded in the log. I also wanted to use the island as a navigation check. I had succeeded in guiding us close enough to St. Helena to see it at close range, but I wanted to do better before we got to Fernando de Noronha, which was even smaller and lower.

We had switched off Prince Henry, our satellite navigator, to save electricity, so twice a day, at 9 a.m. and noon, I looked at the sun through the telescope of my sextant, and turned the knurled knob until its bottom edge rested on the far horizon. That gave me the height of the sun. At that instant, I noted the time to the nearest second. With the help of the nautical almanac, sight reduction tables, and a little elementary arithmetic, I plotted two lines on a blank chart. The point at which they intersected represented our position on the surface of the earth.

Although professional navigators like to build a hedge of mystique around themselves, as though they alone have learned the secret of communication with the cosmos, basic sextant navigation is a fairly simple matter on a vehicle that travels at a little over walking speed. The major problem on a bouncy small boat is knowing when you're looking at the horizon and when you're bringing the sun down to the top of a passing swell instead. Big ships provide high, stable platforms for navigators shooting the sun, but on small yachts being flung about close to sea level it's difficult to take accurate sights. You need two hands to work the sextant, and that leaves none to hang on with, so you have to find a place where you can sit securely, or stand firmly braced against something. Only experience teaches you when to trust your sights. On a calm day, a sight that gives you a fix within a mile of your true position is about as good as it gets. Under normal circumstances, and certainly when you're well away from land, an error of five miles is perfectly acceptable.

Every day at noon, after I had worked out our position, I marked it on the chart, and soon a procession of little dots, about an inch apart, was working its way across the South Atlantic Ocean. It's hard to describe how much those dots on the chart meant to us. They were the only way we knew—or thought we knew—we were making progress. Outside, the sea looked the same everywhere. Day after day, from horizon to horizon, nothing in the seascape changed. There were no milestones, no mountains or rivers by which to mark our journey and to know how far we had come, and how far we still had to go. The sea opened up to allow *Freelance* to thrust her sleek hull through, and closed up again immediately she had passed, leaving no sign of her passage except the white foam of her wake that hissed for a minute and then disappeared.

For us, the dots on the chart were reality, the only tangible sign that we were in command of our own destiny, and not stuck forever in a fading illusion of forward movement. June, Kevin, and I all paused at the chart table several times a day to check on the line of dots heading northwest from St. Helena.

Five days out of St. Helena the trade wind turned nasty. A succession of easterly squalls had us scrambling to pull down the twin jibs and raise the reefed mainsail and a working jib. Heavy showers hissed into the heaving sea, and large cross-seas knocked us west of our course and set *Freelance* rolling viciously. In between the squalls we sat in calms for an hour or two with the hot sun raising steam from the saturated deck, and the pinned-in sails flinging off rainbows of droplets as they slatted back and forth. Every time the wind went light, we had to disconnect the Aries wind vane and steer by hand, watching the compass carefully. The large vane that sensed the direction of the wind would not work properly when the wind speed over its surface fell below about five knots.

It wasn't hard work to steer *Freelance* by hand when the wind was that light, but it was deadly boring and it took concentration. Worse, it bound you to the tiller, so you couldn't move away for more than a minute or so at a time to write up the log or tend to sails. Then, when the breeze first picked up, so that we could hand over to the Aries again, it inevitably toyed with us, pouncing first from one direction and then another, which meant that the Aries had to be set and reset again and again by turning its top bezel and pawls in a series of little clicks. It was Kevin, after one of these frustrating sessions, who christened the Aries "Mr. Klickenfuss," a very apt name.

It was dead calm when June stuck her sleepy head through the hatch at 3 a.m. and looked around.

"Pretty night," she said. She climbed up into the cockpit to sit down close beside me on the teak-planked seat.

The air was cool and fresh from recent rain, and brittle pinpoints of stars poked through the black sky.

"It's OK for the moment," I said. "More squalls on the way, though."

I moved over automatically to give her room, but she pressed against me and felt for my hand. I gave it to her reluctantly.

"How are you doing?" she said.

"Fine, we made three miles in the last hour."

"No, I mean you. How are you doing with all of this?"

"I'm fine."

I didn't want to talk about it. Her closeness made me uneasy. It felt like an intrusion into my working life. This wasn't the time or the place for personal discussions. I was on watch now, and shouldn't be distracted.

I know this reaction will seem very strange to American readers, but like many men brought up in Europe or the colonies I tended to compartmentalize my life. I had a home box, a travel box, and a work box. When I left home, I stepped into my travel box, and I left all household matters behind me. When I got to work, I rarely strayed outside my work box. These were separate, different lives, not to be mixed. June rarely telephoned me at work, except in an emergency. She knew I'd regard it as a jarring interference. She understood that I'd be happier discussing domestic matters when I was safely back in my home box. This is not to say that the boundaries between my compartments were never breached. Our relationship was a close, loving one, and could never be that rigid. Nevertheless, I always felt distracted and uneasy when the world of one box transgressed the world of another.

Now, aboard *Freelance,* I had just one box. I was stuck in my work box. My work was to get my boat and my family safely to America. It was serious work, probably more than I should ever have taken on, and until it was finished I would have no other box to go to.

I stood up and moved away from June, pretending to adjust the mainsheet. She put her arm around me, kissed me on the cheek, and started to go below.

"I love you." She said it softly, but there was a note of sadness with it.

"Me too," I replied.

It was true. I did love her. But that was in another box somewhere. There was no place for that box out here on the ocean. It wouldn't help us get to America.

"Man's love is of man's life a thing apart," I thought.

"'Tis woman's whole existence."

Byron knew what he was talking about.

As we drew close to our next landfall, Ascension Island, Kevin and I took particular notice of the swells. We wanted to know if we could see or feel the difference in the swell that a nearby island makes, just as the ancient Polynesian, Melanesian, and Micronesian navigators could. Centuries before white men explored the Pacific, the ancient navigators were making regular voyages across the Pacific basin, one third of the earth's surface. They had no sextants or compasses, only the stars, the planets and an extraordinary understanding of the sea and the weather in all its moods.

Many of their secrets were recorded by Dr. David Lewis, a New Zealand-born physician and small-boat sailor, in his book *We, the Navigators*. He sailed the Pacific with skilled island navigators who were still versed in the old arts of navigation that had been passed by word of mouth from generation to generation.

Lewis maintained they could detect the presence of a low island from as far as thirty-five miles away by a change in the pattern of swells. A boat running dead downwind toward an island, as we were, could expect to feel swells reflected straight back from land.

"I feel the sea hit the canoe—shake him, like move him, go back," said one of the Polynesian experts.

Kevin and I soon discovered that if you haven't spent a lifetime studying them, it's very difficult to detect the patterns of swells in the open ocean, especially when they're confused by breaking waves.

Swells are interesting in their own right, of course, because they're the remains of waves from storms that have died out in the far distance. They are still transmitting power, and they seem to march forward, but in fact neither swells nor waves move any water forward, except for a small amount from breaking crests. It's like shaking a length of rope: the undulations move forward along the rope, but the rope itself doesn't move forward. The energy of the swells just carries on until it meets resistance—usually the coast—where it is expended in a great show of power and noise as the swells trip over their own feet on the shallowing sea bottom and plunge down their steepening faces.

Kevin and I could easily detect a regular swell running in the same direction as the wind, roughly southeast, which was no surprise. But it took us an hour or more of close observation to realize that a smaller but persistent swell was running almost at right angles to it, coming from the southwest. It was presumably the remains of large swells generated in the Roaring Forties, many hundreds of miles to the south of us. That was why *Freelance* was rolling so much. This secondary swell came at her from the side.

No matter how hard we looked, we couldn't detect any sign of a reverse swell coming back toward us from Ascension Island.

"Perhaps the sea's too rough," said Kevin. "It was difficult enough to pick up the southwesterly swell, never mind a faint one from ahead."

"Maybe we're not heading for the island," I said. The eternal self-doubt of the navigator had enveloped me again.

We stopped looking and concentrated on *feeling* instead, waiting for a swell to lift the bow first, check *Freelance's* forward speed ("shake him"), and then pass aft to lift her stern.

We felt, sitting with our backsides on the cockpit seats, and we felt standing with our hands braced against the rim of the dodger, but we felt in vain. Our senses detected nothing. *Freelance* simply lifted her tail, rushed down the face of the swells, settled gently back into the hollow for a moment, and did it all over again.

And then, at 3:20 p.m., I sighted the island fine on the port bow—as good as dead ahead. Once again, a wonderful feeling of relief swept over me. I might not be able to navigate by swells, but my sextant was doing just fine.

At sunset, as we ran into shallower waters, we caught a barracuda on our fishing line. I held him up proudly for the cook to see. June had already prepared our supper, but the thought of fresh fish was too much, and she started all over again as soon as I'd cleaned and gutted our catch. Soon the delicious smell of frying barracuda steaks filled the cabin and we all happily agreed that there was *nothing*—absolutely nothing—half so much worth doing as simply eating barracuda straight from the sea.

We ran down the eastern side of the island shortly after nightfall, and I called Ascension Radio on VHF Channel 16 to report our position and say we were en route to Fernando de Noronha.

"You're not stopping, sir?" the operator asked.

"No, we don't stop where we're not welcome."

"Sir?"

"They told us at St. Helena that yachts are not welcome here."

"Oh no, sir, you're very welcome."

"Well that's what the police told us, so we'll just carry on."

"I'm sorry, sir. Have a safe passage."

We were tempted, for a minute or two, to stop and explore the island after all, but we decided it would be better not to waste any more time en route to the West Indies. Besides, it gave us a nice feeling of moral righteousness to sweep right past the anchorage and the little town behind it with our noses in the air, even if they couldn't see us in the dark. Very few private yachts would have done that.

I was pleased with our progress, too. Despite the calms and squalls, we had taken only six days for the passage from St. Helena to Ascension, the same as the Hiscocks in *Wanderer III*. Henry Wakelam and little *Wanda* had done it in seven days, and Bernard Moitessier had taken nearly nine. Frank Wightman, who had hit extensive calms in *Wylo*, took twelve days, and his biggest daily run was only 87 miles. Ours was 132. For a bunch of newies, we weren't doing badly.

Ascension is an uninvitingly rocky island about seven miles long and eight and a half miles wide—a tiny dot in the immense expanse of the South Atlantic. It's barren and supports no vegetation, hardly even a blade of grass, except for a central green peak of two thousand feet that gets plenty of rain. But, unlike St. Helena, it is colorful. Some forty cones of gray and red ash rising from plains of dark lava, cinders, and pumice stone contrast strongly with the white beaches and blue skies. Frank Wightman described it as having a gaudy, barbaric quality—"gaudy without life."

At Clarence Bay, on the northwest coast, lies the best anchorage, with the nearby small settlement of Georgetown housing a population that fluctuates according to the needs of the island's main employers. The British Broadcasting Corporation has relay transmitters there. The U.S. Air Force and NASA operate satellite and missile tracking stations there, and Cable & Wireless Ltd. maintains telecommunications networks with Europe, Africa, and South America.

Like St. Helena, Ascension is a volcanic peak of fairly recent origin, geologically speaking. It rises ten thousand feet from the seabed, but its great advantage over St. Helena is that it has an airfield.

During World War II, in March 1942, the U.S. 38th Engineer Combat Regiment landed fifteen hundred men and eight thousand tons of equipment there. In little over four months they had constructed a three thousand-yard runway named Wideawake Field after the nickname for the local birds. In short order, hundreds of aircraft were refueling here en route from Brazil to Africa. When NASA later began operations, the runway was extended fifteen hundred yards.

For those arriving by sea, the only landing place was a set of steps at a small stone landing stage, and they were unusable if The Rollers set in, so passengers from visiting ships were not encouraged to go ashore lest they became stranded there.

The fifteen-ton crane at the end of the landing stage was the one Frank Wightman had heard about in St. Helena, and it was certainly capable of handling *Wylo's* weight. She was still leaking moderately from an unknown source, even in the light weather she had experienced on the way from St. Helena, and Wightman was worried that the leak would get worse if they ran into heavy weather. Wightman received permission to use the crane to inspect *Wylo's* hull, but the large swells rolling through the anchorage made it too dangerous to bring the boat so close to the rocky shore. He and Graham Young waited several days for the swell to die down, but it did not cooperate. They decided, with some misgivings, to take a chance and sail on to Trinidad, more than three thousand miles to the north.

My old friend Bernard Moitessier arrived at Ascension in a despondent mood. The gods had whispered in his ear that the calm weather was offering him a good opportunity to climb to the top of the mainmast and see *Marie-Thérèse II* from above, drawing her three-knot wake through the dark-blue South Atlantic in all her glory. But when he got there, he found more evidence of his shoddy boatbuilding and maintenance. The masthead was crumbling with rot. He was devastated.

The rot posed no immediate threat, because the rotten portion was above the point where the standing rigging attached, but it meant he'd need a new mast fairly soon. Worse, it was an indication that his jerry-built boat was not likely to last much longer, even though she was only a couple of years old. He had already replaced five planks in the hull. Now the mast. And goodness knew how much rot was lurking out of view beneath the concrete he had poured into the bilges. He was beginning to realize how dearly he would have to pay for the haste with which he'd built his boat in Mauritius.

His friend Henry Wakelam was already anchored in Clarence Bay when Moitessier arrived, and it didn't cheer him up any to hear Wakelam call him a lazy bastard for being so slow.

When Eric and Susan Hiscock dropped anchor there and made themselves known in their usual polite manner, the resident magistrate, Mr. Harrison, invited them to stay with him and his wife in their house. Harrison declined to offer that courtesy to the bearded, fierce-looking Wakelam, however.

"I rather think the Cable & Wireless people are a bit suspicious of passing yachts," Wakelam warned Moitessier, "they must have seen plenty of bums in their time."

But they were pleasantly surprised when they went ashore. Harrison invited the vagabond and the pirate home for lunch. And there they sat entranced, not knowing which was better, the first decent meal they'd had in weeks, or the presence of their host's ravishingly beautiful eighteen-year-old daughter.

Once they had feasted their stomachs and their eyes, their scavenging instincts came to the fore, and they secured a permit from Harrison to collect two dozen eggs each from the nests of the noisy little sooty terns known as wideawake birds. That was the standard allowance for St. Helenians working on Ascension under contract, who sent eggs back to their families when the regular ship called. Harrison was concerned that this unique and isolated bird population would be fatally depleted if more eggs were collected, especially because they hatched only one egg at a time.

Moitessier and Wakelam promptly went out and collected four hundred eggs each, smashing and discarding many more whose embryos had started to develop. The eggs were about two-thirds the size of a hen's egg, and they coated them with petroleum jelly to preserve them. They also met a worker from the American base and talked him into providing them with a free case of bully beef, bottles of Coke, cans of beer, and new flannel shirts. The scavengers were in fine form, and congratulated each other on their cunning.

Harrison, knowing none of this, made them very welcome, took them on a jeep tour of the island, up to the heights of Green Mountain, and even ordered special bread from the island bakery for them when they left. He didn't know that his friendship had been betrayed until years later, when Moitessier wrote in *Sailing to the Reefs:* "I hope he will forgive us." With their plunder safely stowed below, the pirate and the vagabond set sail for Fernando de Noronha.

For two days after we passed Ascension Island the trade wind blew steadily as we chased the sun. It was now north of the equator, where we needed to be, too. *Freelance* sped along nicely, occasionally causing clouds of flying fish to flee frantically before her churning bows. It was easy sailing as the row of dots on the chart now pointed toward Fernando de Noronha, the tiny island two hundred miles off the "elbow" of South America.

I never tired of watching the sea and the way *Freelance* handled herself on it. The regularity of the swells, and her forward rush down their faces, was almost hypnotic, and I spend many hours lying on the foredeck in the shade of the sails, watching her brilliant white bow wave rise and fall on the warm blue water. On easy passages like this, small things assumed great significance. On March 22, for instance, there was an entry in the official ship's log that said: "Passed green wine bottle floating in the sea." That was a measure of our sensory deprivation. The fact that a single piece of garbage could stimulate me to jump up and point and call to June and Kevin is indicative of just how empty and characterless the ocean appears on the surface day after day. We talked about it for a full five minutes, speculating how long it had been there, why it was still afloat, whether it had come from land or a ship, who had drunk its contents, and so on.

Later that same day, June saw a freighter passing astern of us, and when it became dark I spotted the lights of another ship on the horizon. We were obviously crossing a shipping lane. When Kevin came on watch he reported seeing two more. For us, it was almost like stumbling upon a freeway in the sea.

The next night we ran into fishing boats, too. Kevin spotted the first group in the dark hours before dawn and maneuvered *Freelance* around them. He had strict orders to wake me if he spotted any kind of shipping during his night watches because he was color-blind and couldn't easily tell port lights from starboard lights. But he deliberately didn't call me, and I discovered his transgression only when he wrote it up in the log at the end of his watch.

"Why didn't you call me?" I asked. "You know the rule."

"No need to wake you," he said. "It was easy to go around them."

"But you can't tell which way they're going if you don't know which is a red light and which is a green."

"I can figure it out, dad," he said reassuringly. "I took bearings on them."

I found it disconcerting to have my standing orders disobeyed so casually, but there was no gainsaying the fact that he had safely avoided a collision, so I left it there. My little boy was growing up, flexing his muscles. I had to learn to trust him, color-blind or not.

We wondered what on earth fishing boats were doing out there in the vast wastes of the South Atlantic, which Moitessier had declared to be devoid of fish. But they obviously knew their business better than the French vagabond did, and, as if in confirmation, a fine bonito took our trailing lure at noon. Our gastric juices were running freely at the thought of a meal of fresh fried fish, but I lost him when I tried to pull him over the stern, and the hook pulled out. I set out straightaway to make a gaff from an old broomstick and a large fish hook.

Halfway between St. Helena and Fernando, five days after we had passed Ascension, we ran into calms again and had to steer *Freelance* by hand for several hours. It didn't take long for depression to set in. As always, we began to experience the irritation and short tempers that a calm inevitably generates on a small boat at sea.

To overcome that feeling of helplessness and frustration, I invented what I called the calm bonus system. It worked on the principle that our average speed would be one hundred miles a day. That was the arbitrary figure we used for all planning purposes. So, at noon every day, after I had calculated the day's run, I would note in the log the number of miles we'd covered in excess of one hundred under the heading "Bonus."

Thus, after two days of one hundred and thirty-mile runs, we'd have sixty points as a bonus, which meant we were running six-tenths of a day ahead of schedule. It was a good morale builder, but it came in even more useful in calms. If we covered less than one hundred miles a day, the difference was subtracted from our bonus. But the remaining bonus was inevitably positive, because under normal circumstances we easily did more than one hundred miles from noon to noon. So, if the two days of one hundred and thirty-mile runs (add sixty to bonus) were followed by two days of only eighty-five miles (subtract thirty miles from bonus), we could see at a glance that the bonus was still thirty points. In other words, despite the gloom and frustration of calm weather, we were still about a third of a day ahead of schedule. That thought kept us sane.

The calm didn't last long. After a few frustrating hours, during which we raised and lowered the twin staysails as the breezes came and went, the trade-wind weather changed into doldrums weather. Fierce, dark clouds came charging over the horizon and enveloped us in squalls and heavy rain showers. We handed all sail, changed into our swimsuits, and washed ourselves all over while *Freelance* drifted unattended. The rain was cold, but it felt wonderful to get the salt off our bodies and out of our hair. In total overcast and atrocious conditions we ran all night under bare poles, leaving Mr. Klickenfuss to do the steering while we huddled in the scant shelter of the dodger.

During the night we caught a puffer fish on our lure, one of those ugly yellow fish with spikes that we kids in Simonstown used to call *blaasoppies* (which, literally translated from the Afrikaans, means "blow-uppies"). They blow themselves up with air or water to make themselves look bigger and more ferocious than they really are. When I shone the flashlight on it, this one looked like a miniature mine about to explode.

With its bulging eyes and lips, and its tiny vestige of a tail and fins, it looked quite comical and out of place, not the sort of thing you'd expect to find in mid-Atlantic. It also looked like the last thing in the world I'd want to eat, but in fact its flesh is so delicious that thousands of people are prepared to risk death for a small taste of it, for this is the infamous fish that the Japanese love so much, the one they call fugu.

The fugu's ovaries, skin, muscles, and especially its liver may contain a deadly poison similar to curare for which there is no known antidote. The lethal dose for a human being, one or two milligrams, could fit on the head of a pin. Despite this, fugu has been eaten in China for thousands of years and in Japan for centuries. The Japanese eat tens of thousands of tons of fugu every year, prepared by government-licensed fugu cooks who must take intensive courses, extensive apprenticeships, and written exams. Even so, traces of the poison sometimes escape detection. Between seventy and one hundred people die every year from fugu poisoning.

No matter how delicious it might be, I didn't want it served up as sushi or puffer stew, and I didn't want to deal with it in the dark in that weather and risk getting stabbed by a spike, so I left it to drag at the end of the line. But at dawn there was nothing to be seen. Both fish and lure had disappeared, presumably into the stomach of some bigger fish with a constitution more robust than mine.

The barometer fell quite ominously from its usual reading of 1014 millibars to 1008 and we wondered what was in store for us. A fine sprinkle rained on us from high cloud as the wind went into the east and then the north, but the threatened gale did not arrive. Quite the opposite. We drifted into calms again.

Kevin spotted a nearby whale on his afternoon watch, but didn't call me, for which I was thankful. I didn't trust them and didn't know how to deal with them. I knew at least one boat, the thirty-foot Cape Town sloop *Pionier,* that had been sunk in midocean by killer whales, otherwise known as orcas (which are really dolphins, despite their common name). It happened during the Cape-to-Rio Race in January 1971. I had also read of many other yachts that had been severely damaged by accidentally plowing into ordinary whales. One slap from a big whale's tail would be enough to sink us.

That night, while we were still more than three degrees south of the equator, June spotted what she called the Big Dipper low on the northern horizon. It was the constellation of Ursa Major, of course, the Great Bear, which I knew better as The Plough. No matter what it was called, it was June's first sighting in more than twenty-three years of the constellation she had known so well in her childhood in Utah and Idaho. She was so excited that she wrote in the official log: "Saw the Big Dipper for the first time."

Later that night, torrential rain and lightning forced us to take in all sail at 3 a.m. We put a chain over the stern, attached to the backstay, to ground the mast in case we were struck by lightning, and we lay ahull all night, drifting broadside on to the swells as the wind lashed us. In the middle of it all, a large bird that cawed like a crow landed on the main boom and rested there for half an hour. Then, when I wasn't looking, it disappeared, and I cursed myself for not observing which way it went. I presumed its presence meant land was getting near, and I wanted to know the direction. I hoped it wasn't nearer than I thought. I didn't want to run into Fernando de Noronha, or one of its surrounding islands, in the pitch dark of a vile night like this. I went below and checked the noon fix, and the distance we'd come since then. By my reckoning, we were still one hundred and fifty miles away, but with all the insecurity of a neophyte navigator approaching land, I sat in the cockpit and stared ahead into the blackness of the night, just in case.

Light switchy winds ushered in the dawn and the rain showers drifted off over the western horizon, leaving us with high light cloud and a warm steady breeze. I sounded our main water tank during the morning, the one we had taken all our fresh water from, and discovered that we had used about 1.6 gallons a day in total for the three of us—or about half the amount usually recommended.

We didn't shower, of course, except on deck in the rain. We usually washed our bodies all over with salt water and detergent, then dipped a washcloth in fresh water and rubbed ourselves all over to remove the salt. June used seawater for cooking whenever possible. The only other fresh water we used was for brushing our teeth and drinking—there was no restriction on how much we drank. We carried about eighty gallons in three separate tanks, two under the settee berths and one in the bilge, so we had supplies for fifty days or more, and we could have caught a lot of fresh water with buckets during the rain squalls, when water poured off the mainsail near the gooseneck in a steady stream.

That night, when Fernando de Noronha was only fifty miles or so over the horizon, we were stunned by a display of phosphorescence or bioluminescence of a kind we'd never seen before.

Phosphorescence is one of the finest shows the sea ever puts on, of course, and there were nights when the ocean water seemed to crackle with light of such crisp beauty and such great abundance that our eyes had trouble taking it all in. We experienced the strange feeling that our other senses ought to be able to appreciate it, too. We longed to hear it, or taste it, or *feel* the extraordinary sensations we were witnessing so inadequately. In a small boat like *Freelance,* you could dip your hand over the side, touch those glittering lights, and bring your hand up covered in tiny sparkles.

In his famous account the *Voyage of the* Beagle, Charles Darwin said phosphorescence was caused by the decomposition of organic particles "by which process (one is tempted to call it a kind of respiration) the ocean becomes purified."

When waves scintillated with bright green sparks, it was generally due to minute crustacea, he believed—presumably plankton. "But there can be no doubt that very many other pelagic animals, when alive, are phosphorescent," he added.

Phosphorescence can also be very frightening. I was badly scared one calm night off the southern tip of Africa when two dolphins suddenly raced toward *Freelance's* side, carving hollow undulating tubes of brilliant underwater fire. My immediate thoughts turned to torpedoes, but at the very last moment they dived under us and glowed away into the distance. I felt very silly when I realized what they were, and I was thankful that I hadn't had time to shout for June and Kevin. Nevertheless, it seemed hours before my heart stopped pounding.

But an even greater surprise awaited us that night as we approached Fernando de Noronha. Thin oval disks about ten feet long and five feet wide exploded into brilliant light as *Freelance* approached slowly, flashing like photographer's electronic strobes. The disks lay scattered at odd angles to each other about six feet under water. Each disk erupted instantaneously in an eerie greenish flash that lit up our white sails, and sometimes several would go off together. We watched them in silent fascination.

Darwin had seen the same phenomenon at this very spot 148 years before, and had no explanation for them. "Near Fernando Noronha [*sic*] the sea gave out light in flashes," he noted. "The appearance was very similar to that which might be expected from a large fish moving rapidly through a luminous fluid. To this cause the sailors attributed it; at the time, however, I entertained some doubts, on account of the frequency and rapidity of the flashes."

In *Life on Earth,* the explorer and zoologist David Attenborough mentions that some fish living in the stygian depths of the ocean have cultures of phosphorescent bacteria in special organs with flaps of skin over them that can be moved to expose or conceal the bacteria in a series of winks and flashes. But that didn't explain what we had seen. This was no series of winks. This was pure underwater lightning.

And that's exactly what the ancient Polynesian and Micronesian sailors called it. David Lewis, in his book *We, the Navigators,* says they knew it as *te lapa,* and used it to locate land from eighty to one hundred miles away.

"It comprises streaks, flashes and momentarily glowing plaques of light, all well beneath the surface," Lewis says. "Exactly like lightning, it flickers and darts and is in constant motion. It occurs a good deal deeper down than common luminescence, at anything from a foot or two to more than a fathom."

Apparently, its flashes dart out from the direction of the nearest land, or else flicker to and fro in line with that bearing, so that among the Polynesians it was customary to steer by it, particularly on dark rainy nights when it was very marked.

The breathtaking display stopped abruptly after an hour or so, but we felt very privileged to have witnessed a show that Nature keeps secret from most small-boat sailors. One of the few circumnavigators to write about it was Bernard Moitessier, who at the time was racing Henry Wakelam from Ascension to Fernando de Noronha.

He said *Marie-Thérèse II* was making four knots and leaving a phosphorescent wake, sharp and clear, but here and there he could see large phosphorescent patches that shone for a few seconds and disappeared. He tried to find an explanation for the "numerous transitory phenomena," these sudden bursts of blue-green light, but like mightier minds before him, he failed.

Before we left Durban, a former commodore of Point Yacht Club, Bob Fraser, had told us that our landfall on Fernando de Noronha would be unmistakable, even though the island was only five miles long and two miles wide. "You'll see a huge finger of rock pointing up out of the sea to show you the way," he said.

He was right. After lunch on Monday, March 30, fifteen days out of St. Helena, we spotted Bob's finger, a towerlike mountain called Pico, poking up over the horizon ahead. A fair breeze was pushing us toward it fast.

"I wonder what adventures we'll have there," said Kevin.

"I don't care if we don't have *any,*" I replied. "I'm just happy to have found the place."

"Knock on wood," said June. "We're not there yet. We're still twenty-five miles away."

11

A TROPICAL JEWEL

We approached Fernando de Noronha nervously, wary of being set on to the cluster of small islands and rocks to the east of the main island. A warning note printed in livid purple on the chart said: "Caution—Current flows toward the west with variable intensity between 0.7 and 1 knot. Navigators heading into anchorages, and those approaching or circling the archipelago from the east, must use great caution."

I had plotted on the chart a clearance position five miles east of the archipelago, but late in the afternoon we could tell from compass bearings that the current was indeed pushing us sideways toward the land. We headed up twenty degrees to compensate, but still we were less than two miles offshore when we rounded up in the lee of the island at 6:30 p.m. I was thankful that the weather was fair and the wind moderate.

Darkness fell rapidly after the sun set, for there is very little twilight in the tropics, and by the time we arrived off our intended anchorage in San António Bay I was reluctant to close with the shore.

From a distance of a mile offshore we could see no landmarks to position ourselves accurately. The two lighthouses, one at either end of the archipelago, were perfect for bearings if you were out at sea, but we couldn't see the western light from where we were, and one light is not enough for a position fix in darkness.

We could see nothing in the spot where we presumed the anchorage to be, but someone there spotted our navigation lights and called us on the VHF radio. He was an American singlehander, and he offered to guide us into the anchorage. The entrance was very easy, he said, and there were no rocks or reefs in the way.

It was a kind offer and I probably should have accepted, but I was born on the border of Devon and Cornwall and I knew all about the Cornish wreckers who used to lure cargo ships onto the rocks with beckoning lights. I told the American that we had already decided to heave to offshore for the night and anchor in the morning. I expected to hear some protest from June and Kevin. After all, we had been at sea on continuous watch for nearly sixteen days and the temptation to find a calm anchorage and enjoy a full night's sleep was almost overwhelming. But, to their credit, neither challenged my decision so we headed out into the pitch-black sea for a couple of miles in the lee of the island and hove to under a reefed mainsail and a backed working jib. *Freelance* lay quietly with her head under her wing, pointing toward the island, but drifting slowly sideways through the water toward the west.

There was little for the watchkeeper to do that night, except keep track of our drift. When I came on watch at 2 a.m. I discovered that Kevin had indeed taken bearings every half hour, and had plotted our position on the chart with hypnotic regularity. But he didn't seem to connect the spiderweb of lines on the chart with the reality of our position.

"We're being swept westward much too fast," I said. "Look—we're already three miles past the western end of the island and heading for Brazil. Now we're going to have a helluva time fighting back against the wind and this current. Why didn't you call me?"

He shrugged. "We seemed perfectly safe out here," he said.

"For goodness' sake, Kevin, use your common sense," I snapped. "We're supposed to be in the shelter of the island, not out here at sea."

"Sorry," he said quietly.

"I should think so."

I am ashamed of that little episode now, when I think about it. Poor Kevin. He didn't deserve that. It was *my* insecurity that was showing.

I let the foresail draw and started *Freelance* back toward land, close-hauled on the port tack, and Kevin went below quietly. I heard June talking to him sotto voce, presumably asking him what was going on, but I couldn't hear what was said.

Progress against the current was very slow, and at dawn we were still about eight miles from the anchorage, so I started the engine and we handed the foresail so that *Freelance* could point higher into the wind, using both power and mainsail. The wind had increased at dawn and was now blowing at twenty knots or more, but the seas smoothed out as we approached the island again and we were able to make reasonable headway against the wind and current.

June and Kevin joined me in the cockpit in the morning sun, and soon we were gazing with awe at the giant's finger of Morro do Pico (Peak Hill) pointing straight upward for almost one thousand feet from the beach.

Then the smell of the land hit us. It came in heavenly puffs on the blustery trade wind, the sweet, fecund smell of damp warm tropical earth and perfumed blossoms. It was the joyfully seductive scent of promise and ease that only sailors coming in from the sterile deep sea can properly appreciate. We sniffed slowly and deeply and smiled at each other.

"It's like frangipani," said June. "Like the tree in front of your mother's old house in Durban."

I knew it well, and remembered the sweet, cloying fragrance of the waxy white blossoms.

"It smells like heaven," I said.

We made our way slowly against the wind and current past beautiful palm-fringed beaches of blindingly white sand and dropped our anchor in San Antonio Bay in thirty feet of water in the lee of a small hill topped by an ancient wooden church. The water was as clear as gin and we could see the links of the chain making tracks in the fine white sand on the bottom as *Freelance* settled back on her anchor. We had taken sixteen days and seven hours for the passage from St. Helena.

The singlehander had left at dawn, and the only other vessel in the anchorage was a small sloop flying the Swedish flag, but there was no sign of life aboard. We presumed they were all ashore.

It was bliss to be in still water again and to have time to relax and take in our surroundings. The bay was a shallow crescent, entirely open to the north and west, but as long as the wind remained in the southeast it was adequate shelter.

A large old fort, with cannons still in place on its ramparts, dominated a high knoll at the western end of the bay. There, a huge Brazilian flag streamed stiffly in the breeze. It was the Forte dos Remédios, built in 1737. The Portuguese obviously placed tremendous strategic importance on this little island, just ten square miles in area, two hundred and fifty miles off the mainland, for they built ten forts here during that period. This was the main one, overlooking the only decent deepwater anchorage. It was subsequently used as a prison and as headquarters for the army, but was now abandoned—as, indeed, the whole island seemed to be. We hadn't seen a soul anywhere.

Fernando de Noronha is not as isolated as St. Helena or Ascension but it's still one of the world's lonely places. Like Ascension, however, it has the advantage of a good airstrip, and almost all the requirements of the sixteen hundred inhabitants are flown in from the Brazilian mainland.

Just off the northeastern tip of the main island, near where we anchored, were five small islands. The nearest one, Ilha Rasa, attracted our attention immediately. In the narrow gap between it and the main island, two lines of surf approached each other at an angle, each one leaping over the whole length of the other in a spectacular display of glistening spray and foam, backlit by the early morning sun. We had never seen anything like it before, but here it was non-stop and just part of Nature's grand show.

I got out our yellow-and-green Brazilian courtesy flag and sent it up to the starboard spreader. Something about it worried me, however, and I wondered for a moment if I'd confused it with another country's flag. But no, it was definitely the Brazilian flag. Then I looked across the bay at the Brazilian flag flying from the fort and I knew what was wrong. The colors had been reversed. Where there should have been yellow, there was green, and vice versa. I cursed the color-blind flag maker at the Canvas Construction company in Durban, who had made it for me, and hauled it down. It would be better not to display a courtesy flag than to insult Brazil with this crazy aberration.

After the long passage I was quite happy to sit back quietly and feast my eyes on the beauty all around us. I was in no hurry to go ashore. What I wanted to do was pat *Freelance* all over, pretty her up, thank her for a good trip, tidy up the coils of rope, and get everything shipshape and Bristol fashion. Furthermore, as the trip went on, I found myself increasingly reluctant to leave *Freelance* unattended while we had a cargo of Krugerrands on board.

But Kevin and June had spotted a large building next to a smooth beach that looked like a natural landing place for a dinghy, so we retrieved the orange Metzler inflatable dinghy from the V-berth and pumped it up on the foredeck.

I wished June and Kevin could go ashore and leave me to potter around quietly on my own, but neither of them had any experience of landing a dinghy through surf. And in any case, most countries will allow only the skipper to go ashore until the boat and its crew have been cleared by customs and immigration. I didn't think they'd be too fussy about that particular requirement on this little island, however, so we all piled into the dinghy. Because we could be upset in the surf at the landing place, our passports were in plastic bags and we were dressed in swimsuits. We carried our shoregoing clothes in plastic bags inside a backpack.

I started the little outboard, motored out a few yards, and stopped to look back at *Freelance*. I never tired of seeing her lying peacefully at anchor. It gave me a thrill just to see the sweet curve of her sheerline, and the elegant but purposeful lines of her cabintop. At the very top of the long mast her scarlet-and-white Point Yacht Club burgee fluttered in the tradewind breeze, and at her stern her national ensign flapped lazily. *Freelance* at anchor was a sight that made my heart leap. But June and Kevin, quite understandably, were focused on the land, so we motored over to inspect the landing place.

There were about four lines of breaking surf, but nothing too ferocious, and after hanging around beyond the surf line for a few minutes in an unsuccessful attempt to find an incoming set of swells that was smaller than normal, I drove her bow into the first breaker and we flew in toward the shore like an arrow loosed from a bow, with spray flying high on either side. As she hit the sand with a thump, we jumped out into knee-deep water and dragged her up on to the warm sand, out of the reach of the waves.

We put on our best clothes—long pants for Kevin and me and a dress for June, not shorts, because we knew the Brazilians were formal dressers, even in the tropics—and walked up to the large building.

The building turned out to be a fish-processing and refrigeration plant, and the engineer there gave us a friendly greeting in Portuguese. He turned out to be the island's customs and immigration officer as well, and after he had gravely inspected our passports he handed us a photocopied form in atrocious English, the gist of which was that our stay would be limited to three days, and that we would not be permitted to buy any provisions on the island. Everything had to be imported by air, and there was only enough for the local residents. The island was a military base, and all it produced on a commercial scale was guano and salt. They caught fish for local consumption and grew some fruit and vegetables. Other goods were scarce and expensive, and not available to visitors.

I tried to ask him if the ban on purchases included fresh produce such as lettuce, tomatoes, and potatoes, which we would dearly have loved to buy, but he understood very little English and we spoke no Portuguese. I tried my smattering of Spanish on him, which brought the usual result—he understood perfectly and came back at me in a torrent of unintelligible Portuguese. It was a trap I'd fallen into before. If you speak a few words of Spanish to a Brazilian, the presumption seems to be that you will understand Portuguese. In fact, many *written* Portuguese words are easily translated by a Spanish-speaker because of their common Latin heritage, but the difference in pronunciation is so great that it makes the spoken word impossible to understand. Who would guess, for example, that the letters "oes" in Portuguese are pronounced almost as "*oinsh?*"

I understood perfectly well, though, when he produced a Brazilian courtesy flag, pointed at my boat, and held out his hand. We paid in U.S. dollars and it seemed like quite a lot, though I have no idea of whether that included a fine. I tried to explain that we had not intended to insult Brazil. We had had a flag specially made up for us, because no Brazilian flag was available in Durban, but some idiot had reversed the colors and . . . but it wasn't any use. He didn't understand a word, so I shrugged and paid up.

From what we could gather, there was a small hotel and a few other buildings in a tiny settlement toward the middle of the island, about two miles away. June wanted to phone her sister Carol in America to report our progress, and we presumed we'd be able to do that from the hotel. We found a road leading that way and started trudging along in the hot sun.

After about a mile or so, a small bus came up from behind us and stopped alongside. It was empty, except for the driver, who waved us in. Not knowing what the fare might be, and having no local money, we shook our heads and said no thanks, but he insisted and after a moment or two, by some sort of mental osmosis, we gathered that this was the island's free bus service.

"Hotel?" I said.

"Hotel," he confirmed.

Blocking the entranceway was a large basket full of fish. The driver indicated we should leap over it, or just step in it if that were more convenient. Kevin and I managed the leap, but it was too wide a stride for June, so we had to help her levitate by lifting her as she leaped.

Then, full of smiles on all sides, we set off for town. We were dropped off at a low, nondescript building set among a gaggle of similar structures resembling a minor military base. We entered the cool lounge where a few people were sitting around tables, and ordered drinks. None of the locals stared at us, but nobody smiled or came to speak to us, either. We got the feeling that visitors to this military island were a nuisance. They were not geared up for tourism.

June's lengthy negotiations with the hotel management to make her phone call were totally defeated by a combination of the language barrier, an obvious amazement that anyone would want to telephone the United States from here, and connection problems to the Brazilian mainland. We gathered that it might take a week to organize a long-distance call like that, if it were possible at all.

So we slowly walked back to the anchorage, wishing vainly that our friendly bus driver would appear again because our legs were weak from disuse after sixteen days at sea. When we finally limped up to our landing spot we found a scene of great excitement.

Three fishermen were working the surf, throwing out baited hooks on long lines and simply hauling them in with small fish on the end. It seemed a ridiculously easy way to catch fish. But all around them, as they stood up to their waists in the water, were dozens of screeching frigate birds doing their own brand of fishing, diving breakneck into the crashing surf, sending up great plumes of tumbling water, and grabbing fish in their beaks. Frigate birds, with their long forked tails and angular wings look like miniature pterodactyls. They're extraordinary to see in flight, large birds, all arms and legs and elbows sticking out, and they move like lightning—that is, quickly and erratically. They seem to be either permanently out of control or deliberately reckless and abandoned, but they can certainly catch fish. They're also experts at chasing and harassing other seabirds until they cough up in midflight the fish they've just caught. They should really be called pirate birds.

I was worried about getting back out through the surf in the dinghy. Coming in is one thing, going out is quite another. You have to pull the dinghy into water deep enough for the outboard motor's propeller, so you can start the motor before you get in the boat. But when you're in water that deep, the bow of the boat is being pounded by incoming surf, which tries with surprising force to push the whole boat back on the beach.

We stripped down to our swimsuits near the engineer's building and then I got Kevin and June to walk out into the water and hold the boat in place, one on each side about halfway back. I stood at the stern, and while the whole boat bobbed up and down with the passing of lines of surf, I lowered the outboard and got it going in neutral.

At my shout, just after a row of surf had passed, we all three pushed forward mightily and flung ourselves into the boat, which is not as easy as it sounds. Before the next line of surf could smack us sideways and capsize us, I put the engine in gear and revved it mightily. It was only a five-horsepower model but it battered us out slowly in a cloud of spray as the boat tried to stand on its tail with each passing swell, and then, suddenly, we were beyond the break and in calm water.

"Whew!" said June, laughing and still hanging on tightly to the safety lines. Her wet hair was plastered tightly against her face in pretty, tight curls. "Quite a ride. Thank goodness the water's warm."

We did that ride again several times in the next few days. The fish-plant engineer told us we could help ourselves to fresh water collected from the roof of his building and stored in a tank near the beach. There was a large outside sink there, obviously intended for cleaning fish, but we used it to wash our bed linen, towels, and clothes. They hadn't been laundered since we left Cape Town. It took the three of us a long time to do everything by hand, and we felt guilty about using so much fresh water, but we knew it would be quickly replaced by the frequent rain showers ushered in by the steady southeast trade wind. We took it back to *Freelance* in large plastic bags and spread it over the lifelines to dry in the hot sun, making us look like a floating gypsy encampment for an afternoon.

We explored the ancient fort with its fascinating dungeons, bronze cannons, and an orchard still producing tropical fruit. The whole structure was in a remarkable state of preservation, presumably kept in good shape by the military, although it had no practical use in these times. Standing on the high ramparts looking out to the north and west, it was easy to imagine galleons and men-o'-war beating into the anchorage two hundred years before.

Nearby, in the shade of tall trees, was a large church, Nossa Senhora dos Remédios, that was built in 1772. It, too, was well preserved but we gathered from notices in the high, cool interior that it was to be restored to original condition within the year.

We walked a mile or so west to the magnificent beach beneath Pico, the Praia de Conceição, and on the way we passed a few small houses where children playing in doorways looked at us shyly and smiled. No adults were visible anywhere.

I have seen some of the great beaches of the world, including Copacabana and Ipanema, but nothing compared with the beach lining the Baía do Pico.

More than half a mile of fine white sand was backed by dense thickets of brilliant green coconut trees. Crashing, thundering surf turned a translucent green
ocean into white foam against a blue horizon decked with cotton-ball clouds.
And just behind it, Pico's extraordinary finger of dark stone extended one thousand feet into the sky where mist swirled away in short streamers. It was elegant,
dramatic—and quite empty. We were the only souls there. It was the deserted
tropical island beach of everybody's dreams.

I sat in the cool shade of a coconut palm and watched the slim figures of
June and Kevin cavorting happily in the surf. I was glad that June was enjoying
herself. If only she could have enjoyed living on *Freelance* half as much, life
would have been perfect.

Extraordinarily, that beach was just one of sixteen wonderful beaches on
Fernando de Noronha, many of them more protected from the ocean and more
suitable for scuba diving or snorkeling. The water was so clear that scuba divers
were said to be able to see for one hundred and twenty feet.

Much of the little archipelago is a protected marine park, and on our way
back to the boat we climbed the little hill above the anchorage and looked
down on the other side of the island where there is a dolphin nursery in the
Enseada da Caieira (Dolphin Bay). This is where the remarkable rotator dolphin *(Strenella longirostris)* comes to breed.

The rotator is normally found only on the high seas, where it sometimes
puts on a spectacular show for passing ships. It's usually about seven feet long
and weighs two hundred pounds—not the biggest dolphin in the sea—but it
can jump more than seven feet into the air, and as it does so it twists round and
round. Nobody knows why they do this. There is speculation that it might con-
fuse a predator, and some people think the rotators perform the corkscrew motion simply for fun, but the real cause of this unique display is a mystery.

Groups of rotators come in from the sea at sunrise and spend the day in
Dolphin Bay, returning to the ocean to hunt at night. These dolphins, like many
cetaceans, use echo-sounding for navigation and to locate underwater obstacles
that are out of sight. But this handy apparatus also allows them to perceive two
heartbeats in one body, so they can tell if a female is pregnant.

The Brazilian government, knowing that scientists hope one day to be able to do the same with females of other species, became involved in a fascinating experiment involving research into communication between rotator dolphins and human fetuses. With the backing of French and Belgian scientists, Brazilian researchers went to work in Dolphin Bay with three pregnant woman attended by gynecologists and obstetricians.

Just what they expected to prove is not clear. Even if a rotator dolphin could tell you if you were pregnant or not, how would you hold it to your tummy long enough for it to make a diagnosis? The Dolphin Bay experiments apparently lead to a lot of head shaking and speculation among the islanders. For as long as any of them could remember, they'd had their own ways of knowing when a woman was pregnant, none of which required the use of a rotator dolphin.

From our vantage point on the little hill, we could see that while the island was covered in thick tropical bush, like much of Africa, there were few trees, apart from bananas and coconuts. This was because the Brazilian government cut down every tree they could lay hands on when the island was being used as a penal colony. They feared that the prisoners would use the wood to build boats in which to escape. Only the region near the Sapata headland in the far west retained its original forest, but Sueste Bay, a shallow natural harbor on the southern side of the island, still had stands of spindly mangroves—the only ones on an oceanic island in the South Atlantic.

On the second day of our stay, a small wooden boat rowed by three teenage boys came alongside *Freelance*. It seemed to be the local bumboat. They offered us fish, but what we wanted most was fruit, vegetables, eggs, and beer. This simple list was not at all easy to communicate, for they spoke only Portuguese, of course. They seemed to understand about the fruit easily enough, but when it came to eggs they had no idea of what the Spanish word *huevos* might mean. So in the end I did a little pantomime of a hen flapping her wings, cackling, and laying an egg, which caused great mirth among them but seemingly created some degree of comprehension. Then I held up my fingers to show that I wanted two dozen eggs. That caused much consternation and head shaking, but after a short powwow they rowed off purposefully toward the beach, indicating that they would return later.

"What do you make of that?" I asked June.

"Oh, I expect eggs are scarce here," she said.

"I suppose we're not likely to get two dozen, then."

"Who knows?" she said, laughing. "Anything could happen."

She was right. They came back with no eggs at all. They were proudly holding up a dead chicken.

Kevin could hardly contain himself. "Maybe you need acting lessons, Dad," he snorted.

"You're lucky they didn't bring two dozen chickens," said June.

My failure as a communicator was not absolute, however. They did have some fruit, a sweet, soft tropical fruit they called *sucos.* And I gathered that while they were not permitted to buy beer, they might be able to barter for some if I had a bottle of whiskey. I wasn't a whiskey drinker, but there was in fact a bottle of Johnny Walker on board for the purpose of bribing port officials if necessary, and I was prepared to swap it for beer, even warm beer, as we had no way of cooling it.

So the bumboat boys went off again with their chicken and a picture of an egg that I had drawn for them on a piece of paper, with the number 24 written beside it. They returned the next day with six eggs in a brown paper bag, two of which were broken, and more fruit. We gave up, and paid them in U.S. dollars, but the negotiations for the beer/whisky swap were more complicated and protracted. I wanted twelve beers for my bottle of whiskey but in the end the head bumboat boy, a hardened bargainer, beat me down to six cans of Brazilian beer and even managed to make me feel grateful.

We never did get any vegetables, but I consoled myself with the thought that we'd done better in Fernando de Noronha than my friends Bernard Moitessier and Henry Wakelam had. Those seasoned scavengers met their match on this little island. They weren't able to add anything at all to their stores of provisions, and even had to pay for an expensive meal they didn't want, having been invited as guests (or so they thought) at the local hotel. Apparently they had discovered the habit prevalent in some Latin countries whereby strangers are cordially invited to come and participate in a friendly lunch or dinner. "And then," as Moitessier put it, "click! up comes the bill, with a charming, unaffected smile: and that's because in some countries, that's the normal way to behave."

I think poor old Bernard was more surprised than bitter at this turn of events. He'd been having a bad run. He had raced Henry Wakelam to Fernando de Noronha from Ascension, and lost—again.

As if it weren't bad enough finding the wickedly grinning Wakelam already peacefully at anchor when he arrived, he was depressed at finding more evidence of wood borers in his boat. *Marie-Thérèse II* was literally being eaten by rot and borers. Furthermore, Moitessier's plan to stock his boat with lizards had failed, too.

Both their boats were infested with cockroaches. They're detestable creatures at the best of times, but they're particularly loathsome in the close confines of a small yacht. Moitessier had decided that lizards were the answer. He would catch lizards and take them aboard, where he hoped they would eat his unwanted stowaways.

He and Wakelam rowed in through the surf and, without a care for local sartorial customs, set off the for village in shorts and singlets to check in with the police chief, who handled customs and immigration procedures at that time. They were carrying their sandals ("so as not to wear them out," Moitessier explained) and planned to put them on before they reached the village.

Along the way they found lizards all right, quite large ones, from four to eight inches long, and it was easy to catch them as they dozed in the hot sun, so Moitessier stuffed six of them in his shorts pocket. He took off his singlet and jammed it into the mouth of the pocket to prevent the lizards from escaping.

When they neared the village, Moitessier donned his formal dress. He put on his singlet and his sandals. He borrowed Wakelam's handkerchief and used it with his own to keep the lizards in place.

In the village they spotted the first person they'd seen on the island, a young woman. She fled without further ado. Then they saw on old woman sitting on a doorstep. She went into her house and slammed the door.

They walked down the deserted street while doors opened behind them and heads appeared, but could make no contact. Eventually they knocked on a door and a man answered. But he couldn't understand their request to be directed to the police station until Moitessier used the Italian word *carabinieri,* upon which a gaggle of small children led them to the office of the chief of police. He interviewed them briefly, stamped their passports, and then wanted to discuss the writings of the French author Gide.

Moitessier didn't like Gide. He didn't want to discuss Gide. He wanted nothing more than to get out of the police chief's office because one of his lizards had escaped and was slithering down his bare leg.

He and Wakelam got out of there without the police chief's noticing anything untoward, apparently, but by the time they reached the hotel there was only one lizard left in Moitessier's pocket, and he was on the point of dying so he was left under a bush to recover.

It was the police chief, incidentally, who introduced them to the charming manager of the hotel, who, in turn, "invited" them to lunch against their will, and presented them with the bill afterward. So, in a strange way, perhaps justice was done. The pirate and the vagabond set sail for Trinidad shortly afterward.

As for the others who had gone this way before us, wiry old Jean Gau didn't stop at Fernando de Noronha. He hardly stopped anywhere, as a matter of fact. He loved long passages, and he sailed *Atom* directly from Mossel Bay to Puerto Rico, covering six thousand miles in 123 days.

The Hiscocks didn't stop there in *Wanderer III* either, because they were making for the Azores, and needed to keep to the east. Frank Wightman, still bothered by a leak in *Wylo,* decided to bypass the island and head straight for Forteleza, on the Brazilian mainland, where he hoped to find a marine railway that could haul his boat out of the water for repairs. Joshua Slocum had sailed past the island at night, several miles south of it, in May 1898, during his record-breaking solo voyage. Thus, very little had been written in the yachting literature about this fascinating island.

We knew we were supposed to leave after three days at anchor, but the fourth day happened to be a Friday, and I refused to start a passage on Friday. I thought about the admonition implicit in my letter from the U.S. Consulate, that we should get ourselves to the United States with all possible dispatch, or face the possibility that my expired immigration visa would not be accepted, but I didn't think one extra day would make any difference.

Besides, the authorities on Fernando de Noronha weren't urging us to leave, despite their written instructions. The Swedish boat that was here when we arrived was still anchored nearby, and nobody had been near her. The fish-plant engineer had indicated that she had a problem with her rigging, and they needed time to fix it.

"I don't see anything wrong with the rigging," Kevin said, "except that they've loosened one rigging screw."

"I bet they're gorgeous, helpless Swedish blondes," I said bitterly. "No doubt they're being entertained by the governor or the military commander or whoever's in charge here. I bet he sent a damned car for them."

"They're probably sleeping in air-conditioned bedrooms," said June mischievously, "eating caviar and sipping champagne."

I glared at her. "I'm not jealous," I said, "not at all. But why does the governor always ignore *us?*"

During the morning, our old acquaintances from Mossel Bay arrived aboard *Ev-a-Dene.* They anchored alongside and invited us over for drinks. To my astonishment, they produced a cold beer for me, the first I'd seen since St. Helena. It was eleven o'clock in the morning, and no beer ever tasted better.

Ev-a-Dene was a large ketch, four times the size of *Freelance,* manned by two South African couples, Dave and Ardene, and Errol and Evelyn. The women were sisters and the boat was named after them. After the cramped accommodation in *Freelance, Ev-a-Dene,* with its separate sleeping cabins, seemed like a luxury liner.

"You must come over and see how we slum it on *Freelance,*" I said.

It didn't take them long to inspect our boat, but unexpectedly we won high praise in one department.

"How do you keeping your toilet smelling so nice?" Evelyn asked. "I've never known a boat toilet that smelled so clean and fresh."

"Oh, it's just always been like that," I said airily, glancing at June, who had cleaned the toilet just that morning and poured it full of liquid freshener.

"You should give guided tours of your toilet," said Ardene. "It's an example to us all."

High praise, indeed. But I should have knocked on wood. Little did I know then what trouble that toilet was going to cause us in a few days.

Our bumboat boys came back that afternoon with an offering of fish that we didn't really want, a bucketful of needlefish and sardines. Without refrigeration, we couldn't keep them fresh. We gave the boys some more dollars anyway, and an extra $5 to mail three letters, which, sad to say, were never received.

The next day, April 4, we sailed at 11 a.m. for Bequia, in the West Indies. We waved good-bye and shouted good luck to our friends on *Ev-a-Dene*. The Swedish yacht, we noted, was still swinging to her anchor, unattended. *Rigging problem, indeed,* I thought. *Damned governor.*

TOP *Freelance* hauled out for bottom painting at Point Yacht Club in Durban.

BOTTOM Our furniture goes up in flames in our auction house, Durban, just before we set sail to the USA.

June Vigor in *Freelance*'s cabin before the start of the voyage,
pondering where to store everything.

Leaving our home port, Durban, in *Freelance*.

John Vigor in Port Elizabeth, with *Pink Maru Maru* and
Freelance at right.

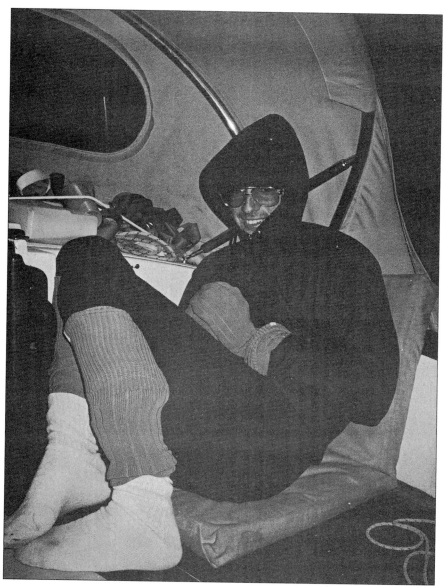

Rounding Cape Aghulas—Kevin Vigor on night watch in the cockpit, trying to keep warm.

June Vigor on top of Table Mountain, Cape Town. The faint dark patch in mid-horizon is Robben Island, where Nelson Mandela was jailed for twenty-three years.

With John Vigor at the helm, Freelance departs from Cape
Town harbor as a tablecloth spreads over Table Mountain.

In the heel of the southeast trade winds, we conduct our first trial of
the twin staysails and their remarkable twistle yard.

TOP On her fiftieth birthday, in mid-South Atlantic, our
ingenious Ship's Welfare Officer produced this delicious loaf of bread,
baked over a kerosene stove in a pressure cooker.

BOTTOM The crude landing steps at St. Helena Island, where the sea
level rises and falls constantly.

LEFT A noddy bird finds a perch to rest on for several hours in mid-South Atlantic. It ignored us completely.

ABOVE June reads unconcernedly in the cockpit as Atlantic swells break along *Freelance*.

Delicious fresh fish for supper. John holds a fine dorado caught on *Freelance*'s trailing feather lure.

Nature's own signpost in the South Atlantic, the dramatic 1,000-foot tall
finger of Pico, guides us to the tiny isolated island of Fernando de Noronha.

Passengers perch wherever they can between items of deck cargo as the West Indian inter-island schooner *Friendship Rose* plies between St. Vincent and Bequia.

Warm, clear water and cloudless skies make for an enchanting tropical anchorage in Wallilabou Bay, St. Vincent.

TOP A drug-busting team from the U.S. Customs Service shepherds
us into port in Fort Lauderdale, Florida, in the Cigarette boat, *Blue
Thunder*.

BOTTOM June and Kevin aboard *Freelance* in Fort Lauderdale,
Florida.

12

FERNANDO DE NORONHA TO BEQUIA

Much as we liked Fernando de Noronha, we didn't find it difficult to say good-bye. We watched Pico disappearing over the horizon astern with a mixture of anticipation and excitement because our next stop, 1,880 miles away, would be in the West Indies, every cruising boat's dream destination. It was the stomping ground of the privateer Drake and the pirate Blackbeard. It was the romantic background for Robert Louis Stevenson's *Treasure Island.* It was also where I hoped to turn our gold Krugerrands into American dollars. If we couldn't do it there, it wasn't likely that we'd have another chance before reaching the United States, where it was illegal to import them. I didn't even want to think about what my choices would be in that case.

We planned to make a landfall on St. Vincent Island, and then backtrack a few miles and anchor at charming little Bequia Island, the first in the chain of the Grenadines. I had deliberately chosen St. Vincent as our landfall because it was high, clear of obstructions, and easy to identify for a vessel approaching from the southwest. In theory, it should be visible from twenty or thirty miles away, so that even a nervous navigator like me ought to be able to find it. I set a straight-line course to take us right there, parallel to the coast of Brazil, two hundred miles out at sea.

With the twin jibs pulling strongly, we kept a sharp lookout for the light on the Atol das Rocas, an extensive coral reef in shallow water just thirty miles to leeward. It was apparently a beautiful spot, but the site of many shipwrecks in the old days when sailing ships caught in the calms of the doldrums were driven onto the reef by the strong sideways current we had already experienced on approaching Fernando de Noronha. Kevin thought he may have seen the loom of the light on the western horizon during his midnight watch, but it was too indistinct to be sure, and by next morning we were clear of the danger.

For two days we loafed along in the tail end of the southeast trades but at the 10 p.m. change of watch on the second night out we had to haul down the twistle yard in a flurry of wind and spray as a fierce squall warned us that we were nearing the equator and the unsettled area of doldrums where we could expect anything from dead calms to torrential rain and ferocious lightning storms. The first squall was brief, just a warning shot across our bows, and we were soon under way again under the mainsail and a poled-out working jib, but conditions were very uncomfortable as we rolled excessively in a steep little cross swell.

We were still bouncing around the next day in light airs and hot humid weather when the toilet broke down. That was not good news. I investigated the cause of the stoppage, and found that salts from the seawater flushing system had calcified inside the discharge pipe. Our toilet was suffering from arteriosclerosis. The buildup on the inside of the pipe wouldn't have mattered much, since it hadn't yet reached critical proportions, but the excessive motion of the yacht, and particularly the hammering she was taking from swells slamming into her sides, had shaken the calcification loose. It had all dropped back down the pipe into the Henderson pump mounted on the bulkhead, and jammed it solid.

There was only one thing to do: strip the pump completely, and remove and clean out the discharge pipe. During the next twenty-four hours, I began to understand why plumbers and sewage engineers are able to command such rich rewards for their work.

By dumb luck or expert planning (I'm not sure which) I happened not only to have a service kit for the Henderson pump, but I was also able to find it in one of *Freelance*'s crammed lockers.

Then came the hard bit. First I had to bail out into a bucket the contents of the toilet that had refused to pass through the pump. The toilet was, of course, no longer smelling as sweetly as it had been when *Ev-a-Dene's* crew had inspected it a few days earlier. Next, I had to remove the discharge pipe and unbolt the pump from the bulkhead. It was hot and airless in the little cubicle that served us for a bathroom. The ship's motion was severe. Time seemed to pass very slowly. Eventually, however, I was able to take the pipe and the pump to the cockpit, where I sloshed bucketfuls of sea water and disinfectant over them.

To get inside the pump, I needed to undo about a dozen nuts and bolts. Ashore, it would have taken no more than five minutes. But out there in the middle of the ocean, *Freelance* was heeling over and bouncing around so badly that I didn't dare set down a nut or bolt on the cockpit seat for fear it would be flung off and lost immediately.

It took two of us, Kevin and me, a lot of pondering to think up a system that would allow me to place the nuts and bolts safely in the exact pattern in which they came off. We used dabs of a bilious-looking yellow plastic putty called Prestik, carefully stuck down to the cockpit seats. Kevin pressed one nut or bolt into each dab as I removed them from the pump.

Once it was apart, the pump was easily cleaned and reassembled, but the discharge pipe, a ribbed plastic affair, was more recalcitrant. In the end, we whacked it against the teak cockpit coamings and shook out the soggy lumps of smelly calcified salts from its sclerotic interior. We didn't get it all out, but I figured that if it didn't come loose with the whackings we gave it, it would be OK in the bathroom.

All this took time, of course. We still had to run the ship, navigate, and get some sleep, so after the pump and pipe were in working order again, Kevin took over the watch on deck while I went below to catch up on my sleep. We didn't get around to fixing them in place until the next day. The toilet was out of commission for a full twenty-four hours, in fact, and meanwhile we had to use a bucket in the cockpit instead, which was simply emptied over the side after use.

That wasn't as easy as it sounds because the bucket kept skating across the cockpit floor with the violent motion of the boat, bouncing off the sides like the ball in a pinball machine. It became a serious challenge to place the bucket and sit down on it fast enough to pin it in place; and even then, with your weight on it the slippery plastic bucket tended to give you a wild ride by careering the length of the cockpit as you tried vainly to hang on to the seats. For June, it was all too much of a challenge, and I had to hold the bucket firmly in place while she used it. She was mortified, of course. No amount of reassurance on my part could convince her that this was just a normal part of a sailor's life, or that I would love her just as dearly afterward. In any case, we gave her the privilege of christening the throne once it was working again, and she was very, very grateful.

For eleven days we were assailed by ill-tempered northeasterly trade winds, hot and cranky after a long trip across the South Atlantic. They heaped up waves that pounded us from just forward of the beam, and for all that time the motion was so violent that we couldn't stand up on deck. When we needed to go forward to the bows we had to crawl on hands and knees, or scoot along the side deck on our bottoms. *Freelance* crashed and bashed her way into fast-moving swells under a reefed working jib and a double-reefed mainsail. Heavy flying spray covered the boat from bow to stern, and for the first time since we'd had her, the portlights on the starboard side started to leak. This was intensely annoying for June, who was getting dripped on while she tried to sleep on the settee berth beneath.

The cause of the leaks was a puzzlement. They had never leaked before, even in the storm off Cape Agulhas. But I eventually realized that *Freelance* was heeled so far over that powerful blasts of solid water were hitting the *underside* of the portlight surrounds and forcing their way inside under great hydraulic pressure. The cure was easy once I'd figured out the problem. I caulked the bottom of the portlight surrounds from the outside with plastic putty, the same Prestik that had helped us repair the toilet pump. It was a temporary repair, naturally, but like many other temporary repairs on small boats, likely to be there forever. But June was able to sleep again, and that was all that mattered.

Few people really understand how viciously a small sailboat gets tossed around at sea, even in the trade wind belts, which are usually regarded as benign.

June was astonished at her first experience of rough water the day after we sailed from Durban. In a letter to friends she wrote:

"Looking back, I am amazed that I thought I knew what I was getting into. I'd read lots of books about cruising, of course. I'd talked to people who had crossed oceans in small boats. And we had done some offshore sailing that we considered fair practice.

"All this had given me a picture of beautiful blue water, blue skies, sparkling white foam, fluffy white clouds, and us swooping along gracefully in a boat that combined all the best attributes of a bird and a ballerina. And for background music: the galloping parts of the New World Symphony.

"There were times like that, of course. We'd had lots of them, sailing off Durban on Sunday afternoons. But we hadn't had any of the rough times.

"When we left Durban, neither Kevin nor I had ever spent a night at sea. I kept suggesting, while we were getting ready, that we ought to go to Richards Bay, eighty miles or so up the coast, or somewhere, to get overnight experience, but John kept saying we'd get lots of experience once we were underway. He admits now that he was afraid a short run like that would just put us off, and we were already too committed for doubts or second thoughts. He was right on both counts.

"We learned, on our first night out, that nothing in normal experience prepares you for the nonstop, totally unpredictable movement of a small yacht. It's like being tossed in a concrete mixer with several tons of your possessions.

"When it got dark, the wind began to blow quite hard. It was still OK until it got time to go to bed. I went below and stood for a moment, clinging to the overhead grabrails with both hands, trying to work out how to get undressed. I could only let go with one hand and I couldn't work out how to lift even one foot from the floor without falling over, since the boat was heeling and pitching.

"My stomach allowed just ninety seconds for pondering before it gave warning that I had better get horizontal, and fast. Time enough to clean my teeth and my face and put on my pink pajamas tomorrow. So I flung myself into my bunk and found that it levitated, in separate parts and directions, underneath me. The only way to keep from being thrown off was to hook up a heavy canvas leeboard that was attached to the side of the bunk underneath the cushion, and fasten it across my body to hooks on the side of the boat. The general effect was like being in a straitjacket.

"I began to realize that the bouncing, the swaying, and the rocking was not going to stop at bedtime. And then it really hit me that we were just going to keep on sailing, all night and all day, and all night and . . .

"Our carefully stowed provisions and equipment began to bang around the shake loose. Everything rattled, and clanged, and thumped. Pans crashed against locker doors. Tins rolled with the rumble of an avalanche in the bins under the bunks. The toilet door unhooked itself and began to slam to and fro with every roll. The bottles in the grog locker clanked together every five seconds. I have never experienced such a feeling of chaos—and all in total darkness.

"I began trying to quiet things down. That meant thrashing and struggling out of the straitjacket, finding hand and footholds, and listening hard to find out where a noise—a particular noise—was coming from. I decided to tackle the grog locker, but I made the mistake of opening the door when that side of the boat was on the uphill part of a roll. Two bottles, several glasses and a corkscrew fell out, and I somehow managed to catch them with my free hand. That left me with no hope of catching anything else. I knew I had five seconds before the next roll dropped the rest of the stuff on me, so I flung it all back in, willy-nilly, shoved a towel in after it, and slammed the door shut. Then my stomach said: 'Lie down!' and I did.

"That's the way the rest of the night went. I got up, shoved whatever I could lay hands on into the noisy lockers, and flung myself back into my bunk. I lost pieces of clothing that night that we never did locate again. It took three tries to tether the toilet door. Everything had to be done in forty-five-second bursts. I had spells when I just huddled in my bunk and told the damn boat to shake itself to bits—and see if I cared. But then I'd have to get up and try again.

"John discovered the hard way that if you relaxed for one second while you were sitting on the throne, the boat would pitch you headfirst into the hanging locker opposite. Kevin woke up with his knee caught under the shelf beside his bunk and his head wedged under the chart table. He thought the end had come. I managed to get my elbow jammed in the towel rail.

"But things were better by the third day. I had managed to restore some order down below. I started the stove and produced some soup. I had the feeling you get after a long illness, when you begin to get up and move around—a sense of pride and achievement in the smallest everyday things. I put on my pink pajamas and went to bed with a feeling of immense triumph.

"Then we arrived at Port Elizabeth in the middle of the night and all hands were needed on deck in a hurry, so I arrived at our first port of the journey wearing pink pajamas and an orange anorak. I tell you, sailing is full of indignities, and triumph slips through your fingers with great ease."

Now, after three months of living aboard *Freelance,* June no longer got her elbow stuck in the towel rail, and Kevin no longer got his head stuck under the navigation desk. And even though we were being bounced around mightily by an ill-tempered trade wind, nothing rattled loose in the lockers any more. June had her department firmly under control.

Surprising things were still happening in the sailing department, however. One afternoon when I came down below into the cabin I noticed the bottom portion of the mast swaying backward and forward. It was a result of the pounding the hull was taking. The wedges that held the mast in place where it came through the deck had come loose, and several had fallen out. Not only was the aluminum mast now appreciably weaker though lack of support at deck level, but it would fail from metal fatigue if it went on bending like that for long.

It was an extended, awkward job to get the hard rubber wedges in place from below. Normally, they're hammered in place from above. But to do that, I would have had to remove the mast boot, which stopped water pouring down the mast hole, and I wasn't going to remove that boot while the decks were running with water. I did my best to hold on to the mast with one hand while I held a wedge in the other hand, which left no hand to hammer it into the hole over my head. But somehow on occasions like these, things get done on small boats at sea with the aid of sheer desperation, despite the apparent impossibility of the task, and this one got done, too.

I did wonder, though, if there was something I could do to alleviate *Free-lance*'s wild motion, which was causing all our present problems. I wondered if there was something I should be doing to the boat, some basic trick of seamanship that had evaded me. I recalled a passage by the famous author E. B. White, who was obsessed with sailboats, and couldn't stop himself from setting sail even when he became old and afraid of the wind and the sea.

Lacking instruction as a newcomer to sailing, he invented his own ways of getting things done, he said. When he was more than seventy years old, he admitted that he had never learned to sail properly, even though he'd done it all his life. He was thirty before he learned to hang a coiled halyard on its cleat. "I was always in trouble," he said, "and always returned, seeking more trouble."

I, too, was self-taught. I had never been to university. I had never had a lesson in sailing or navigation. Everything I knew I had taught myself from books, or learned from experience. But I was ahead of Mr. White in at least one respect—I knew how to hang a coil of halyard line on a cleat so it wouldn't fall off when the boat heeled. I read it in one of Eric Hiscock's books.

Alone in the cockpit at night for four hours at a spell, there was plenty of time to think, but I couldn't come up with a solution for *Freelance*'s wild motion, except to slow her down. I was loath to do that because we had a date with June's sister in the British Virgin Islands, and we needed all the time we had. Besides, slowing down might make only a small difference to our comfort. The real problem was the shape of the seas, steep waves rucked up by the contrary Guiana Current that flowed southwest at between one and two knots, parallel to the coast, and the angle at which the seas were hitting us. There was nothing I could do about that. And so we plowed on, sometimes under jib only when the wind rose to over twenty knots, notching up splendid noon-to-noon runs of 131 miles on occasion.

What we were experiencing here was a lack of seakindliness, not seaworthiness. There is a difference. "Seaworthiness is basically the ability of a boat to live in heavy weather without swamping, capsizing, breaking up, or being heavily damaged while underway," wrote Howard I. Chapelle in *Yacht Designing and Planning*. He was a professional naval architect and Historian Emeritus in the

Department of Industries of the U.S. Museum of History and Technology, Smithsonian Institute.

Seakindliness, on the other hand, refers to a boat's motion at sea. A seakindly boat has a slow, easy roll and pitch, with no sudden stops. Such a boat is kindly to her crew. *Freelance* was hopping around like a cat on a hot tin roof, literally leaping up and sideways on the heaping seas. She was far from seakindly under those particular conditions. But I learned later that it wasn't her fault. No small boat can be seakindly if she is also to be seaworthy.

"Unfortunately, boats under forty feet that give an easy roll and pitch can rarely be designed," Chapelle explained. "Usually they require such a range of stability, through low weights, and such buoyancy, through form and location of weights longitudinally, in order to live in the relatively exaggerated wave heights a small boat meets, as compared to a large vessel, that comfort of occupants is very slight indeed.

"It is generally impossible to stand or walk in the cabin of a small cruiser, power or sail, in heavy weather, if she is a safe design for such conditions. However, this very characteristic of quick motion required in a small boat may prevent her from shipping solid water or much spray if she is properly designed, and is required if she is to live through very severe weather."

In other words, if a boat under about forty feet in length is to be seaworthy in heavy weather, she cannot be seakindly. She will bounce around like a demented ping-pong ball and drive her crew crazy, but at least they'll survive.

We each found our own ways of surviving. June, unable to keep pots from being thrown off the stove, improvised meals brilliantly with sprouts for salads and precooked meat and vegetables from cans. Kevin learned to draw his knees up and wedge himself in the narrow quarterberth so he wouldn't be thrown around while he slept. I whiled away the hours on watch by trying to remember suitable music to accompany our wild ride and wishing we had a music center on which to play it. There was Gustav Mahler's scherzo, for example, in his First Symphony in D Major, the *Titan,* where the brass and violins kick up a wonderfully insistent, repetitive fanfare: Here we come! Here we come! Out of our way!

And there was that wonderful driving, throbbing theme from Franz Schubert's no. 9, *The Great:* DAH dah dah dah, DAH de dah de dah de dah de . . . bashing its way forward recklessly just as *Freelance* was, stopping for nothing, only just under control.

On the day that we crossed the equator, Kevin wrote in the log:

"Sea very confused, motion violent. Cloud cover complete and heavy rain, but making good progress." It was just one of many similar entries.

It was 10:45 p.m. when, by my calculation, we actually crossed the line but despite the miserable conditions we all gathered in the cockpit to open a present that our Durban friends Dave and Gem Trompeter, of the yacht *Inyati,* had given us. It turned out to be a box of very special chocolates, which we fell upon with much gusto.

At noon the next day, April 8, we sat in the cockpit again in our swimsuits for the official crossing-the-line ceremony, clinging to the cabintop and the cockpit coamings. We had all been over the equator before, but never under sail, so by tradition there had to be a dousing of the crew and a sacrifice to Neptune and the god of the winds, Aeolus. That would transform three pollywogs into three shellbacks. There was no question of my standing up with a bucket of seawater and pouring it over anyone's head with *Freelance* bouncing around so badly, so I had made another plan. Somewhat to the surprise of Kevin and June, I opened one of my precious cans of beer and sprayed it over them. In the startled silence that followed, I dropped a second, unopened can over the side for the gods. I then made a short but fitting speech beseeching the gods for a little mercy in the form of reduced wind and waves in return for the great sacrifice I had made.

I'm afraid the ceremony wasn't a great success. June and Kevin weren't greatly amused at being covered in warm, sticky Brazilian beer, and the gods of the wind and sea ignored my plea entirely. My slitty-eyed crew went off to wash their hair, a difficult job under the circumstances, and refused to talk to me for a couple of hours. Our wild ride continued unabated.

Strangely enough, when Bernard Moitessier had come this way many years before us, he had enjoyed wonderful weather most of the time. He and Henry

Wakelam had sailed from Fernando de Noronha on February 19 and we had sailed about six weeks later, on April 4. We followed exactly the same track, so I don't know if we were just unlucky with the weather, or if the tradewind pattern had changed over the years.

Marie-Thérèse II experienced no rain and no squalls on the way to Trinidad. Her forward hatch was kept open day and night. Moitessier reported runs of one hundred and fifty and one hundred and sixty miles with the aid of the Guiana Current, and spent only a couple of days beating in choppy seas. Wakelam, who was racing little *Wanda* against the bigger *Marie-Thérèse II,* enjoyed the same weather, of course, and kept pace with Moitessier although they were out of sight of each other.

It was scant consolation for us to remember that Frank Wightman, in *Wylo,* had also experienced continuous heavy weather on this leg. He, too, was heading for Trinidad because he'd failed to find a boatyard in Fortaleza, on the Brazilian mainland, where he could have *Wylo* hauled out so that her leak could be located and fixed.

Two hundred miles off the mouth of the Amazon—where we were now—*Wylo* ran into an area of very rough and confused water. "The blue seas were marching down on the great volume of outthrust river water, and there they piled up and thundered over in a three-hundred yard strip of breaking seas. It looked like seas running in on a rocky coast," said Wightman.

After surfing through this barrier in hair-raising fashion, Wightman and his companion, Graham Young, found themselves in water of a different color, more gray and brown than sparkling blue. They tasted it and found it was nearly fresh. By the next day, in fact, they could drink it—two hundred miles out to sea. They also began to pass some floating trees and branches, some of them uncomfortably large.

A few days later, *Wylo* ran into a large tree at night: "As she was sliding down the face of a sea, she struck something that stopped her as if she had hit a wall." Both men were knocked down in the cockpit. Wightman jumped overboard and tried to walk the tree along *Wylo's* side. After some minutes of pounding, the little yawl floated free.

By now there was water over the floorboards, but after some frantic work at the pump handle, Wightman determined that there were no holes through the hull. Nevertheless, it took him almost an hour to clear the bilges. Within a day, the wood had taken up, and the pumping was down to ten minutes every two hours. They changed course and headed for Georgetown, in British Guiana, about one hundred and fifty miles away. But even there they were unable to find the facilities they need to check her underwater planking properly, so they set sail for Trinidad once more.

We never came across those lines of surf at the confluence of the Amazon and the Atlantic, nor did we hit any floating trees, but we did notice one day that the water had changed from blue to green, and both the sea and the air seemed cooler. It also seemed that the current was no longer with us, so we changed course for a night and by noon next day we were back in the blue water.

Two weeks after we'd left Fernando de Noronha, on Easter Sunday, the sea finally calmed down enough for June to produce a hot meal. The wind was still blowing hard enough that we needed two reefs in the mainsail, but the swells had lengthened and smoothed themselves out, so that *Freelance* was much steadier.

Kevin and I could hardly believe our eyes when June, after a burst of activity in the galley, produced a magnificent three-course lunch, a belated crossing-the-line celebration. We started off with *Equatorial Tomato Bisque,* followed by *Fried Shrimp Rice à la Neptune* and *New World Fruit Cocktail à la Robin.* The latter, named after my brother-in-law in Durban, Robin Harrison, consisted of litchis, mandarin oranges, cream, and nuts doused in a South African orange liqueur called Van der Hum. Robin had given us the fancy cans of litchis and mandarins. The meal was nothing short of a gastronomic sensation for palates jaded by two weeks of cold concoctions straight from the can, and we toasted the Ship's Welfare Officer with some more Van der Hum.

The wind started to ease off that day, and even looked as if it were trying to come from astern. Kevin and I discussed raising the twistle yard and the twin jibs, but decided to give the weather some time to settle down.

That night, after I'd been asleep for an hour or so, I was awakened by the noise of thumping overhead. I recognized it as Kevin running across the cabintop.

Soon there was the noise of aluminum yards clanking together, and halyards being sweated home, and I could feel *Freelance* responding to the powerful pull of the jibs. It was the first time either of us had managed to raise the jibs alone.

I felt a flush of anger, not because I'd been woken, but because Kevin hadn't called me to help with the sail change. Once again, he had broken my standing orders. I could hear from the way he was lurching overhead, that he wasn't fastened to the boat with a safety tether, and every time he ran back to the foredeck after tending the helm I lay rigid until I heard some other noise that indicated he was still on board and working the rig.

When, after a long period of dozing and waking, I went up to take over the watch, I shoved my head through the hatchway, looked forward, and evinced surprise and delight that the twins were up and pulling well. Kevin wasn't taken in. He knew that I knew what was going on. But he looked quietly pleased as he went below to catch up on his sleep. He had passed another important milestone in his young life.

One afternoon when I was on watch there was a loud bang from astern and I noticed that the log spinner was missing, presumably taken by a shark or a large tuna. The spinner was a small propeller on the end of a long thin line, and as it screwed its way through the water it turned the gears on the Walker taffrail log, so that we knew exactly how many nautical miles we'd come. The propeller was painted black, but after weeks of being towed behind us the paint had started to wear off, and the metal underneath was shining through. This seems to be irresistible to some fish, because log spinners are frequent victims to voracious predators, and the Walker patent log always comes with a spare spinner and line tucked away in its little wooden box. I fitted the spare spinner and replaced the line with thicker stuff, since there was no knowing how much it had been strained by this encounter.

Of course, the proper fishing lure—the one that we wanted a nice bonito or dorado to take—was completely ignored. We didn't manage to catch any fish at all on this passage. Kevin reported in the log one night: "Tuna jumping about boat." But I wasn't too sorry that we didn't catch a tuna, since they are big fish and we couldn't keep one for long because we lacked refrigeration.

My old friend Jean Gau had the same problem aboard *Atom,* and he told a curiously chilling story about a time when some dorados had followed him at sea for more than a week. He eventually caught one of them on a very short line baited with a white rag that fluttered alongside *Atom* and gave the illusion of a flying fish.

It was a big fish, and Gau couldn't keep it because he had no refrigeration, so, like the good chef he was, he cut a neat fillet from its side and threw it back into the sea. The next day he happened to glance overboard and there was his dorado, swimming alongside again with the huge open wound in its side. And there it continued for the next few days. Gau didn't say how he felt about that, but if it had happened to me I wouldn't have been able to eat another fish in my life.

The day after our memorable meal, we started to pick up music on the radio that could only have come from the happy-go-lucky Caribbean. It turned out to be Barbados, and we were now to windward of Trinidad, where Moitessier and Wakelam arrived after seventeen days. We had taken only fifteen days to cover the same distance, and I began to wonder about Moitessier's claims of having done 150 and 160 miles day, since I knew the farthest we'd run in twenty-four hours was 131 miles, which included help from the current. And I doubted that Wakelam's little twenty-five-footer, which kept up with him, was capable of sustaining an average speed of more than six and a half knots for that length of time.

No matter. Moitessier anchored near the yacht club at 10 p.m. Next day, he sailed to the Customs House to report in, and found *Wanda* already there. She had come in an hour earlier, straight from the sea. So who won the race? Moitessier generously decided to call it a draw.

We parted tracks with my old friends here. Within a few weeks, Moitessier was to fall asleep on watch and lose his boat on a reef near the island of St. Vincent. It was a disaster startlingly similar to the one in which he lost the first *Marie-Thérèse* on Diego Garcia.

Stranded, penniless, and deeply depressed, he begged for drinks in bars, but eventually was offered a job on a tanker bound for Europe. Back in France, he wrote a book about his adventures. It became a best seller and earned him enough money to have built a thirty-nine-footer called *Joshua,* which brought him worldwide fame and established him as one of the elite bluewater sailors of the world. He later lost *Joshua,* too, of course, on the shores of the Sea of Cortez, so his record was complete, but the world ignored his failures and reveled vicariously in his triumphs, of which there were many.

While the vagabond was washed up on shore, the pirate plodded on to Europe in *Wanda.* Henry Wakelam never came back to live in Durban, and I lost touch with him, but for many years I had an address for him in Fort-de-France, on the Caribbean island of Martinique. I believe he married and did very well for himself. He certainly ended up owning a much larger boat.

Neither of these men ever knew the influence they had on me, of course. They were unlikely heroes, and I was not cast in the mold of the pirate or the vagabond. They were larger-than-life characters, carefree and confident, whereas I was more introspective, less certain of myself, and given to serious doubts about my capabilities as a sailor. Yet I admired them, learned from them, and let them lure me to sea.

Now, as *Freelance* branched off on her own from the course they had pioneered for us, I was able to take stock of what I had accomplished so far. It pleased me mightily to realize that I had followed in their tracks and done what they had done in my own quiet way without drama or plunder. It's true that I had started off with a great deal more trepidation than either of them had ever felt, but I found it very satisfying to discover that even anxious, cautious sailors like me could cross oceans in a safe, seamanlike fashion. You didn't have to be a card-carrying pirate or a happy-go-lucky vagabond to sail around the world. Ordinary people like me could do it, and do it well. It was a discovery that bolstered my confidence no end—but perhaps a little prematurely, in view of what was about to happen.

By about 8 a.m. on Tuesday, April 21, we should have been able to see the high mountains of St. Vincent, some thirty miles away. The highest, Richmond Peak, had an elevation of 3,524 feet. There was no sign of them. By 10 a.m. we should have been twelve miles closer, but there was still nothing. I began to worry. What had started off as a minor anxiety now became the cause for major concern.

At noon, I shot the sun for a latitude sight that did nothing to solve the problem. The position line showed that we were within twelve miles of the island. My eyes told me that we patently weren't. There was nothing on the horizon in any direction. The sea and the sky joined each other seamlessly, and no land, high or low, interrupted their circumference. We were completely lost. We could be anywhere.

With my stomach in a knot I got Kevin to fire up Prince Henry, the satellite navigator, and an hour later it produced a fix that indicated we were within six miles of the island. Well, we plainly weren't. It was a fine sunny day and any land would be visible farther away than that. I didn't care what Prince Henry thought. "I don't trust that thing," I said.

We had a nervous lunch while I tried to decide what to do.

"Let's just keep our course," said Kevin. "We've got plenty of food and water. We have to hit land somewhere in the next few days."

"But what if the compass has gone wrong?" I said. "What if we've been steering a wrong course for weeks? We could be in mid-Atlantic. Perhaps that explains the rough weather."

We all peered suspiciously at the Sestrel compass set into the cockpit bulkhead.

"It's just after noon," said June. "The sun should be roughly in the south, shouldn't it? Does the compass show that?"

"Yes," I said. "Roughly."

"What about your hand bearing compass?" said Kevin. "Does it agree with the steering compass?"

I hadn't thought of that. I stood as far back as I could get in the cockpit, so that one compass couldn't affect the other, and called off the ship's heading on the little compass. Kevin confirmed it from the steering compass. "Within two degrees," he said. Good enough.

We went over the known facts again. The compass was accurate. The sextant sight agreed with the satellite navigator. We were now about five miles from where the island was shown on my chart. But it obviously wasn't five miles away or we'd see it. What could we deduce?

"Can the chart be wrong?" I said.

None of us could answer that.

"If it isn't, the island has disappeared," said Kevin.

"Is it volcanic?" June asked.

We looked at each other, startled by the suggestion in each of our minds. Could St. Vincent possibly have been blown off the face of the earth? Wouldn't we have heard something? Wouldn't there be rescue ships and planes congregating here? And wouldn't the water be discolored and hissing with gases? No sign of that.

And so we sailed on, worried and perplexed, until just after 2 p.m., when I noticed a bright flash in the sky up on my right. I thought it must have been a far-off plane, but a couple of minutes later it flashed again, and suddenly I could see that it was a window shining in the sun, a window on a house high up on a mountainside. The island of St. Vincent suddenly appeared all around us. It enveloped us, and loomed over us, and seemed so close that I instinctively jibed the boat and reversed course to avoid running aground.

"My god," I shouted, as much in relief as astonishment, "look at that. We're right up under it."

We all gazed at the brown mountainsides and the rich green vegetation in amazement, hardly believing our eyes. We could see houses and roads, and even a vehicle moving in a cloud of dust.

"So Prince Henry was right," said Kevin defensively.

I was only too pleased to admit it. "I take it all back," I said. "Prince Henry is wonderful. Everything is wonderful."

When our excitement had subsided, and we were on a new course for the nearby little island of Bequia, we worked out that we were within three and a half miles of St. Vincent before we sighted it. We learned later that we were deceived by a heavy salt sea haze that often occurs at that time of the year. It cuts visibility to less than five miles, but it gives no indication of its presence. The only clue, to those who have experienced it before, is that the horizon, the meeting of the sea and the sky, is less distinct than usual.

It was getting dark when we dropped anchor in Admiralty Bay, Bequia, sixteen days and three hours out of Fernando de Noronha. The trade wind was blowing hard, and on shore, in the town of Port Elizabeth, the coconut palms were thrashing and bending to the gusts. There were many yachts in the anchorage, probably about fifty or so, and we had to anchor in deep water to leeward of them all. Our thirty-five-pound CQR anchor dragged, and we had to drop the kedge as well. I decided to keep an anchor watch, and it was just as well, for we dragged again a couple of times until *Freelance* settled down.

We didn't get an awful lot of sleep that first night in Bequia. But we didn't mind. For the first time in two weeks the boat was still. You could put a mug down on the table, and it would stay there. You didn't have to brace yourself against the bulkheads in the toilet. You could stand upright in the cockpit and not be tossed overboard. It was too marvelous.

13

THE WEST INDIES

When we all came on deck shortly after dawn on the day after our arrival in Bequia, the first thing we noticed was that the town of Port Elizabeth seemed to be on fire. Lazy flames licked at a long section of the waterfront, and dense clouds of black smoke were billowing downwind toward the anchorage.

We waited to hear the wailing sirens of fire engines and police, but nothing stirred. We wondered if we were the first the spot the fire. Perhaps we should raise the alarm. I was about to send out a VHF radio broadcast when I spotted a man moving in the cockpit of a yacht ahead of us.

I shouted and pointed excitedly at the waterfront.

"Garbage," he said calmly, as if that explained everything.

We looked at each other. Garbage? Garbage?

"Is it OK?" I shouted.

"It's OK," he confirmed.

Then it dawned on me. "They're burning their rubbish on the foreshore," I said. "It must be how they get rid of it."

"Well, it's a good job we're not moored any farther in," said Kevin. "The boats near the shore must be getting covered in flying ashes and dirt."

"The smell must be something, too," I said. "Roast rotting garbage. Imagine."

"That's enough," June said quickly, "or there'll be no breakfast for you two."

We didn't want to stand out in any way from the crowd of foreign yachts anchored in Admiralty Bay, Bequia, so we stayed at the back of the bunch. Despite the fact that our passports were British and American, we were wary of being labeled as South Africans.

At that time, South Africa was a pariah state in the eyes of many Caribbean nations because of its policy of apartheid. South Africans were often refused permission to go ashore. They were even denied access to mail and fresh water, especially in those nations farthest south in the chain of islands stretching from Trinidad to St. Maarten. I didn't think there was any chance at all of changing our gold Krugerrands into cash in this little corner of the West Indies.

We went ashore and checked in with the local police. They gave us temporary clearance, but said we'd have to go to the capital, Kingstown, on the island of St. Vincent, nine miles away, to complete the formalities. That wasn't a problem because there was a local ferry that made the trip several times a day, and we wanted to see St. Vincent anyhow.

To celebrate our arrival in the West Indies, June and I treated ourselves to a night ashore at the Frangipani Hotel, an attractive two-story waterfront establishment with an open-sided dining room. We left Kevin to guard *Freelance,* but we knew he'd be heading for the local nightspots as soon as we'd turned our backs, so we hid our precious cargo of Krugerrands in the bilge, just in case somebody decided to break into the unattended boat. We gave him fifty dollars to spend and warned him to keep a sharp eye on the rubber dinghy and the outboard.

The Frangipani was expensive, and even the best rooms were not air-conditioned. Not that it mattered to us. Our room had a ceiling fan, which we much prefer in tropical climates, not only because it's silent but also because it's less of a shock to walk from your room into the heat of the day outside.

We reveled in the space and the luxury. We took our first freshwater showers in nearly four months, and June caught sight of herself in a full-length mirror.

"Oh lord," she groaned, "I look gaunt and haggard. My bottom is drooping. My hair's out of control. It hasn't been cut since Cape Town." She had, in fact, lost fifteen pounds since the beginning of the trip, but I thought she looked just fine, and told her so. We had drinks in the bar and a slow, delicious dinner. We talked to strangers and we laughed.

June said: "This is wonderful. Civilization is marvelous. We get to sleep tonight in a comfortable bed that doesn't try to throw you out every few minutes. We'll have cool clean, white sheets." She looked very happy.

I, too, was happy, but at the back of my mind some little imp was suggesting that this jaunt might have been a mistake. Even after one day in luxury ashore, it would be a wrench for June to go back to the primitive life aboard *Freelance,* and the isolation—especially the isolation. I didn't mind the isolation, and was content with the Spartan life. *Freelance* was a little part of my beloved South Africa, the only permanent thing left in my life. But I started to get the feeling that we wouldn't be on the boat for much longer. My plan to live on board in the United States while we found work (and maybe even longer, much longer) was going to fall apart. In short, the two loves of my life were beginning to seem incompatible. But I wasn't prepared to admit it yet.

Bequia (pronounced *BECK*-way) was a small island, only five miles long and half a mile wide. It supported a permanent population of about five thousand and was known throughout the Caribbean for its capable boatbuilders, a vestige of former times when whaling was the mainstay of the economy for more than one hundred years.

It was a pretty island, compact, green, and hilly. White sandy beaches fringed most of the bays and coconut palms grew everywhere. Bequia was the first link in a chain of islands known as the Grenadines, which, with the island of St. Vincent, formed an independent nation. This was once a British colony, and they still spoke English, though we found it difficult at first to make any sense of the thick local dialect.

The major industry appeared to be tourism, and if the number of visiting boats in the harbor was anything to judge by, it was doing well. We were astonished to hear people on boats calling the local bakeries on their marine VHF radios, and ordering bread and pastries to be picked up later. If you wanted a taxi, you could either take a chance on finding one in the official spot—under the almond tree in Port Elizabeth—or you could simply put out a call on Channel 68 VHF and order one in advance. Such casual use of the radio was unheard of in South Africa, where you could lose your transmitting license for this transgression of the international laws.

Just a few miles south of Bequia, the little island of Mustique formed another link in the Grenadines chain. It was where Princess Margaret of Great Britain had a holiday home, but we had no plans to go there. We had already been pointedly ignored by petty little governors on remote South Atlantic islands. We didn't need to be snubbed by royalty.

The three of us clambered aboard the local ferry, a wooden, eighty-foot auxiliary schooner for the trip to St. Vincent. The *Friendship Rose* carried cargo and passengers from Port Elizabeth to Kingstown. The passengers perched anywhere they could, including all over the cargo. Using her gaff sails and motor, the bluff-bowed old gal took an hour and a bit to complete the nine-mile trip across the warm blue sea. We were interested to note that we could see St. Vincent from Bequia this time—the dense haze that accompanied our arrival in *Freelance* had disappeared.

St. Vincent was named by Christopher Columbus in 1498, but it had been inhabited since long before that by various indigenous peoples. The fierce Caribs were firmly in possession when Columbus came along, and they were tamed only in 1762 when the British established a settlement there. It became a fully independent state in 1979.

Kingstown, the capital of St. Vincent and the Grenadines, was a small but bustling town that had a faintly seedy third-world look about it. It fronted a broad, deepwater bay between two promontories, and in the background the island rose steeply to rugged mountains covered with lush forest.

Everyone was friendly, and after we had completed the ship's business without any problems, we hiked off through town in the hot sunshine to find the road to the world-famous botanical gardens. It seemed to be a long uphill walk, especially for a trio who'd been confined on a small yacht for weeks, but it was in fact only a mile or so.

Surprisingly, the twenty-acre natural preserve is said to be the oldest botanical garden in the Western Hemisphere, and harbors many rare plants and animals. A beautiful breadfruit tree was the direct descendant of one brought there in 1793 by a certain Captain Bligh, of *Bounty* fame, to provide food for slaves. It made me quite homesick, for there was also a large breadfruit tree in the garden of my childhood home in Durban. It bore large fruits, the size of small melons, but since we didn't own any slaves I had never tasted the pulp, which you can dry and grind to make a nutritious flour for bread and puddings. We wandered around the cool and pleasant gardens until late afternoon, and then ambled back to the docks for the return trip to Bequia in *Friendship Rose*.

After five days in Bequia we sailed north to Wallilabou Bay, on the island of St. Vincent, and there we made one of my lifelong dreams come true: we anchored in a calm bay off a beautiful tropical beach with a stern line to a coconut palm ashore. The water was blood warm and as clear as air. The bay was deserted, but the faint sound of a steel drum came drifting through the palm trees now and then. Shortly after lunch, another yacht arrived and anchored nearby. June and Kevin joined her friendly crew ashore to walk to a picturesque waterfall, leaving me to take pictures and tinker happily with *Freelance*. I doubled our stern line, taking it around the palm tree and back to *Freelance's* stern, so we could cast it off and leave at any time we liked without having to go ashore.

For the best part of a week we worked our way north through the entrancing chains of the Leeward and Windward Islands. The Caribbean was an intimate sea after what we'd been used to, and with the next island always in sight, the navigation was easy. We took the gentleman's way north—in the lee of the islands, where we were protected from the sometimes fierce blast of the trade winds. This meant we had to motor in some calm patches behind high islands, but I decided I could bear the criticism of the sailing purists, who insisted on taking the blustery route well to windward of the islands, because we could see, hear, and even smell much more of the land as we crept along close to it in the quiet lees.

We stayed a night in picture-perfect Marigot Bay on St. Lucia, and passed close by Fort de France, on Martinique, where Henry Wakelam had lived for many years. In a dead calm, we motored past sinister-looking Dominica at midnight, and by early morning we were looking for a new marina on the French island of Guadeloupe, the one shaped like a butterfly.

Our guide book said the marina was in Basse-Terre, the left wing of the butterfly, near the bottom, but we couldn't find it. From the description in the book it appeared to be somewhere between the southern harbor of Vieux-Fort and the town of Basse-Terre a little farther north. When we were quite sure we had passed it, we turned back. After retracing our course and still not finding any sign of a marina we decided there was no such place, so we gave up and turned north again. After a few minutes, a small powerboat appeared from nowhere in front of us, seemingly having emerged from a featureless coastline. So we nosed in cautiously and, sure enough, a small marina materialized before our skeptical eyes.

It was crowded with boats inside, though there were no people around, and we moored awkwardly in a berth that was too small for *Freelance* while I went to find someone who could tell me where to moor. I eventually did find a man in an office, but he spoke no English, and none of the ten words of French that I knew seemed either adequate or appropriate, so after we had looked at each other for a few moments, smiled, and shrugged hopelessly, I left him to his business and he left me to mine.

I decided to take the bull by the horns and move *Freelance* into a vacant slip of the proper size, hoping that it didn't belong to a boat that was out fishing or day-sailing. Then, as it was lunchtime, and this was a small portion of France, we went to find a restaurant.

There was only one place open, and it was almost deserted. We soon discovered that they wouldn't or couldn't accept a traveler's check. We counted the few Eastern Caribbean dollars remaining from Bequia, and after much squinting at the French menu, decided we could just afford something simple.

Once again, nobody spoke English, so I did my best to translate the menu for June and Kevin. June had a small salad, which she enjoyed, but Kevin and I ended up sharing an omelet of unknown origin. The exact translation had defeated me. Inside it was a sort of gray mush with gritty bits. We tasted it cautiously. We knew the French reputation for springing gastronomic surprises such as snails and frogs' legs. But the gray mush didn't taste much of anything, so we ate it all. Only later did we figure out that it must have been sea urchin. Luckily, by then we had digested it.

We spent the night quietly on board without seeing another soul in the marina and left without regret next morning for the port of Deshaies, also on Guadeloupe, but about twenty miles north.

People were much friendlier in the little village of Deshaies. After we'd anchored in twenty feet of water in the protected bay we went ashore to explore and buy a little fresh produce at the lively open-air market. There seemed to be no problem about language here. Everybody understood my French (or maybe it was just the pointing and smiling) and they accepted U.S. dollars without hesitation.

June prepared a splendid meal for us that evening and we ate it together in the cockpit. The breeze was balmy, and there was just enough of it to keep us cool. It was a beautiful setting, with the island in the background and a few other yachts around us. We raided the grog locker and opened one of our last bottles of South African wine. June passed around the first course of the meal—smoked oysters on crackers.

I laughed. "What would we be doing right now if we were rich?" I asked. "I mean, really stinking rich."

"We'd be sitting on our own private yacht in the Caribbean, drinking imported wine, eating oysters, and watching the sunset," said June, joining the laughter.

"Right. People pay millions for a view like this," I added. "In fact, money couldn't buy a home with a view as nice as this. And we enjoy it all the time for nothing."

"We're millionaires," said June. "In a manner of speaking, anyway."

I picked up my wine glass. "I have a toast," I announced. We all clinked our glasses. "To our financial advisor: The hell with him."

"The hell with him," came the chorus. We drank heartily and laughed a lot more.

I had sought financial advice in Durban when we first felt the need to emigrate to the United States. I sat down with a serious man in a gray suit and gave him a list of my assets. It didn't take him long to read it.

"What are your short-term and long-term goals?" he asked.

"They're basically the same," I explained. "I want to buy a yacht and sail around the world."

He looked startled. "What about work? Income?"

"Well, you can't work if you're sailing around on a yacht."

"But what will you live on? If you purchase a yacht, even a modest yacht, there will be very little capital left to invest—certainly nowhere near enough to retire on."

"I hadn't thought of it as retirement," I admitted.

He looked at me pityingly and did some rapid sums on his calculator. "I'm sorry to say it's impossible," he said. "I'm afraid you've left it too late. You and your wife would need to work at least another twenty years and save fifty percent of your present salaries before you could buy a yacht and retire."

That was the safe way to do it, of course. But after the ANC sprayed graffiti in my backyard and we had come to the sad conclusion that we could no longer bear to live in South Africa, I chose the other way, the reckless way. I resigned from my work as a newspaper columnist and used my pension money to buy a boat. We sold our house and moved aboard *Freelance*. Life was for living now, we decided. You get only one chance. Let the future take care of itself.

Some of our friends and family members were as startled as our accountant had been. We had a reputation for being very conservative and responsible, always doing the right thing. "The worm has finally turned," I told them, adding ominously, "Every worm has a turn."

For the three worms reveling in a warm sunset in Deshaies Bay, it was the kind of glorious evening that our gray-suited accountant had forecast would never come. But it had, and nobody could ever take the memory away from us.

We set sail early next morning for St. Maarten, the Dutch portion of an island that was shared with the French. The wind sprang at us from all directions in teasing puffs, so we proceeded under power and mainsail until about

8 a.m., when a nice breeze filled in from the east-northeast and we could turn off the engine.

We sailed all day and all night, maintaining our normal seagoing watches. We passed islands whose very names bespoke the magic of the West Indies—Montserrat, Antigua, Barbuda, and St. Christopher—and early on May 5 we found ourselves approaching Groot Baai, the Great Bay, in St. Maarten, or St. Martin, as the French spelled it.

There was a large white cruise ship maneuvering in the bay and blocking our passage. I didn't know whether to pass in front of her or behind. She seemed to be trying to anchor, shunting back and forth as if to set her ground tackle in the sea bottom.

I called her repeatedly on VHF Channel 16, saying I wanted to keep out of her way, but got no reply. I didn't mind. We had been ignored by nobler personages all through the South Atlantic. It struck me that mighty cruise ships probably didn't deign to talk to pesky little yachts anyway, so we handed the mainsail and crept up on her slowly under power.

The night before, we had cursed several other cruise ships that we had come across circling aimlessly at low speed on the open sea. It was impossible to guess what their true course was, and all we could do was divert from our course to keep miles out of their way.

Kevin eventually figured it out. "They're pretending for the passengers' sake to be making a romantic night sea passage," he said. "They're actually killing time between islands. It can't take them more than an hour to get from any one island to another, so they wander around in large circles in the dark as if they were crossing an ocean, pleasing the passengers and confusing innocent yachtsmen."

Most of the cruise ships we saw were shaped more like apartment blocks than ocean liners, slab-sided and top-heavy with swimming pools on the highest decks. With all that top hamper, they must have been hell to handle at slow speeds in any kind of wind, and the only concession they made to seaworthiness was brute size.

Our present bête noire did indeed have an anchor cable running from the bow, so I felt fairly safe in squeezing through the gap ahead of her and making straight for the town of Philipsburg a short distance away. As we passed her, I conjured up one of my sternest glares and fired it up at what I imagined to be the ship's bridge in that mish-mash of gleaming chrome and modern architecture but unfortunately no one was looking at us, so my well-deserved jolt went astray.

Just after 9 a.m. we dropped a stern anchor and made our bow fast to a jetty in Bobby's Marina, Philipsburg. June and I grinned at each other. It was an exciting moment, not because the island was particularly worth visiting for its natural beauty, but because this was where we hoped to perform the second part of our Krugerrand miracle.

St. Maarten was the only completely duty-free island in the Caribbean. It was completely dependent on the tourist trade. Some six hundred thousand tourists a year poured off five hundred cruise ships, wallets at the ready, to jostle each other mindlessly for what they thought were bargains in Philipsburg's two main streets. It was not a place we would have visited, had it not been for the freebooter atmosphere and the possibility of selling our Krugerrands there.

The island covered thirty-seven square miles, and was divided between the French, who had the larger northern portion called St. Martin, with a resident population of about thirty-two thousand, and the Dutch, who had the southern portion called St. Maarten, with a population of about thirty-five thousand. St. Maarten was not only economically liberated but also more politically flexible than the other Caribbean nations we'd visited, for some eight hundred South Africans were living there semipermanently, we were told.

All this bustle and economic prosperity was deceptive. The third world still lurked behind a first-world facade. When we explored Bobby's Marina we were surprised at the range and quality of the products on sale in the boating store— all the best imported stainless steel and bronze yacht fittings, and the latest electronics from Europe and the United States. We hadn't seen a selection like that since Cape Town. This would obviously be a good place to fit out a boat, I thought. But when I rushed off with great eagerness to try the coin-operated showers, I was bitterly disappointed. The water was rationed to about ten gallons, and it all poured out in one thirty-second deluge, leaving me high and dry before I had even soaped up. Apparently the art of plumbing was lagging far behind the art of making money from tourists.

There were a couple of young South African men working at Bobby's Marina, and I asked them in a roundabout sort of way if any yachts ever brought Krugerrands to St. Maarten to be sold. I didn't want the word to get around that I had some on board *Freelance*. But they looked vague and shrugged, so I didn't press the matter.

June, Kevin, and I walked the short distance from the marina to the town. Philipsburg's business center was sandwiched between the sea and a large inland salt pond, and on this narrow strip of land there were two main streets, Front Street and (appropriately enough) Back Street.

Front Street, the closer to the tourist landing, was lined with stores offering expensive fancy goods from all over the world—watches, perfume, gold, jewelry, cameras, and electronic goods.

As we wandered down Front Street, someone handed me a brochure from the local chamber of commerce. I scanned it carefully. "In Philipsburg," it said, "opening a bank account is easy. You can open a bank account with a personal check, cash, traveler's checks, or even gold. And the currency in use is U.S. dollars." *Or even gold.* Those words made my heart leap. Another miracle. We were home and dry.

We hurried back to *Freelance* and I got dressed in my business attire—a short-sleeved shirt, long trousers, and leather shoes. I dug out our forty, one-ounce gold Krugerrands and put them in my disreputable plastic briefcase with the broken zipper.

"Just going to see a man about a bank account," I said to June, grinning. "Back soon, I hope."

I should have known it wouldn't be that easy.

Philipsburg's Front Street was hot and dusty in the heat of early summer. Tourists jostled for space on the narrow sidewalks. The air was humid. The noise of traffic was loud in my ears after the long sea voyage.

I found a large branch of Barclay's Bank, a familiar name to me because I'd been a customer of Barclay's in Durban for years. I got in line for the teller.

"Sorry," he said, "but we don't accept South African Krugerrands. Other gold coins, yes, but not Krugerrands. We agreed not to support apartheid."

That was two kicks in the teeth I didn't need.

I protested: "But the brochure says . . ."

"Sorry, but I'm not responsible for the brochure."

My blood was running hot now. I decided I'd like to see the person who *was* responsible for the brochure. Back in Front Street I found an information kiosk.

"Who's the chairman of the chamber of commerce?" I asked.

An assistant told me.

"And where do I find him?"

She pointed across the road at a casino, one of many on the island.

In fighting mood, I walked out of the bright street into the cool darkness of the empty casino. I found the chairman of the chamber of commerce near one of the gaming tables with another man.

"I've come to complain about your misleading brochure," I said.

He looked startled at first, then puzzled.

I waved the brochure at him. "It says here that you can open a bank account with gold," I said. "Well, you can't. Not if the gold is Krugerrands. This brochure is misleading."

"Yes," he admitted, "a decision was taken to support the trade boycott against South Africa."

"Then you should say so in the brochure," I said. "It's not fair."

He shrugged. "You want to sell some Krugerrands?"

"Yes."

He walked over to where a bright overhead light was shining. The other man lurked in the shadows. When I followed him to the light, he looked at me very warily, trying to sum me up. It obviously wasn't every day that someone wandered into his casino trying to sell gold.

"I may know a customer," he said eventually. "Do you have a sample?"

I reached into my bag and pulled out all forty in their plastic jackets. He whistled in surprise. "Do you always carry all these around with you like this?"

It was my turn to shrug.

"Come back tomorrow, same time," he said. "Maybe I will have a buyer."

I walked out into the heat and crowds again. I tried my luck at two Indian jewelers' shops. But the owners weren't there and the clerks weren't authorized to buy gold coins.

On impulse, I went back to Barclay's Bank. I felt I deserved better treatment as an old customer. This time I demanded to see the manager.

They made me wait fifteen minutes, but I was grim-faced and determined. "I want to convert these into dollars," I said, slapping the coins down on his desk.

He looked at them for a long while. Then he asked me where I was from, and where I had got the coins. He asked how much I wanted for them. I told him $375 each. Eventually he said: "I have a customer who might be interested. I'll call him."

I sat and waited in his office. After a while a young Indian woman appeared. "She will choose three samples at random for testing," the manager said.

"Go ahead," I said as casually as I could.

Was I being taken for a ride? I had no way of telling. I hoped that testing for purity didn't destroy the coins.

Twenty minutes later, an Indian man in a business suit came into the office. The manager introduced us.

"I'm a jeweler," said the newcomer. "These appear to be genuine."

"Yes, they are," I assured him. "I brought them directly from South Africa."

"They're in very good condition."

"They're uncirculated," I said. "They're sold by stockbrokers. Some are in mint condition."

He looked at me uneasily. "Why do you want only $375 each?" he asked.

Apparently the price had gone up since I had last been able to check. Well, good luck to him. I wasn't good at negotiation and intrigue. I just wanted to get this over and done with.

"It's what I paid for them in South Africa," I explained. "I can't take them into the United States and I don't want to make a profit. I just want dollars for them."

He pulled out a pen and wrote me a check for $15,000.

I went downstairs, opened an account, withdrew it all in dollars, closed the account and exchanged my cash dollars for dollar traveler's checks.

When I got back to the boat June said: "You were a long time."

"Yes," I laughed, showing her the traveler's checks and hugging her. "It took a bit longer than I thought."

14

ST. MAARTEN TO THE BAHAMAS

"How does it feel to be able to transmute gold into paper?" Kevin asked one evening as *Freelance* ghosted along between St. Maarten and the British Virgin Islands.

"I guess King Midas would have thought me crazy," I replied, laughing, "but I'm very relieved." Exchanging our South African Krugerrands for traveler's checks that could be legally accepted in America had indeed taken a great weight off my mind. "And *you* should be relieved, too," I added pointedly, since the total proceeds from my transaction would go toward paying his college expenses in the United States.

"I am, Dad," he said earnestly. "And grateful, too."

"Good," I said, "a little gratitude doesn't come amiss."

"Of course," he added mischievously, "I suppose this means I'll definitely have to go to college now. And I did so much want to be a garbage collector." He chuckled and disappeared down the hatchway to get some sleep, leaving me alone in the cockpit.

It was an overnight sail to Tortola, the largest of the British Virgin Islands, where June's sister Carol would be joining us for a few days. She would be flying in from Idaho. We had the twin staysails up in a light breeze from the east, and *Freelance* was bustling along quietly at three knots with another three-quarters of a knot of current helping her on her way. The wind was a trifle too light for Mr. Klickenfuss's liking, so I had taken over the steering from the wind vane. The tiller quivered gently in my hand, and as I looked up at the billowing blue-and-yellow headsails I thought of the two Swedish sea captains who had built *Freelance* and ordered those sails. I wished they could have experienced this delightful night of sailing in the warm tropics, where the stars were so brilliant that they made a faint shadow if you held you hand over *Freelance*'s white deck, and where the wind was as warm and gentle as a lover's caress.

One star that was brighter than the rest caught my eye and startled me when it resolved itself into two and seemed to be plunging steadily toward us. My heart beat faster for a minute or two until I identified it as an approaching aircraft with its landing lights on. I didn't know where it was going, but it did make me realize how disengaged we'd become from civilization over the past few months. I had spent many hours under the open sky every night, watching planets and constellations come and go, and never once after Cape Town had I seen a plane in the night sky until now.

There were other strange lights abroad that night, too, but I knew what they were—more hideous cruise ships wandering aimlessly in large circles to kill time. They were menaces. Ships of that size ought to be required to maintain a straight course, so that small boats know best how to avoid them. Their ever-changing courses were just inviting a collision. I worked *Freelance* well to the north to keep clear of them, but even as I cursed them I couldn't help thinking how nice it would be to be lying back in a deck chair in the cool night with a cold beer at hand and a waiter at my beck and call. Not to mention a wide bed with crisp linen sheets to go to. The Caribbean was making me soft.

Shortly after daybreak we sighted Virgin Gorda, the Fat Virgin, on the port bow. The island was named by Christopher Columbus, who was apparently amused by its shape, which, from a distance, appeared as a silhouette of a reclining pregnant woman. Just before 1 p.m. we crossed the Sir Francis Drake Channel and made fast in Village Cay Marina in Road Town, on Tortola, the largest of the British Virgin Islands (BVI).

June and Kevin took the ferry for twenty-five miles to Charlotte Amalie, on St. Thomas Island in the U.S. Virgin Islands, to meet her sister Carol Stoddard when she flew in from Idaho. I would have liked to go with them, but didn't want to complicate my already precarious immigration status by entering that sleepy outpost of the United States with an expired visa, so I stayed with *Freelance* and was quite happy to have her to myself for a night.

On the way back aboard the ferry next day, who should sit down next to June but Dr. Benjamin Spock, the famous pediatrician and author. When June was editor-in-chief of South Africa's largest parenting magazine, she had flown halfway around the world to Camden, Maine, to interview Dr. Spock on a summer cruise aboard his modest little yacht.

"He's now living on a bigger yacht in the BVI," June told me.

But Dr. Spock was getting on in years. "He didn't remember me at all," June said wryly, "not even when I reminded him of our interview. But he was charming and I was very glad to see him, since that interview was one of the high spots of my career, if not his!"

With Carol as a new crew member, *Freelance* toured the sheltered waters and many islands of the BVI—what June called "little humpy volcanic blobs crammed full of palm trees and thick vegetation, so you couldn't see the rock, just the volcanic shapes and outlines." The plants and trees were all much like ours back home in Durban. The beaches were dazzling white and the water an amazing translucent blue.

I wondered quietly how the reality was measuring up to Carol's expectations. Sailing on *Freelance* was not the glamorous yachting vacation advertised in the glossy magazines. Our accommodation was Spartan—perhaps primitive would be a more accurate description—and privacy was nonexistent. It was hot and stuffy down below at night in port and the berths were narrow.

Inevitably, we had acquired some cockroaches in the Caribbean, and although June had cleaned ship as much as was humanly possible to impress her sister, a few of these detestable insects had managed to escape her onslaught.

"Carol mustn't see one," she had warned Kevin and me before Carol arrived. "They don't have cockroaches in Idaho. She'll die of fright. If one appears when she's around, make sure she doesn't see it. Do anything. Squash it with your hand, if you have to."

Kevin obviously wasn't concentrating very well when June made that plea. During her first night on board, Carol was helping Kevin with the washing up in the galley.

"By the way," he said by way of polite conversation, "did you get the instructions about the cockroaches? You have to squash them with your hand."

June was mortified, but Carol was a good sport and a hardy Westerner. She never once complained as we wandered from one beautiful island to another, anchoring overnight, and like June, she spent many hours in the water, snorkeling over coral reefs and marveling at the brilliant colors of the fish that clustered around her without fear.

June was so hooked on snorkeling that time escaped her completely, and more than once I had to help her clamber back into the rubber dinghy, blue and shivering. I would never have believed you could suffer from hypothermia in those warm waters, but if you spent as much time snorkeling as June did without a wetsuit, it was obviously possible.

The waters of the BVI reeked with history, and it was thrilling to think that *Freelance* was sailing among the islands that had sheltered so many famous pirates and privateers in the late seventeenth and early eighteenth centuries, including the infamous Blackbeard (Edward Teach); Black Sam Bellamy, the self-styled prince of pirates; and that gentleman privateer Sir Francis Drake, who plundered and pillaged so ruthlessly with the blessing of his queen.

Columbus was the first white man to see the Virgin Islands. He sighted land on November 17, 1493, on his second voyage to the New World. In his usual circumlocutory manner, he named the islands "Santa Ursula y las Once Mil Virgenes"—Saint Ursula and the Eleven Thousand Virgins—in memory of a saint slain by the Huns, together with eleven thousand virgin martyrs, in Cologne during the Middle Ages. But Spain apparently thought little of these islands, located so strategically on the trade-wind highway to the Caribbean Sea and the riches of the Spanish Main, so they eventually fell into the hands of the British.

Soon they became infested with pirates attracted by Spanish galleons ballasted with gold and silver.

Of all the pirates, I felt the greatest kinship with Drake, for no better reason than the fact that he and I were born in the same county of England, and I had stood on the bowling green on Plymouth Hoe where, in 1588, Drake received from an excited messenger news of the approaching Spanish Armada. He is supposed to have muttered nonchalantly that there was time to finish the game before he dealt with the Spaniards. And deal with them he certainly did. Officially, Drake wasn't a pirate, of course, but he wasn't a wholly admirable character either. He was a privateer. It was a subtle difference, for a privateer was nothing but a government-sanctioned pirate whose "letters of marque" protected him from being hanged if he were captured.

But before the famous sea battle in which the Spanish Armada was destroyed, and after it, Drake was busy in the Caribbean, snapping viciously at the heels of the Spaniards he hated so much. In 1585, he passed through the Virgin Islands with an enormously rich cargo wrested from the Spaniards, for which a delighted Queen Elizabeth rewarded him with a knighthood.

Ten years later, in 1595, Drake visited the BVI again in company with his cousin, Sir John Hawkins. They assembled their fleet of twenty-seven ships and twenty-five hundred men at a splendid natural anchorage in Gorda Sound, surrounded by six islands. A twenty-year war between England and Spain had erupted, and they were preparing for a surprise attack on the Spanish at Puerto Rico, less than one hundred miles to the west.

The beaches of the BVI delighted us with their cleanliness and lack of crowds. In this prime tourist area we expected anchorages to be jammed with boats, and the beaches to be covered with litter. There were some anchorages where we had to do some reconnoitering before we found a good spot among the charter boats, whose occupants were not overly concerned with tidy anchoring, but those anchorages were few.

We were all lolling around beneath the palm trees on an otherwise deserted white beach one afternoon when a cruise ship arrived and hove to in the entrance to the cove. Bays opened in her sides and disgorged launches that rapidly filled with people dressed in bathing suits and floppy hats, and then sped them to the beach right in front of our noses.

We watched the antics of these white-skinned northerners as they splashed around in tight little groups, emitting happy little shrieks and totally ignoring us. After an hour they were all swept back to the ship in the launches again, and the ship disappeared. We were once more alone and shaking our heads in disbelief. The beach was still unlittered, and it was as if nothing had ever happened.

We spent a day and a night at Norman Island, where people still searched for loot buried by pirates. It was supposed to be the *Treasure Island* of Robert Louis Stevenson's book, and our thoughts turned to Ben Gunn, and the black spot, and pieces of eight. Just two or three miles away was Dead Chest Island, where the pirate Blackbeard is said to have marooned fifteen mutineers with one bottle of rum.

In Gorda Sound we stopped overnight at Drake's Anchorage on tiny Mosquito Island, where pelicans did impossible high-speed belly-flops into shallow water and came up with beaks full of fish. They looked so panicky and out of control on their dives that we burst into laughter every time we saw them do it.

There had been so little development since Drake's time that it was easy to imagine a bustling anchorage filled with ships and men preparing for war, the air sharp with the smell of tar and powder, and the atmosphere filled with the prickly tension that precedes action.

When we had dinner in the open-sided restaurant at Drake's Anchorage, it occurred to me that Mosquito Island would make a marvelous setting for a children's adventure novel. It was exactly the right size for an adventurous bunch of kids. I little imagined then that one day I would actually sit down and write it.

June was the eldest of seven children, so she and Carol naturally had a lot of family talk to catch up on, much of it to do with her father, Thouis, whom she dearly loved. Her mother, Mabel, had died suddenly many years earlier when we were struggling journalists trying to raise a family in Durban, and to June's great distress we couldn't afford the air fare for her to attend her mother's funeral in the United States.

It should have been plainer to me that all this talk was making her itch to get home to the Western states she knew so well, Utah and Idaho, where her family lived. She had been separated from her family for twenty-three years. But I was consumed by my own concerns. I began to fret about the amount of time we were taking to get to Boston, where they would accept my expired immigration visa. My precious letter authorized by the State Department stipulated that we were not to make any stops "other than those required for obtaining fuel and supplies or made necessary by inclement weather en route to Boston." So far we had complied with those stipulations, but I wasn't sure I could justify Carol's cruise around the British Virgin Islands. It was only a few days, to be sure, but it wasn't strictly necessary in terms of a delivery voyage.

When Carol left, June and I talked things over and decided that it might be better to call at the nearest port on the U.S. mainland, rather than waste more time trekking another fifteen hundred miles or so north to Boston. Fort Lauderdale, in Florida, seemed to be the obvious place. It looked to be quite a big city, and would have daily newspapers where we could work while we lived on *Freelance*. We could hire or buy a camper and head west to settle Kevin in college in Salt Lake City, where June's sisters could keep an eye on him, and then come back home to *Freelance*. And if they wouldn't accept my visa in Fort Lauderdale, we would simply have to continue north; but the big thing was for me, the only foreigner in my family, to be legally accepted into the United States.

I had chosen Boston as our arrival port in the States simply because I thought I might have a better chance of finding a job on a newspaper there. I knew that the *Christian Science Monitor* had no bias against South Africans, for instance, because John Hughes, one of my predecessors as back-page columnist on *The Mercury*, in Durban, had become editor of the *Monitor*. I wasn't a Christian Scientist, but I was sure that wouldn't matter.

But the more I thought about calling at Fort Lauderdale, the more I realized how difficult it would be for us to tear ourselves away from there and sail to Boston. June would want to be reunited with her family as soon as possible. Carol's visit had crystallized June's thinking about cruising. June knew then that she didn't want to go on living aboard *Freelance*. I had to face the fact that the two loves of my life were incompatible. I had to make a choice between them.

When I suggested tentatively that we might want to sell *Freelance* as soon as we arrived in Fort Lauderdale, June and Kevin agreed immediately. I was taken aback and a little hurt at the speed and enthusiasm with which they accepted this idea. There was no discussion, just relief on their part. But I knew in my heart that it was the right thing to do, even if the thought of selling *Freelance* made me feel like a traitor.

June later explained her feelings poignantly in a letter to friends in South Africa:

"The long ocean voyages became too monotonous for me ever to want to go to sea again. Of course, there are lovely days and great moments—but there are also long stretches of just sitting and watching the water, when you feel that you are not moving at all, just bobbing up and down in the same place.

"I read a lot, but the days still got very long and the pattern of each one is so similar that they all run together and you lose track of time. I began to feel that I was suspended in time and space, accomplishing nothing.

"But worse than that is the feeling of isolation that goes with living and traveling on a yacht. I felt that we were a small, totally detached cell, moving and existing entirely independently, and that other people on other yachts were equally separate, isolated cells.

"I felt very cut off. We did meet a few people along the way, but the next day they would be gone, or we would, and it was very lonely. Even on our boat there was a sense of isolation. Each person had their own duties, their own time to sleep, their own concerns, their own reactions and feelings.

"The watch system meant that there wasn't much time when the three of us were on deck together and we all found our own ways of filling our time and our thoughts. And so, although we shared an adventure where we all needed each other, it was a very individual experience.

"Even when you get to a port, you aren't part of the life there. You are just passing through, and so many yachts are sailing around the world now that the locals really aren't interested, even in the most remote islands. And so, although solitude can be very refreshing, this was just too long a dose. I found I didn't want "to get away from it all"—I *need* it all, especially the people, and work to do.

"And so, although I would be happy to spend a week or two cruising among sunny islands in the future, I'm not planning on crossing any more oceans."

On June 1 we left the British Virgin Islands and found ourselves heading north on the deep ocean again, with no islands in sight. The wind was very light from the east and it spread out over the flat blue water in little cat's-paws, making the sails fill gently and then fall limp again.

When I came on watch to relieve Kevin at 10 p.m. there were long periods of calm when *Freelance* lay quivering in her own moonlit reflection, and I recalled with a shiver down my spine the most frightening experience I'd ever had at sea. Strangely, it was in the middle of a calm.

I was one of a crew of four racing across the South Atlantic from Cape Town to Rio de Janeiro on a home-built, thirty-three-foot, wooden sloop called *Diana K*, owned by my friend Dave Cox. My watchmate, Eddie Howard, had gone down below to rest, for we weren't moving and there was nothing for him to do on deck. I sat alone in the cockpit and watched the pinprick lights of a thousand stars wobbling over the greasy surface of the dark water. The lights touched and crossed and joined each other as if some cosmic spider had spun a giant web all around us. It was startlingly beautiful in its fragility.

Then I started wondering if the fish and sea mammals could see this wonderful show from beneath the surface. I wondered how far the light of a star would penetrate into the clear water of the South Atlantic, and without thinking I grabbed our powerful deck flashlight and shone it over the side. The narrow beam drove deep down, bending in elongated green spirals, and there was no telling what depths it reached.

Then I was seized by a sudden feeling of dread. I burst out in a cold sweat. I realized I had just signaled our presence to every monster in the sea below us. And by monster, I meant squid. I had a sudden vision of a giant squid enveloping our little thirty-three-footer in its tentacles and dragging us under in one swift flick.

It sounds melodramatic to relate it now, but my fear at the time was well based and absolutely genuine. As we weren't moving, we were a sitting duck hundreds of miles from the nearest land. It was dead silent and very calm. The sea was not even sucking at the transom as it usually did. It was a hot humid night, but I started shivering, and got down on my haunches in the empty cockpit.

After a minute or two of near-paralysis I crept down the companionway steps to fetch the fireman's ax we kept down below for emergencies. There was nothing else on board that could sever those tentacles.

I clutched the handle of the ax and waited with my heart racing. I don't know how long I waited like that, listening intently. Time stood still. But eventually I felt a faint breeze, and I sprung into action.

I freed the mainsheet and trimmed the sheet of the big genoa jib. I crouched over the tiller, willing the boat to move forward, out of the danger area, back into the anonymous blackness of the sea. No racing helmsman ever sailed better than I did at that moment. I felt the pulse of every zephyr that wandered along, easing and trimming sheets, anything for speed and distance, never mind direction.

Eventually we were free and clear, and I could breathe easily again. I never told the others about my fear because I thought they'd scoff, but I knew my alarm was justified.

Few people ever stop to consider that the lightless zone of the ocean, which includes everything below about three thousand feet, constitutes more than 90 percent of all life on Earth. Because the abysmal depths are so dangerous and expensive to explore, we know next to nothing about them or the creatures that inhabit them. But there are squids down there.

David Attenborough says in *Life on Earth:* "Squids grow to an immense size. In 1933, in New Zealand, one was recorded that was twenty-one meters (sixty-nine feet) long, with eyes forty centimeters (nearly sixteen inches) across, the largest known eyes in the whole animal kingdom."

Even so, Attenborough concluded, we are unlikely to have discovered the biggest squids that exist because they are extremely intelligent and swift-moving. They have no trouble avoiding man's attempt to catch them in nets or clumsy deep-sea dredges.

Sperm whales, which are among the biggest creatures on the sea, dive and hunt for squid. They frequently return to the surface badly scarred, with wounds that suggest they have been battling creatures with suckers five inches across.

"So it is by no means impossible that the kraken and the other legendary sea monsters that are said to be able to rise from the deep and wrap ships in their tentacles, really exist," Attenborough says. I, for one, have no difficulty believing him.

Thor Heyerdahl, the Norwegian ethnologist who drifted forty-three hundred miles across the Pacific in 1947 on a balsa-log raft called *Kon Tiki,* agreed with many marine scientists who held that most of the sea's creatures dived during the day. "The darker the night was, the more life we had around us," Heyerdahl told the famous biologist and author Rachel Carson. He added that at night his raft was literally bombarded by squids.

Oceanographer Richard Fleming is quoted by Carson in her landmark work, *The Sea Around Us,* as saying that off the coast of Panama it was common to see immense schools of squid gathering at the surface at night, and leaping upward toward the lights that were used by the men to operate their instruments.

Not all squids are giants like *Architeuthis,* of course, but all seem to be highly intelligent sea creatures. The most commonly found squid is about six to eight inches long, and is mainly sold as fish bait or eaten as calamari.

Michael Greenwald, an amateur sailor who wrote *The Cruising Chef* cookbook tells of an occasion when he was becalmed in mid-Atlantic. He discovered his fishing line had some sort of dead weight on it, making him think he had hooked a plastic bag. But when he reeled it in he was confronted by a three-foot squid, thicker than a man's leg and weighing perhaps thirty pounds. It was a brilliant, angry red in color.

As Greenwald attempted to pull it on board "it took one look at me with enormous eyes and squirted me in the face and chest with a powerful acid, and quick as lightning wrapped a tentacle around my hand and pulled with amazing force, nearly taking me over the side.

"I screamed in pain from the acid, struggled free, and rushed to the sink to wash my face. By the time the pain was gone, my woolen sweater had burned away where the acid had hit it. I returned to the deck and cut the line."

That was a three-foot squid. Imagine what an *Architeuthis* could do. Sixty-nine feet long. More than three times the length of *Freelance*. Sixteen-inch eyes—each as big as a car wheel. I shuddered at the thought of it, and was very careful not to shine any more lights down into the sea.

The weather stayed light as we worked our way north to the Bahamas, and on the second day out of Road Town, shortly after dawn, two American sailboats, *Pendragon* and *Escudo,* came motoring past us, traveling in company to Fort Lauderdale.

We overheard them talking about us on their VHF radios. They apparently couldn't understand why we didn't start the engine when the boat's speed fell below five knots, as they did. There was a lot of discussion about how much ice they were making, with their engines running all the time. I began to realize we were truly entering a new and fast-moving world.

The wind hauled aft just before the yachts disappeared over the horizon ahead of us, and we were able to raise our twistle yard and the twin foresails.

"What do you know?" said the radio. "That guy's got his spinnaker up at last."

"Yeah, slow thinker," came the reply.

A few hours later, in midafternoon, I heard U.S. Navy vessel P28 calling the two yachts, warning them to keep clear because it was conducting gunnery practice. P28 then put out a call to all ships in the area, asking for their positions. I called on Channel 16 and gave them our position, which they acknowledged.

By the next morning we were about two hundred and fifty miles northwest of Puerto Rico. June was doing her 6 a.m. to 8 a.m. shift on deck when the radio burst into life again.

"Sailing vessel four miles on my starboard bow, this is the USS *Wainwright*. Please identify yourself."

I leaped out of my bunk and flew up the companionway steps. June and I looked around the horizon and could see nothing.

A few minutes later, the radio message was repeated, and suddenly we saw her, an enormous warship racing at us down the path of the rising sun. I didn't know it then, but P28, the *Wainwright,* was a 547-foot-long guided missile cruiser capable of thirty-four knots. She was once the most decorated surface ship in the U.S. Atlantic fleet. In any case, to us on that morning she was an ominous, intimidating sight.

She closed in on us, and the radio ordered us all to gather on deck in the cockpit while they observed us through binoculars. I roused Kevin from his bunk and he staggered on deck rubbing his eyes.

"What right do they have to accost us?" I asked June. "We're in international waters. This is not America."

June shrugged. "I don't know."

The radio asked if we were armed. I said no, and wondered if they were about to send a boarding party. I went white as I remember my expired visa.

"Do you know where the prescription is for our Scopolamine seasick patches?" June asked.

"No," I said. "Is that a listed drug?"

"Don't know. Just trying to get prepared. They can confiscate a boat if they find drugs aboard."

They demanded to know where we had come from and where we were going. They asked for our names and nationalities. I told them, and added that I had an immigration visa. I didn't say it was expired. They asked if we had a cargo. I said no.

The questioning seemed to go on and on. I began to resent being grilled by an armed warship when I was peacefully minding my own business on the open ocean. This was undoubtedly bullying and harassment. But I was too scared to object. I had too much to lose.

Eventually they seemed satisfied. They said they would move off and not steal our wind. They came astern of us and passed along our port side, some two hundred yards off. There were sailors and what appeared to be Marines formed up on the decks.

Then the VHF spoke again: "You've got a line trailing astern. Can you identify it."

"Yes, I said. "It's a log line with a spinner on the end. A Walker taffrail log."

There was a long silence. Obviously the modern navy had forgotten all about taffrail logs. They probably thought we had thrown a stash of drugs overboard when we saw them coming.

"Can you pull it in and hold it up for us to see?"

"Yes," I said. "Stand by."

Several pairs of binoculars appeared on the *Wainwright's* bridge as I hauled in the log line and held up the little black spinner. Lord knows what the sailors and Marines on deck thought I was doing—boasting about my fishing prowess, probably—but it made me feel very foolish. Then the eagle-eyed officers of the *Wainwright* pronounced themselves satisfied, and they steamed off at high speed to the southeast.

There was no question of going back to bed after that encounter. The adrenaline was still coursing through our veins, so we all sat in the cockpit and nursed *Freelance* along on course while we wondered aloud how many ordinary people in America knew what their government was doing in their name. If America was the land of the free, where no home or vehicle could be searched without due cause, that freedom certainly wasn't extended to others. The Ugly American epithet was well earned on the open ocean.

Even before we had left Durban, we had heard several stories from round-the-world sailors about how yachts had been harassed and searched by the U.S. Coast Guard operating not only in international waters but in the waters of other sovereign states, such as the Bahamas.

Bob Fraser, a former commodore of Point Yacht Club, and the man who had told us how to find Fernando de Noronha, once skippered a small sailboat that was closely stalked at night in the Bahamas by a large unlit powerboat. "We were very scared," Fraser told me. "We had no idea who they were or what their intentions were." When he finally challenged them by radio, they identified themselves as a U.S. Coast Guard cutter. They said they would now board his boat; but Bob had more guts than I had, and told them it would be too dangerous at night in the heavy seas then running. They held off. But many others had been boarded and searched for no good reason whatsoever, except to justify America's strange war against drugs, which wouldn't have been necessary at all if Americans themselves were against drugs, and didn't buy them so willingly and use them so enthusiastically.

We were rather shaken by our encounter with the *Wainwright.* We felt intimidated, even though we had done nothing wrong. Whether you're in the right or not doesn't matter when you're confronted in mid-ocean by a missile cruiser. We didn't even dare take a photograph of the ship for fear the action would provoke a boarding. We wondered apprehensively how we would be received in the United States.

It was a quiet ship and a very thoughtful crew that drifted slowly onward over a calm sea toward the Bahamas and Fort Lauderdale.

15

THE BAHAMAS TO FORT LAUDERDALE

Seven days out from the British Virgin Islands, in sunny weather and a perfect wind from the east-northeast, *Freelance* gave us our first sight of land at low-lying San Salvador Island, otherwise known as Watling's Island. We were immersed in history once again, for this was where Admiral Christopher Columbus made his first landing in the New World in 1492, according to many scholars.

The docile, friendly inhabitants referred to their thirteen-mile-long island as Guanahani, but that wasn't good enough for the excited Columbus, who arrogantly informed them that he was taking possession of their island in the name of the King and Queen of Spain, and promptly renamed it San Salvador. Little did the inhabitants realize the import of Columbus's arrival. Within about thirty years they had been annihilated. Those who weren't captured as slaves died from diseases they caught from the Europeans.

Columbus, meanwhile, was beside himself with joy because he thought he had at long last discovered the East Indies. The more phlegmatic British, in their turn, gave Guanahani the name Watling's Island, and included it in the Bahamas group; but they had a change of heart in 1926 and gave it back its old name of San Salvador.

Unfortunately, Columbus was unable to ascertain the latitude of his landfall accurately, and his description of the island was imprecise. Over the years, learned scholars have suggested nine possible islands as the one Columbus landed on, but historians have more recently narrowed the list of serious candidates to two—San Salvador and Samana Cay, some sixty-five miles southeast of San Salvador.

We had already passed Samana Cay in the night without seeing it, so whichever it was that Columbus landed on, we had definitely crossed his wake of five hundred years before, and we experienced a very tangible connection. It's silly, of course, to regard the wake of the *Santa María* as if it were a groove carved into the ocean forever, but it's surprisingly easy for voyagers under sail to imagine its existence and to be awed by it.

Man has never managed to change the face of the sea, as he has the land. There are no ancient pyramids at sea, no medieval castles, no signs at all of mankind's wanderings on its surface over thousands of years. The sea wipes out every trace of man's passing and reverts straight away to the timeless, nascent state it has maintained for uncountable eons. But it cannot erase man's memory, nor his ability to romanticize and relive the emotions of fellow seafarers of ages long past. So while Columbus's wake has gone, it lives on in a very real manner for those who go to sea in small ships.

Columbus Day is still celebrated every October in the United States, and we'd heard that many Americans believed that he discovered their country.

"He didn't miss by much," Kevin observed as we sat in the cockpit together at the change of watch. "He was just a few miles east."

"But he never actually set foot on American soil," I pointed out.

"And just as well," said Kevin. "Otherwise it would be called Columbia and we'd be having to learn Spanish. But as a matter of interest, who did discover America?"

"Amerigo Vespucci," I said confidently. "It's named after him."

"No, no," said June from down below. She knew these things. "There's no proof that he even saw North America. He explored the north coast of South America about 1500, and it was named America after him. Then the term was later extended to North America."

With our store of knowledge thus increased by the Ship's Welfare Officer, we sailed on past San Salvador without stopping except to clear the log spinner every now and then. We had run into a large area of small patches of yellow-brown sargasso weed floating near the surface of the water, which so fouled the log, and produced such false readings of our distance run, that we soon had to hand it and stow it away in its wooden box. After that, we relied on dead reckoning for positions between sextant fixes.

We kept in deep water past the eastern edge of the Bahamas, running one hundred miles or more every day in a gentle northeast trade wind and keeping a close eye on the barometer, for we were now officially in the hurricane season. At the northern tip of New Providence Island we closed with the land and turned west, joining the heavy shipping traffic in the channels between the extensive shallow banks.

We were all excited as we prepared to leave the Bahamas and start on the final leg across the Gulf Stream to Fort Lauderdale under the twin jibs. Shortly before sunset, at about 6:30 p.m. when we were just off the Great Isaac Light, we were startled by the sudden appearance of a low-flying helicopter. It was the U.S. Coast Guard, buzzing us at mast level. I waved at the pilot, motivated more by wariness than politeness, and he gave me a thumbs-up sign.

"What do you suppose that means?" I asked.

"The *Wainwright* obviously told them we're coming," said June. "We're in their computers. They're keeping a close eye on us."

I laid off a course to compensate for the swift Gulf Stream flowing to the north, and *Freelance* flew westward through the night before a strengthening northeaster. By 2 a.m. we were in American waters off Fort Lauderdale, where we stowed the jibs and hove to for the rest of the night.

We all sat in the cockpit, gawking at the myriad lights and bustle ashore, unable to sleep for the excitement of actually being in America.

At 8 a.m. I called the Coast Guard on the VHF radio, and told them we needed customs and immigration clearance. We headed in toward the narrow harbor entrance. Fifteen minutes later, a highly powered offshore racing launch roared toward us. Her name was emblazoned in large letters along her side: *Blue Thunder.* She pulled alongside, her engines rasping at idle in neutral, and spitting water out of her twin exhausts. Two uniformed men wearing dark sunglasses sat on a bench seat in the plushly upholstered cockpit. One was talking on a VHF handset. "*Freelance,*" he said. "No, one word, not two . . ."

The other man looked across at me. "Customs," he said. "Follow us."

I could hardly believe it. Customs? What other country in the world would provide an expensive, exotic boat like this Don Aronow-designed racing machine, specially built by the Cigarette boat company, for its customs service? Cigarette boats, I knew, were favored by smugglers racing loads of marijuana and cocaine ashore from freighters in the Gulf Stream. Had this one been captured and used as a prize? Or was she specially built to outrun and outgun the smugglers' Cigarettes?

No matter: there wasn't time to think about these things. The customs man put his engines into gear and *Blue Thunder* leaped ahead enthusiastically, with her engines still idling. I revved up *Freelance*'s little diesel as far as it would go, but even with a cloud of black exhaust smoke billowing from our transom we could only make five and a half knots at top speed, and *Blue Thunder* consistently pulled ahead, so her pilot kept taking her out of gear and easing her back in again when we had caught up, never once touching his throttles. Together we approached the narrow channel at the harbor entrance in strange procession: a hobbled greyhound leading a tortoise with its tail on fire.

Shortly after we entered the channel we were shaken rigid by the sight of a horde of private sport-fishing boats bearing down on us at full speed, scores of them, fifty or more, all of whom had been bottled up by a road bridge over the Intracoastal Waterway just ahead. I edged *Freelance* over to the starboard side of the channel as the Rule of the Road required, but the frenzied armada came at us on both sides—forty-foot sport fishers with gleaming flying bridges and bimini tops, their twin propellers thrashing the warm blue water into a carpet of white foam, and smaller open Boston Whalers with impossibly large outboard motors, flying out to sea with their hulls hardly touching the water.

I signaled to the men on *Blue Thunder* with my hands, for the noise of the oncoming hordes made conversation impossible. Were we on the right side of the channel? The customs men shrugged. Obviously, nobody cared much about the Rule of the Road. It was every man for himself in this scrimmage, and the devil take the hindmost. I felt very strongly that we were the hindmost.

For five minutes they flashed past on both sides of us, often changing course at the last moment when collision seemed inevitable, and scraping by one boat-length away. Then, suddenly, they were gone, fleeing for the horizon, and it was almost silent again by comparison, with only a low baritone rumble from the greyhound and a tortured soprano squeal from the tortoise.

Within minutes we were in the Intracoastal Waterway and feeling quite overcome by a new tumult of boats on the water and vehicles on land. I watched with fascination as a Volkswagen Beetle flew over a bridge ahead of us, probably doing all of twenty-five miles an hour. Our eyes and senses weren't used to it. For nearly ten days we had watched the sea go by at five or six miles an hour and that had become the norm. Now we were in the middle of a large city, with huge flashy marinas all around us, palm trees growing in white sand, and jet planes screaming overhead.

Blue Thunder led us to a large landing stage where several uniformed customs and immigration men with guns strapped to their hips were waiting. "Welcome to America," Kevin muttered. They ordered us to stand in the cockpit while they searched the boat.

I wanted to ask them what due cause they had for the search, but I didn't have the guts. I showed them my outdated visa, and the letter from the American Consulate in Johannesburg, and they told me to report to an office in the city.

"Anything valuable to declare?" a customs officer asked when they had finished searching and found nothing of interest.

I told them about the traveler's checks, the proceeds from the Krugerrands, but they weren't interested.

"I have some jewels," said June.

She went below and produced a battered Tupperware box, one of many that we used as waterproof containers for important papers and valuables. It housed her lifetime collection of gold rings, bracelets, pendants, earrings, and precious stones.

The customs man took one look. "Is that them?" he asked.

"Yes," said June.

He turned away scornfully, showing no interest.

June bit her lip, not knowing whether to feel relieved or insulted.

Then we were free to go. "You have to leave now," one of the men said. "You can't stay here. This is government property."

I was at a loss for words. We hadn't had time to collect our wits. I had no idea where to go. We were in a strange city in a strange country and our morning had been traumatic.

"Where should we go?" I asked eventually, immediately feeling very silly for having said it.

"Find a marina," he said.

Yes, right, a marina. I had been thinking of a quiet anchorage somewhere, but this was a big city.

We started the diesel and cast off, feeling like abandoned waifs. We edged out into the flow of traffic on the waterway, for which we had no chart, and found ourselves carried along willy-nilly until we came to a forest of aluminum masts and stainless steel flying bridges.

We made fast in slip C80 in the Pier 66 Marina, Fort Lauderdale, Florida. A clean-cut young waiter on a golf cart came zipping down the long finger pier and handed us a bag of ice and three smaller bags filled with soap, shampoo, deodorant, and headed notepaper. "Room service," he announced. "Will you folks be needing a telephone?"

We stared at him for so long in amazed silence that he became uncomfortable. "I'll check back later," he said, leaving abruptly. "Y'all have a nice day."

June was the first to break the silence. "The champagne," she said, "we mustn't forget the champagne."

I dug out the bottle of champagne we'd brought all the way from South Africa for this very moment. It was warm and fizzy but we didn't care. In the heat of the Florida sun in the middle of the morning we sat quietly in the cockpit and drank champagne. We looked around with wide eyes, gradually catching up with the bustling world outside.

"To America," said June, lifting her glass.

"To our new life," I added.

"To *Freelance,* who got us here safely," said Kevin. I drank especially heartily to that.

It was a day we'd never forget, June 11, 1987, two days before Kevin's eighteenth birthday.

When we had showered and made ourselves presentable we discovered that we had blundered into one of the most expensive hotel/marina resorts in southern Florida. The 380-room luxury hotel was set in twenty-two acres of lush tropical vegetation. It had six dining rooms and lounges, at least three swimming and paddling pools of different temperatures, and countless amenities for those whose pockets were deep. The marina fees were correspondingly expensive, so we obviously couldn't afford to stay there long.

But first I had important business with the Immigration and Naturalization Service. I called a taxi that rushed me though wide straight streets built at right angles to each other. It all looked very practical, but quite characterless.

In the INS building I hesitantly handed over my passport and immigration visa to one of two men in a small office. Before he could ask, I told him the visa had expired, but that I had a letter that said my late arrival had been approved by the State Department. And finally, I confessed: "We were supposed to go to Boston, but . . ."

"No problem," said the INS officer affably. He had the long-suffering look of a middle-aged family man whose kids had thrown their pop bottles in the garbage instead of the recycling bin. He called the other man over, and turned to me confidentially. "I'm teaching him how to process permanent residence applications," he said. "We don't get many like this."

In a most casual, friendly atmosphere, we filled in forms. I signed, and they signed, and suddenly in a flurry of stamping it was all over. "Welcome to America," the first man said. "Your green card will be in the mail. Meanwhile, if anybody asks, just show them the permanent residence visa stamped in your passport."

I stood outside the INS building in the hot sun, feeling quite stunned with relief. The contrast with South Africa's authoritarian, power-crazed civil servants could hardly have been greater. They would most certainly have required me go to Boston in accordance with the letter from the consulate. I must have looked quite odd because a man stopped on his way out of the building and asked me if I was all right. After we had talked for a minute, he insisted on giving me a ride back to the marina in his VW minivan, for which I was very grateful.

I jumped aboard *Freelance* in a joyful mood and announced: "I'm legal! We don't have to go to Boston." We celebrated my good news with lunch in the hotel and refreshing dips in the three pools.

One voyage had finished. Another, quite different, was about to begin.

Within three days we had found a calm berth alongside a rental property in a backstreet canal on Hendrick's Isle for $375 a month. It was near a main street called Las Olas, strategically situated between the beachfront and downtown.

Four other cruising boats were moored to jetties alongside us. On the foreshore, in the grounds of the condominium complex, was a large swimming pool and a thatch-roofed open structure that was known as the tiki hut. We had access to these facilities, as well as to an air-conditioned bathroom and shower that we shared with the other cruisers, who had apparently been moored there for some time.

The tiki hut, we soon realized, was the center of the social scene. It was the cruisers' town hall, pub, meeting place, and parliament. The yachties gathered there in the cool of the evening to drink beer and tell tall stories. We met Bob Springer and Susan Oberender who lived aboard a Prout catamaran in the next berth, and they introduced us to the other cruisers. Bob had a perpetual twinkle in his eye and a mischievous smile on his face. He was an expert with computers and worked when he felt like it. Susan was a full-time dental hygienist who wore a more serious mien, as if she were the practical half of the family, the one who kept the other half in line when he was tempted to stray.

We gathered that cruising in southern Florida was a very laid-back affair. Bob, for example, had discovered one breakfast time that a crab who lived in the sand just outside the tiki hut would eat an oatmeal cereal known as Cheerios. So, for the next three days, the mighty brain power of the tiki parliament was finely focused on scientific research, namely, whether crustaceans could also exist on Quaker Oats, Kellogg's Corn Flakes, and Almond Delights.

Captain Crunch, so named because of the difficulty he experienced berthing his Morgan 42, proposed that Twinkies be tested as well, but parliament voted him down. "It's a known fact that Twinkies is not a breakfast food," declared a tanned young man called Ozzie, from the Kookaburra 35. Twinkies would only muddy the research, he declared, and delay or even thwart publication of the scientific paper.

The banter, joking, and teasing was fun, but it was difficult to get any work done. *Freelance* needed some sprucing up after her long voyage, more than a quarter of the way around the world, and we had new lives to start.

Yet, despite the temptation to sit in the sun and watch crabs eat breakfast cereal, we made good progress. I found a documentation agency and an import agency who said there would be no problem about importing *Freelance*. The import duty would be about 1.5 percent of her assessed value, and it was just a question of paying to organize the paperwork. Nobody made any mention of the trade boycott against South Africa, and I certainly didn't bring it up.

June found a part-time job with a small public relations company that would bring in $480 a month. Better yet, they would teach her to use a computer, and the office was air-conditioned. Kevin found a job bussing tables and washing dishes in a nearby restaurant. He kept quiet about his country of birth, because at that stage we were still not sure how Americans regarded South Africans, even though we were refugees from the apartheid state. (He was also an American citizen, of course, although he spoke like a South African.) But one afternoon the restaurant's cook, a large and muscular black man, bore down on Kevin and said: "I hear you're South African."

Kevin, fearing the worst, answered "Yes" in a weak voice.

"Good," said the cook. "Tell me, what tribe do you think I'm from?"

That shaky introduction to the catering trade of America was rather overshadowed a few weeks later, when Kevin found a better job as a clerk at a convenience store. Late one evening a customer pulled a knife on him, and forced him to hand over the money in the till. He wasn't hurt, just shaken and indignant. Nothing like that had ever happened to him in darkest Africa. Fort Lauderdale began to feel even more like the Wild West a couple of days later when he cycled to the downtown library and had his borrowed bike stolen.

Meanwhile, I was searching for a job, too. After much pondering and tapping on our little portable typewriter, I wrote an article about our trip for *Cruising World* magazine. It wasn't easy to find an angle, because nothing had gone wrong. We hadn't broken a mast or lost a rudder, or done any of those interesting things that make such splendidly exciting copy. I eventually crafted a piece along the lines that the cruisers you never hear of, the ones who sail across oceans without any fuss or bother, are the most proficient sailors of all because they have obviously prepared themselves and their boats well, and have maintained constant vigilance. I headlined it "A Family-Sized Adventure," and *Cruising World* bought it. Not only did they buy it, but they splashed it on their cover page, one notch above a story by William F. Buckley, Jr., I was very happy to see.

In a magazine for journalists I noticed an advertisement for a columnist for a daily paper in Evansville, Indiana. Jobs for columnists were few and far between and I couldn't afford to pass this one by.

Hoping to impress the paper with my enterprise, I bought my own air ticket and flew to Evansville, booked into a cheap hotel, researched the area in the local library, wrote two specimen columns, and went to see the managing editor. He wasn't the slightest bit interested in interviewing me, nor did he read my columns. He invited me to lunch rather reluctantly and took me to a seedy hamburger joint, where we chatted in a desultory manner about South Africa, Evansville, newspapers, and sailing. It was pretty obvious to me that he already had made his mind up about his new columnist, and it wasn't going to be me. The post had been advertised purely for the sake of propriety. I had spent $500 for nothing.

I was in a pretty glum mood when I got back to my hotel and entered the dining room for an early supper. Nothing on the menu looked appealing, so I asked the waiter if, by any chance, they could rustle up some fish and chips. I meant, of course, the English dish of battered fresh fish and French fries.

"Sure," he said, "no problem."

Ten minutes later he came back with a large packet of potato chips and two fried fish sticks on a plate.

"You'll need some ketchup with that," he remarked helpfully. "And I'll get you some salsa if you like."

I didn't like. I declined his kind offer, and stoically ate the fish sticks and the whole packet of chips without even touching the ketchup. It is my abiding memory of Evansville.

I had better luck back in Fort Lauderdale, where the *Sun-Sentinel* was looking for a night copy editor. I was given the standard Associated Press exam for copy editors, and apparently passed with flying colors, although the editor who had given me the test said, hardly surprisingly, that he had noticed an Anglicism here and there.

He arranged for me to have a physical examination, a drug test, a hearing test, and so on—the usual run-up to a permanent job—all of which were paid for by the newspaper. I passed all the tests and was given a clean bill of health, but when I went back to the *Sun-Sentinel,* they told me that the man who was about to hire me had been transferred to another department. When I asked what that meant about my job, they just shrugged. Nobody knew. And until he was replaced, they had no authority to hire. I was beginning to learn something about American newspapers and the free market system, something rather disturbing for a person who had always worked for reputable South African and British newspapers, whose word was as good as their bond.

The triviality of life around the tiki hut contrasted strongly with the huge decisions we were taking aboard *Freelance,* and the uncertainties that lay ahead. I began to have private regrets about my decision to sell *Freelance.* Quiet resentment set in. Selling her hadn't been part of my original plan.

The plan had been to live aboard *Freelance* while Kevin went off to university, to move the boat between cities on the East Coast if necessary, while we both found good jobs. Then we could afford to move ashore, into an

JOHN VIGOR

apartment—and eventually a home of our own—without having to sell *Free-lance*. But there was no stopping June now. She had been isolated from her family in Utah and Idaho long enough. She was headed home. She wanted nothing more to do with *Freelance* or Fort Lauderdale. And in any case, I had given my promise to sell the boat.

A few days later, on our twenty-fifth wedding anniversary, June suggested that we have a celebratory dinner at a restaurant. I churlishly refused. I said we couldn't afford it, which was true, since our expenses were already far greater than our income, and we hadn't earned any money for six months or more during the voyage. But that wasn't the real reason. I was still angry.

The next morning, when my friend Bob from the catamaran next door was out offering Cheerios to his crab, we got talking about our favorite foods. I told him about my attempt to order fish and chips in Evansville and he laughed.

"In Florida we know about English fish and chips," he said. "Let me take you to lunch."

At noon, while June and Kevin were at work, he drove me to a restaurant, one of a chain that specialized in seafood, and he bought me a plate of proper fish and chips. It was wonderful.

That evening, when June came back to the boat and heard about my going out to lunch with Bob, she was angry. She thought I had paid for my own meal, right after I had been so mean about buying her an anniversary dinner. In turn, my pent-up anger poured out like the flood from a broken dam, and in the dim lamplight of *Freelance*'s cabin we had the worst row of our entire marriage.

"The deal was to live on the boat and find work," I shouted, "not to sell the boat and move West."

"The deal was that we would *like* sailing," June responded hotly. "It was to be a good adventure."

She was right, of course. I had been fooling myself when I kidnapped my crew back in Durban. June had been tricked into coming along for the trip, but I couldn't compel her to love *Freelance* or to like sailing with a husband who ignored her. That wasn't the good adventure she'd been promised.

242

But my knowing she was right only made things worse. "If you want to leave me and go running off to your family, then go," I ranted. "And good riddance!"

There was a lot of weeping and snuffling that night, and much gnashing of teeth on my part, but by morning I had realized that my indignation was not entirely righteous. We didn't speak to each other for several hours after waking, but maintaining that frigid silence proved impossible.

By afternoon, June and I were talking civilly to each other, after which things quickly got back to normal. Our bond was too strong to be broken by one row, and we both realized that our nerve ends were raw after five months of being cooped up together with no privacy. For me, the row cleared the air and washed away the last traces of my resentment. At long last I was ready to move forward on a new course.

I set about varnishing *Freelance*'s African teak gunwales in the hot summer sun to pretty her up for sale. She wouldn't be easy to sell, I thought. Like many foreign yachts, *Freelance* lacked the luxury features of most American boats. We had led a Spartan life. We had no fridge, no freezer, no shower, no hot water, no pressurized cold water, no watermaker, no oven, no microwave. We didn't even have a washbasin. We used a portable stainless steel bowl. She wasn't wired for shore power. We got along fine with kerosene lanterns.

I determined to sell *Freelance* myself and save the broker's commission. I crafted a brochure several pages long and had copies made. I advertised her in *Cruising World* and other publications as a simple, honest-to-goodness world cruiser equipped with everything necessary for safe passages. Her BMW diesel engine was still almost brand new, with only 323 hours on it. We had added just 103 of those hours during our five-month, seven thousand-mile passage from Durban.

Astonishingly, the third person to look at her bought her. We signed the final papers in the lounge of the Embassy Suites hotel, and I walked out with a check for $30,000—our stake for our new life in America. After my pessimistic forecast of our chances of selling her, I could hardly believe my good luck.

Kevin took himself off to college at the University of Utah, in Salt Lake City, where June's sisters could keep an eye on him. We bought a small used car and loaded it up for the drive across the continent.

I started the engine in the street next to the canal where the boat lay out of sight behind the tiki hut, and put the car in gear.

"Don't you want to take a last look at *Freelance?*" June asked solicitously. She, too, was sad to say good-bye to her.

I shook my head. I didn't need to take a last look. In my mind's eye, I could see her driving west in a smother of foam as the sun set in a blaze of glory in the southeast trades. I could see her bravely resisting the battering of giant waves in a storm off the southern tip of Africa.

I stared straight ahead. *"Just keep driving,"* I told myself, blinking hard. *"Never look back, never regret."* But for a long time the road was mostly a blur.

16

EPILOGUE

I had been wanting to write this book for many years but I needed time to get our flight from South Africa to the United States into perspective. It was the terrorist attacks on the World Trade Center in New York, and the Pentagon—and their aftermath—that eventually spurred me into action.

We fled South Africa in 1987 because of escalating terrorism and the likelihood of a bloody civil war similar to the Israeli-Palestinian conflict. We could see no peaceful future in South Africa for ourselves or our kids.

But after the September 11, 2001, attacks I watched with a great degree of foreboding the attempts by the federal government to assume extraordinary powers, and the apparent complicity of the American public, who were giving away their hard-won individual rights and liberties almost as freely as they distribute candy at Halloween. When the government started secretly arresting hundreds of civilians and holding them incommunicado, I was reminded very forcibly of my former life in South Africa, where civil liberties were suppressed in the name of national security by a government fighting terrorism. Citizens who objected were neatly vilified with one word. They were deemed "unpatriotic."

The events of September 11, 2001, will be remembered in years to come as we remember the Trojan Horse today: a diabolically simple plan cunningly executed with devastating results. But in the early days after September 11, when the whole of the USA was in a state of understandable overreaction, I had to wonder: Did I jump from the frying pan into the fire? Was America rapidly becoming the South Africa we escaped from?

By an ironic stroke of fate, South Africa, in an extraordinary about-face, had since become a democracy. Black people were now in the seats of power. Apartheid, at least the institutionalized aspect of apartheid, had disappeared.

Jonathan Raban, the distinguished British author, read my mind one evening when we were having dinner in a small restaurant on an island in Puget Sound. We were discussing the astonishing metamorphosis of Nelson Mandela from South Africa's most reviled terrorist to its revered state president.

"Aren't you sorry you left, now?" Raban asked.

That was a couple of years before the September 11 attacks, but I was able to answer no. I wasn't sorry then, and I'm not sorry now.

The sad truth is that South Africa is going through a typical early phase of liberation where the people formerly oppressed are now in a position to wield power to their own advantage. The result, as usual, is corruption, greed, inefficiency, a high rate of unemployment, rampant disease, and one of the world's worst crime rates. White people, most of whom are comparatively rich in African terms (although not in American terms) are the natural targets of this crime. Robberies, burglaries, and carjackings are rife and often accompanied by brutal force. Almost every white South African knows a fellow white who has been killed or badly injured in one of these incidents.

When Miss Hudd, my geography teacher, warned us of a revolution all those years ago she was on the right track, but the revolution turned out not to be the anticipated bloody uprising. Instead, it evolved into a long-drawn-out economic revolution, a forced "redistribution of wealth" by armed and ruthless freebooters. While this lawlessness is officially frowned on by the South African government, it continues unabated—not only because the police force is overloaded with work and riddled with inefficiency, but also because the government does not view the problem as one of the country's most pressing. Perhaps, in the view of the black government, the whites are simply getting what they have long deserved. Meanwhile, white farmers are looking nervously over their shoulders at neighboring Zimbabwe, where farms owned by white citizens (even those born in the country) have been confiscated by the black government. South African whites are wondering what they would do if it should ever happen to them.

Anyone who has lived in Africa knows the terrible pull to return, but having tasted liberty and stability in America, I wouldn't want to go back to South Africa now and grow old there. Like the rest of my family, I am an American citizen now, and proud of it.

I am convinced that ordinary Americans have both the common sense and the power to resist attempts to curtail their individual rights in the long run. They may condone some temporary restrictions during a period of crisis, when the country pulls together to fight a common enemy, but I don't believe they will accept them unquestioningly as the majority of South African whites did. The difference is that Americans are taught from birth to think and act as individuals, unlike South Africans (and most Europeans) who are taught to subjugate their personal feelings for the benefit of the tribe.

Furthermore, giving up some personal rights temporarily to preserve a democracy seems a reasonable sacrifice. In South Africa, people were forcibly stripped of their rights by the regime to preserve the evil practice of apartheid.

Nelson Mandela should be a lesson for Americans, though. He turned to terrorism because the South African government wouldn't listen to his protests, let alone act to rectify the oppression of the black majority he represented. He called himself a freedom fighter. We caught him, and had him safely locked up in jail—but in the end he won the Nobel Peace Prize. He shared the honor, of course, with a brave soul called Frederick de Klerk, a true Afrikaner son now almost forgotten by the world, who voluntarily handed over power—an unprecedented act in Africa, and one fraught with grave consequences for him, his National Party, and the Afrikaner people.

Americans might want to ponder the fact that a convicted terrorist won a highly prized international award as a peacemaker. One of the messages here is that it's very important to listen to your enemies, to find out why they hate you, and hate you so much that they are prepared to give their lives to fly planes into your buildings. If Americans have a failing, it's believing that everything American is right, that capitalism, democracy, and the American way of life is superior to everything else, and that anyone who disagrees is either an idiot or a terrorist. There are, in fact, reasonable, peaceful people who might think otherwise. And beware of the label "terrorist." It can be a powerful propaganda tool.

But enough of preaching. I have neither the brains nor the stomach for it. Here is how we fared on our second, longer voyage after our arrival in America:

June and I drove our little car from Key West to San Diego, via Chicago and Seattle, criss-crossing the country from north to south as we went, looking for a place in which to live and work. We had no idea where we would end up. We comforted each other by saying that one evening at sunset we would come to a rise and see the golden glow of a town in the valley below, and our hearts would leap, and we would just *know* this was the right place for us. But it never happened. We visited our sons Trent and Terry in Chicago, and we called on Kevin and June's family in Utah and Idaho. All were doing fine.

Along the way we sought work with newspapers, but the big ones weren't hiring and the small ones were offering wages we couldn't live on.

When we came to San Diego after many weeks of travel from motel to motel, we knew we had reached the end of the road. We decided to hunker down there and earn some money, no matter how. We badly needed to top up our dwindling savings. June found a humble job with a public relations agency, and I laid siege to the *San Diego Union* newspaper. At first, I couldn't get past the front desk. If I didn't have an appointment, I was told, I couldn't go upstairs to the newsroom.

I did, however, manage to extract one bit of valuable information from the impassive faces at the front desk. I found out the name of an editorial secretary, and her extension number. Editorial secretaries know everything and can work miracles.

I called her and was delighted when she offered to meet me at the front desk, escort me upstairs to the editorial department, and introduce me to a section editor.

For several months I dreamed up stories for the gardening pages, and wrote about the advantages of gutters, or plants that didn't need watering every day. I earned a pittance, but every time I went into the paper to drop off my contributions I tried to talk to more people and make myself known.

One day I submitted an op-ed piece about South Africa to the *Union's* so-called rival paper, the *San Diego Tribune,* which shared the same building. The article was published and it seemed to win me a little more prestige.

Somebody suggested I apply for a full-time editorial writer's job the *Union* was having difficulty filling. I got the job and soon found out why nobody wanted it. It was an impossible job because of bitter in-house feuds—though it did give me a chance occasionally to tell President George Herbert Walker Bush how to run America and the world, and to have breakfast with Vice President Dan Quayle. After two years, when Kevin announced that he had a job and could now put himself through college, I quit and went free-lance.

I wrote a book of rules of thumb for amateur sailors, and International Marine publishers of Camden, Maine, bought it. I also wrote a children's adventure novel, which was published by Atheneum in New York, and Carlsen in Hamburg, Germany. Then I noticed an advertisement for the job of managing editor of *Sea* magazine, a glossy powerboat monthly based in Irvine, south of Los Angeles.

I applied and was hired. When the magazine's revenues dropped during a small recession, I was given to understand that I should give a poor performance review to my second in command, a man who had been there for many years, and who was probably earning as much as I was, if not more. He was obviously going to be laid off. He was a very good worker, however, so I ignored the hints and gave him a good review, much to the consternation of the magazine's owners. They solved the problem very quickly, though: they fired me instead. It was a first for me, and quite a jolt.

I had edited many stories about the cruising grounds of the Pacific Northwest and Puget Sound, so June and I took a quick trip to Oak Harbor, on Whidbey Island. It had the rugged Cascade mountain range nearby for June, who loves mountains, and the beautiful sailing waters of the San Juan Islands nearby to satisfy me. We bought a thirty-year-old mobile home in a trailer park for $25,000, which was almost all of the cash we had left.

Within a couple of months, June got a job in the advertising department of the little local newspaper, the *Whidbey News-Times,* at $6 an hour. She later managed to get taken on to the editorial staff, where she became features editor and earned a little more, but the paper was short-staffed and the work very demanding.

I began to write more boating books and was lucky to find some book editing to do. We bought a twenty-eight-year-old Santana 22 sailboat for next to nothing and took thirteen months to restore her and convert her for cruising. She sailed like a little witch, so we called her *Tagati,* Zulu for "bewitched," and we had a wonderful time exploring western Washington state's wonderful system of inland waterways during weekends and vacations, from Tacoma in the South Sound to the Canadian Gulf Islands north of the border.

Tagati was just a little slip of a boat, nothing more than a big dinghy with a lid on top, really, so she had nothing much in the way of accommodation. Living aboard her was like camping on water in a fiberglass pup tent, but we couldn't have been happier to get afloat again. And June just loved it. When she didn't have to cross an ocean, she found sailing and exploring to be great fun.

After a few years, we sold *Tagati* and bought a slightly bigger sailboat, a twenty-five-foot Cape Dory, which we called *Jabula,* Zulu for "happiness." In her we circumnavigated Vancouver Island, the largest island off western North America at about two hundred and eighty miles long. It was a six-week voyage that involved many days of sailing in the open Pacific and was a feat relatively few twenty-five-foot sailboats have accomplished. We felt very proud of ourselves.

When June's job on the *Whidbey News-Times* became unbearable because of staff cuts, she found a more congenial job as a copy editor on the *Bellingham*

Herald, a daily newspaper in the university town of Bellingham, fifty miles to the north. We sold our Oak Harbor mobile home and used the proceeds for a deposit on a modest condo in Bellingham. It was a large step up for us.

There we sold *Jabula* and bought a slightly bigger Cape Dory, a twenty-seven-footer, for cruising in the San Juans and Gulf islands. She's called *Sangoma,* the Zulu word for a natural healer.

In the year 2004, seventeen years after our flight to freedom, I had to admit that our accountant in Durban was right. We still cannot afford to retire. But we are still able to laugh about it. We are surprisingly happy and content with each other and with what we've got. We certainly know there are millions of people in the world with far less than we have. I have also learned to count my blessings, and chief among them is my wife, June, who has supported me and spoiled me for forty years.

As June says, we took our retirement fifteen years in advance, and we're glad we did. It's not such a bad idea to retire at an age when you can still enjoy it, and go back to work later. We're also grateful that we still have the opportunity to work in a country where we have rights and freedoms we never enjoyed in South Africa, and to live in a beautiful city where we can walk the streets at night without having to look over our shoulders all the time. We have much to be thankful for.

There have been some dark days, of course, but always we found ourselves buoyed by the terrific sense of accomplishment we felt from crossing an ocean entirely under our own steam. Our flight to freedom was hard work, but it tested our ability to take care of ourselves and our self-sufficiency. It also tested our commitment to each other. We passed all the tests, which is very satisfying.

June says it made her think of her pioneer ancestors walking and pushing handcarts across the plains. "I admired their courage and endurance and was just as proud of ours. Even if our trip wasn't anywhere near as filled with hardship and deprivation as theirs was, it was still a mighty undertaking."

One of the major freedoms we sailed to was freedom from any doubts that we could take care of ourselves—even starting at age fifty in a new country. That has been an important source of confidence for us, especially in the difficult times of settling in. We always felt (and still do) that we could deal with whatever came at us, and we backed up that feeling with the knowledge that we had sailed thousands of miles across the oceans. For each of us there is an abiding sense of satisfaction and fulfillment.

We also have the great satisfaction of knowing our family is thriving in America. Trent, our eldest son, and Terry, the middle one, are both long established and steadily employed in the commercial printing business. Kevin earned his degree in computer science and never looked back. Trent and Kevin are married and have families of their own now, and have presented us with four grandkids. Terry is a confirmed bachelor and loving it.

Freelance? Oh yes, I still dream about my other love. In 1997, the man I sold *Freelance* to was getting ready to sell her. I flew to Florida to look at her. Perhaps I could buy her and sail her back to Washington state. That would close the circle very neatly.

But I was shocked when I saw her in a berth in Palm Beach Gardens. She had been badly neglected. She was filthy. There was rot inside and out. She had been left in the heat and damp of Florida without ventilation, so that her lockers were black with mold inside. The floorboards had swollen and could not be lifted. The canvas work was rotting. Practically everything that could be taken off and sold had been stripped from the boat, including the life raft, the dinghy, the outboard motor, the radio receiver, the twistle yard, sails, and even an anchor. The Aries vane gear had seized up and the BMW engine was a mass of rust. Even the gear lever in the cockpit had fallen off and had been replaced with an old pair of Vise-Grips. Worst of all, she was literally crawling with cockroaches and stank to high heaven.

I was heartbroken. There was no possibility of sailing her home without a lengthy, expensive refit, and it would have cost me $5,000 to have her trucked overland, so I could work on her at my leisure. I flew home bitterly disappointed and feeling guilty for having brought *Freelance* to this sad state by selling her to a man who neglected her so badly.

When I got home, I offered to buy her for $10,000, but that was less than was still owing on her, so it was refused. Then a friend from Durban, Mark

Cronje, contacted me one day and told me he was now based in Fort Lauderdale. I told him about *Freelance*. He went to look at her and bought her for $12,000. He cleaned her out, restored her, and fitted a new engine. I lost touch with him after that, but, last I heard, *Freelance* was in Grenada. I don't know where she was going from there, but I am very grateful to Mark for rescuing her and giving her a new lease of life. I have a strong feeling we'll meet again one day.

FREELANCE

Freelance's vital statistics:

Length overall	30 ft. 6 in.
Length on the waterline	25 ft. 0 in.
Beam, maximum	10 ft. 4 in.
Draft	4 ft. 9 in.
Designed displacement	11,986 pounds
Sail area:	
Mainsail	220 sq. ft.
Fore triangle	268 sq. ft.

(See lines drawings, page 258.)

Freelance was professionally built of fiberglass in South Africa and launched in 1980. She was one of the Performance 31 class of deep-sea cruising yachts—also known in South Africa as the Morgan 31 class. She was purchased as a bare hull by two retired Swedish sea captains living in Durban. They built her interior of wood.

Freelance was designed by Angelo Lavranos, a prominent South African naval architect now living and practicing in New Zealand. Before branching out on his own, he worked for two famous design teams: Angus Primrose in Britain, and Sparkman and Stevens in the United States.

Although *Freelance* closely resembles the British Camper and Nicholson 31, a design well known for solid seaworthiness, Lavranos says his inspiration for the Performance 31 hull came from a former design he did for Angus Primrose, the North Atlantic 29. All three are fairly beamy, heavy-displacement designs with traditional long keels cut well away at the forefoot. They have transom sterns with outboard rudders.

On deck, *Freelance* had an anchor locker in the bows with a Simpson and Lawrence Seahorse manual anchor winch set down in it. Her bower anchor was a 35-pound CQR that was housed in the substantial bow roller. Her anchor rode was 240 feet of ⁵⁄₁₆-inch chain, and we sometimes needed every foot of it when we anchored in depths of as much as 90 feet. The chain fed down into an anchor locker below the deck locker. Our kedge anchor was a 22-pound Bruce with 30 feet of chain and 210 feet of three-strand nylon rope. The kedge housed itself very neatly on a corner of the after pulpit, and its rode stowed in the stern lazarette.

The cabintop was low and strong, with fairly small fixed ports. Dorade boxes molded into the deck provided dry ventilation below. We carried a six-person self-inflating life raft in a fiberglass container on the cabintop a few feet aft of the mast.

The forward end of the watertight, self-draining cockpit aft was protected by a canvas spray dodger that could be folded flat at short notice and secured in place. Stout aluminum tubes attached the Aries self-steering vane to the transom aft of the wooden outboard rudder.

Freelance's sailplan featured a simple but modern sloop rig of fairly high aspect ratio. Her spars were made of hollow aluminum. Winches were mounted on either side of the mast at waist height for the mainsail and foresail halyards, which ran inside the keel-stepped mast, as did the main topping lift. Her main boom was sheeted to a horse at the aft end of the cockpit. Vertical movement of the main boom was controlled by a four-part vang, or kicking strap. A small winch attached to the boom was used to haul tight the new clews when jiffy-reefing the mainsail.

The mainsail had three sets of reef points. All three reef tacks were hooked over a set of stainless steel horns at the gooseneck. A long track on the forward side of the mast allowed a whisker pole to be stowed vertically. The two 13-foot booms for the twistle yard were also stowed upright alongside the forward lower shrouds.

Freelance carried two mainsails (one a brand new spare) a storm jib, a working jib with a deep set of reef points, a genoa, and twin running staysails.

For a 31-footer, she was very spacious down below, with full standing headroom, a generous galley, and a proper forward-facing chart table. The galley stove used two pressure kerosene burners. Our bilge pumps were both manual—a large Whale pump in the deep bilge alongside the galley, and a smaller one in a cockpit locker that could be worked by the person at the helm. There was plenty of stowage space for staple provisions for three people for a year and enough water in permanent tanks for three people for fifty days at the rate of a half gallon per day each.

As the V-berth in the fo'c'sle was filled with spare sails and our inflatable dinghy, we used the cabin berths to sleep in at sea, and each of the settee berths was furnished with a lee-cloth of heavy canvas.

The little 12 hp BMW diesel engine was situated under the bridge deck. It was cooled by raw seawater. Access to it was quite good when the front of the engine box, which also supported the steps to the cockpit, was removed and set aside. The engine drove a conventional transmission and a fixed, three-bladed propeller.

A 5 hp outboard motor for the inflatable dinghy stowed in the port cockpit locker.

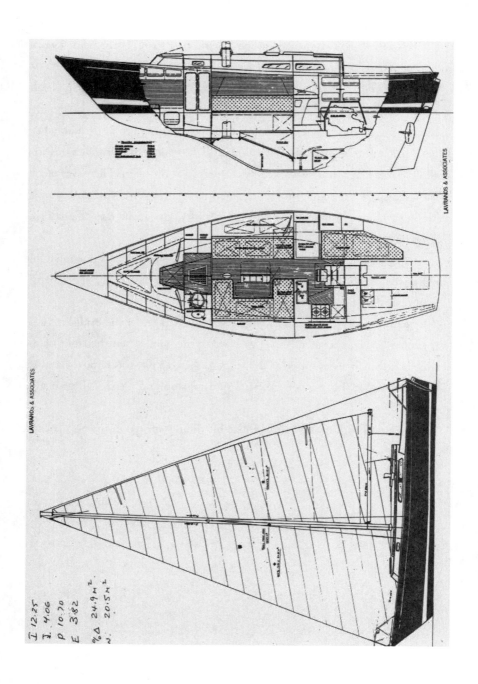

(Reproduced by permission of the copyright holder, Lavranos and Associates.)

The following is a list of the books mentioned in the text, plus a few others I have found useful:

Attenborough, David. *Life on Earth.* Glasgow: William Collins, 1979.

Bardiaux, Marcel. *The Four Winds of Adventure.* Translated by Raymond Johnes. London: Adlard Coles, 1961. Originally published as *Aux 4 vents de l'aventure.* (Paris: Flammarion, 1958)

Beebe, William. *The* Arcturus *Adventure.* New York: G. P. Putnam's Sons, 1926.

Butler, T. Harrison. *Cruising Yachts: Design and Performance.* New York: Yachting Publishing Corporation, 1945.

Carson, Rachel. *The Sea Around Us.* New York: Signet, 1961.

Chapelle, Howard I. *Yacht Designing and Planning.* London: George Allen and Unwin, 1972.

De Neufville, S. *La Navigation sans Logarithmes.* Paris: Société d'Editions Géographiques, Maritimes et Coloniales, 1950.

Fuson, H. Robert. *The Log of Christopher Columbus.* Camden, Maine: International Marine Publishing, 1987.

Greenwald, Michael R. *The Cruising Chef.* New York: Tab Books, 1978.

Guzzwell, John. *Trekka Round the World.* Bishop, California: Fine Edge Productions, 1999.

Hiscock, Eric. *Around the World in Wanderer III.* Dobbs Ferry, New York: Sheridan House, 1987.

Holm, Donald. *The Circumnavigators: Small Boat Voyagers of Modern Times.* Englewood Cliffs, New Jersey: Prentice-Hall, 1974.

Junger, Sebastian. *The Perfect Storm.* New York: HarperCollins, 1998.

Lewis, David. *We, the Navigators.* Honolulu: University Press of Hawaii, 1972.

Marsh, John H. *Skeleton Coast.* Cape Town: Hodder and Stoughton, 1944.

Moitessier, Bernard. *Sailing to the Reefs.* Translated by René Hague. Dobbs Ferry, New York: Sheridan House, 2001. Originally published as *Un Vagabond des Mers du Sud.* Paris: Flammarion, 1960.

Moorehouse, Alan. *Darwin and the* Beagle. London: Hamish Hamilton, 1969.

Paton, Alan. *Cry, the Beloved Country.* New York: Charles Scribner's Sons, 1948.

Slocum, Joshua. *Sailing Alone Around the World.* London: Rupert Hart-Davis, 1967.

Van der Post, Laurens, and Jane Taylor. *Testament to the Bushmen.* Harmondsworth, UK: Penguin Books, 1985.

Wightman, Frank. A. *The Wind Is Free.* New York: Duell, Sloan and Pearce, 1949.

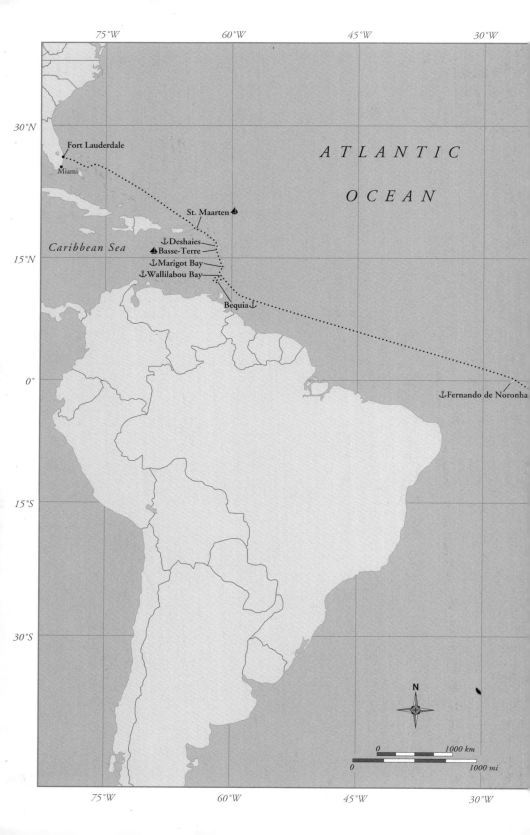

ATLANTIC

OCEAN

30°N

Fort Lauderdale

Miami

St. Maarten ⚓

⚓ Deshaies
⚓ Basse-Terre

Caribbean Sea

15°N

⚓ Marigot Bay
⚓ Wallilabou Bay

Bequia ⚓

0°

⚓ Fernando de Noronha

15°S

30°S

75°W   60°W   45°W   30°W

N

0   1000 km

0   1000 mi